BESTSELLING
BOOK SERIES

Green Home Computing For Dummies®

Cheat Sheet

Quick Ways to Reduce Your Computer's Power

To Do This	Find More Here
Assess the power your computer uses.	Chapter 4
Turn it off when you're away for two hours or more.	Chapter 4
Reduce the number of peripherals you use.	Chapter 7
Unplug unused peripherals.	Chapter 4
Use power management features.	Chapter 9
Get a smart power meter or plog.	Chapter 18
Use smart power strips.	Chapter 4
Upgrade the memory in your system.	Chapter 5
When you buy a new system, buy green.	Chapter 6

Resources to Check before Buying Computer Equipment

- ✔ EPEAT (www.epeat.net)
- ✔ Energy Star (www.energystar.gov)
- ✔ Good Housekeeping Green Seal of Approval
- ✔ Manufacturer's Web site (What is their green policy?)
- ✔ Climate Counts (www.climate counts.org)

Computer Recycling Do's and Don'ts

Chapter 8 covers recycling your computer in detail. Here's the short version:

- ✔ **Do** check a site like 911.com to find green recyclers in your area.
- ✔ **Don't** put your computer out with the trash!
- ✔ **Do** look for places to donate your computer.
- ✔ **Do** wipe the hard disk clean before donating it.
- ✔ **Do** buy computers from manufacturers with green policies.
- ✔ **Do** recycle toner and inkjet cartridges.
- ✔ **Do** share your story so others will recycle too.

For Dummies: Bestselling Book Series for Beginners

Green Home Computing For Dummies®

Cheat Sheet

Tools for Measuring Your CO_2 Emissions

- ✔ The Carbon Footprint calculator at the Nature Conservancy (http://nature.org/initiatives/climatechange/calculator)
- ✔ Makemesustainable.com
- ✔ Edison (www.edison.com)
- ✔ Snap CO_2 Saver (www.co2saver.snap.com)

What's Adding CO_2 to the Environment?

- ✔ Driving your car
- ✔ Taking a bus
- ✔ Flying in a plane
- ✔ Using your computer
- ✔ Buying household supplies and food
- ✔ Heating your home
- ✔ Using electricity in your home
- ✔ Using plastic bags or bottles

For Dummies: Bestselling Book Series for Beginners

Green Home Computing

FOR DUMMIES®

by Woody Leonhard
and Katherine Murray

WILEY

Wiley Publishing, Inc.

Green Home Computing For Dummies®

Published by
Wiley Publishing, Inc.
111 River Street
Hoboken, NJ 07030-5774
www.wiley.com

Copyright © 2009 by Wiley Publishing, Inc., Indianapolis, Indiana

Published by Wiley Publishing, Inc., Indianapolis, Indiana

Published simultaneously in Canada

For general information on our other products and services, please contact our Customer Care Department within the U.S. at 877-762-2974, outside the U.S. at 317-572-3993, or fax 317-572-4002.

For technical support, please visit www.wiley.com/techsupport.

Wiley also publishes its books in a variety of electronic formats. Some content that appears in print may not be available in electronic books.

Library of Congress Control Number: 2009931453

ISBN: 978-0-470-46745-9

Manufactured in the United States of America

10 9 8 7 6 5 4 3 2 1

About the Authors

Woody Leonhard's tree-hugging tendencies date back to his years in the Boy Scouts, where he specialized in whittling divining rods, analyzing pterodactyl droppings, and stammering at Girl Scouts. He's written a whole lotta books, starting with *Windows 3.1 Programming For Mere Mortals,* back in 1992. Somewhat more recently, he's created many *For Dummies* books, in multiple editions, covering myriad aspects of Windows 7, Vista, Windows XP, and Office. Woody's a Contributing Editor for Windows Secrets Newsletter (windowssecrets.com), and he runs his own blog at AskWoody.com, which is tied into a giant all-volunteer computer Q&A site that currently boasts more than 600,000 entries. If you have a question, you know where to go.

A decade ago, Woody moved to Phuket, Thailand, where he now lives with his wife, Duangkhae (better known as "Add"), and his father, George. Together, Woody and Add run Khun Woody's Bakery and three Sandwich Shoppes. If you're ever in Phuket, drop a line — Woody@AskWoody.com.

Katherine Murray's big ambition in life was to be Dr. Doolittle when she grew up, and she's getting pretty close. She writes (mostly) in a home office surrounded by her many four-footed friends, her children (two-footed), and grandchildren. She's been writing about computers, digital lifestyle, home business, parenting, and more since the 1980s, back when IBM PC XTs were cool and nobody had heard anything (yet) about new-fangled software called Microsoft Windows. Since the mid-80s, when she wrote her first books on technology, Katherine has published more than 50 computer books on topics related to digital lifestyle, Microsoft Office, and social and blogging technologies. In addition to her technical book writing, Katherine is the managing editor for *The Educational Forum,* an international research journal in education published by Kappa Delta Pi (www.kdp.org). Katherine publishes a number of blogs, including BlogOffice, where she posts tips and Office miscellanea. A long-time lover of the earth, Katherine was thrilled to be able to work on this project and has grown decidedly greener with every finished chapter. :)

Dedications

Woody: To Add, who put up with all sorts of problems while the books finally took form. To Dad, for providing great inspiration. To Claudette Moore and Ann Jaroncyk, the best agents a guy ever had, and to the editorial and production staff for bringing it all together. Most of all, to Kathy Murray, for doing the (vast!) lion's share of the work to make this book a pioneering effort in an important and all-too-frequently neglected field.

Katherine: To my grandbabies, Ruby and Henry. May they — and all our grandchildren — have beautiful blue skies; fresh, clean air; crystal clean waters; and a healthy, peaceful planet flourishing with life to pass on to the ones they love.

Authors' Acknowledgments

At the heart of the green movement in the world right now is the knowledge that we are all truly interconnected and interrelated. None of us works in a vacuum, and no project — this one included — is ever produced without the vision, talent, creativity, and effort of many people along the way. We'd like to thank the following people who helped take this book from a great idea to the reality you now hold in your hands:

Claudette Moore of Moore Literary Agency, for her support, insight, friendship, and tried-and-true publishing experience;

Becky Huehls, Project Editor, for being this book's champion, shepherding it through the various deadlines and processes that make a book happen;

Joe Hutsko, author, who jumped in and wrote Chapter 10 for us when the deadlines loomed large. Thanks, Joe! (Be sure to check out Joe's green book, *Green Gadgets For Dummies,* Wiley 2009.)

Heidi Unger, Linda Morris, Kathy Simpson, Adam Vaughn, and all the production staff for great line-by-line checking and editing. If you think this book looks great and reads well, their efforts had a lot to do with that.

Katherine would like to thank Woody for the opportunity to work with him on a topic so near and dear to her heart, and for his friendly and encouraging partnership.

And we'd both like to thank you, the reader, for caring about the planet, for believing you can do something about it, and for purchasing this book to begin making that difference.

Publisher's Acknowledgments

We're proud of this book; please send us your comments through our online registration form located at http://dummies.custhelp.com. For other comments, please contact our Customer Care Department within the U.S. at 877-762-2974, outside the U.S. at 317-572-3993, or fax 317-572-4002.

Some of the people who helped bring this book to market include the following:

Acquisitions and Editorial

Project Editor: Rebecca Huehls

Acquisitions Editor: Amy Fandrei

Copy Editor: Heidi Unger

Technical Editor: Adam Vaughn

Editorial Manager: Leah P. Cameron

Sr. Editorial Assistant: Cherie Case

Cartoons: Rich Tennant (www.the5thwave.com)

Composition Services

Sr. Project Coordinator: Kristie Rees

Layout and Graphics: Reuben W. Davis, Timothy C. Detrick, Andrea Hornberger, Jennifer Mayberry, Christine Williams

Proofreaders: Laura Albert, Evelyn W. Gibson, Jessica Kramer

Indexer: Potomac Indexing, LLC

Special Help: Linda Morris, Kathy Simpson

Publishing and Editorial for Technology Dummies

    Richard Swadley, Vice President and Executive Group Publisher

    Andy Cummings, Vice President and Publisher

    Mary Bednarek, Executive Acquisitions Director

    Mary C. Corder, Editorial Director

Publishing for Consumer Dummies

    Diane Graves Steele, Vice President and Publisher

Composition Services

    Debbie Stailey, Director of Composition Services

Contents at a Glance

Table of Contents

Part V: The Part of Tens *341*

Chapter 18: Ten Best Ways to Make Your Computer Greener......343

Chapter 19: Ten (Plus) Online Resources for Green Info, Action, and Products 351

Introduction

● ●

*W*elcome to *Green Home Computing For Dummies!*

It's the first step in making a great green change for the planet.

As you've no doubt noticed, green is all over the news. Green jobs, green products, green programs, green people. Well, maybe not green *people*. Yet.

But you don't have to look far to see that the U.S. is — finally, some would say — waking up to the realities that our planet needs our attention and care. For decades, we've been pumping unhealthy chemicals into the air, using valuable resources as though there were no tomorrow, mowing down trees, and sinking drums of toxic waste in the middle of the ocean, thinking that the consequences of these actions were not our problems.

Today, we know that kind of "not my problem" thinking *is* the problem. And by picking up this book and resolving to make a green difference by making earth-friendly choices about your computer use, you have become part of the solution. Congratulations!

About This Book

Green Home Computers For Dummies is all about making good choices that reduce the wear and tear that our computing practices have on the planet. This book helps you learn about the power your computer, peripherals, and other tech equipment — like your game systems, PDAs, and mobile devices — are consuming right now, and puts it all in context so you can clearly see why that matters.

After you have a sense of the impact you're making — called your *carbon footprint* — you learn a variety of ways to reduce your power consumption by changing your practices, upgrading your system, buying green, and much more. You'll also learn how to dispose of old computer equipment in a way that is kind to the planet and find out how changing the way you think about work (telecommuting, anyone?) may be one of the greenest home computing possibilities around.

Foolish Assumptions

As we wrote this book, we envisioned you, the reader, as a person we were sitting with, sipping organically grown, free-trade coffee in a funky sidewalk cafe (that of course went all green long ago). We chatted about ways we can green the planet by expanding our awareness and exercising our choices about the way we use our computers. We made some assumptions about you and the type of information that would be most helpful to you as you start greening your home computing:

Our first assumption is that you care about what you're hearing in the news about global warming, deforestation, water worries, species extinction, and more — and you're wondering what you personally can do, through your computing choices, to help turn the tide. That's a good place to begin!

We also assume that you know something about computers, but it's not necessary to know a whole lot. In this book, you'll find examples for a collection of operating systems, from Windows XP to Vista to Windows 7 and Mac OS X. You'll find lots of good green info, a huge range of resources, great practical eco-friendly ideas, and techniques, tips, and suggestions for greening your computing practices from the inside out.

We also assume you want to know how to modify the system you already have and perhaps either upgrade it or recycle it and buy a new greener system. You'll find that information in Part II.

We also assume that you want to understand how personal technology in all its forms — PCs, laptops, mobile devices, game systems, and more — contributes to our planetary challenges. You'll find ways to evaluate the impact you're already making, find practical ways to reduce that impact, and discover ways to reuse and recycle what you can.

How This Book Is Organized

Green Home Computing For Dummies is designed to give you the big, global picture (what is global warming and how are we contributing to it?) and then take you into the small stuff (how do I set up power management in my PC?); but you don't have to approach any of the topics in a particular order. Each chapter stands on its own right, and if it contains the information you're looking for most, just jump right in — the water's reasonably warm.

Here's a quick look at what you'll find in the various parts of the book:

Part 1: Getting a Little Green Behind the Ears

Part I starts the book by exploring why greening your computer practice is important for the environment and helping you see how much of an impact you're already making. In this part, you calculate the size of your carbon footprint and see how your power consumption contributes to the gas bubble that is warming the planet.

Part II: Choosing Your Green PC Path

Part II helps you take an up-close-and-personal look at your own computers and peripherals and get a sense of how many resources you're using. Here you get practical information on how to upgrade your computer to make it greener, shop for a new green system, choose earth-friendly peripherals, and ultimately, recycle the computers you've got in a way that's good for all of us.

Part III: Greener Under the Hood

Part III takes a closer look inside the computer for ways to reduce power consumption and cut down on other resources like paper, water, and time. In this part, you learn to set up power management in your computer, green your mobile devices, reduce the resources you use in printing, and use home networking to share resources throughout your house.

Part IV: Telecommuting, Teleconferencing, and Teleporting

Part IV explores ways in which you can green your practices by, first and foremost, using technology to work from home, which reduces your travel time, gas costs, and CO_2 emissions right off the bat. This part also shows you how to set up a green home office and use cloud computing, teleconferencing, and other communication tools to be successful at work no matter where you're working.

Part V: The Part of Tens

Finally, Part V provides sets of quick items to make your computer greener, find reliable green tech sites, and shop for green electronics online.

Icons Used in This Book

The Tip icon marks tips (duh!) and shortcuts that you can use to make green computing easier.

Remember icons mark the information that's especially important to know. To siphon off the most important information in each chapter, just skim through these icons.

The Technical Stuff icon marks information of a highly technical nature that you can normally skip over.

The Warning icon tells you to watch out! It marks important information that may save you headaches or keep you from heading into waters that are more *greenwashing* than really green.

Part I

Getting a Little Green Behind the Ears

"I asked for software that would biodegrade after it was thrown out, not while it was running."

In this part . . .

*O*ur computers are hungry. Like most of the people you know, some computers (and mobile devices, and peripherals) have bigger appetites than others. This part of the book introduces you to green computing and shows you how you can start to get a handle on the natural and energy resources that get gobbled up when you use your computer, when you open the fridge, when you drive to the store. For every action there is a reaction, as you'll see in this part of the book, and in some cases, those actions are turning up the temperature on global warming. The good news is that awareness is the first part of positive change, and you'll have lots of opportunity for that in this part of the book. Today is a good day to find out where all that energy is going and choose to manage it wisely (so it doesn't manage you!).

Chapter 1

What Is Green Computing?

Contrary to what Kermit the Frog says, today it's pretty easy to be green. Take a look at any media channel — TV, Web, or print — and you're sure to see an ad about the latest must-have green product for your home, car, kitchen, or office. Organic is *in* and consumers are spending more and more on items that manufacturers promise are earth friendly.

Computer manufacturers are right there in the mix. Dell is offering a laptop made of 95 percent recycled materials; Apple is touting its greenest MacBook yet; and most hardware vendors are busy producing four-color glossy marketing materials that tell you how environmentally conscious they are and how good you can feel when you write that check or sign the credit card slip.

This chapter gives you a quick look at what green home computing is — and isn't. (Hint: It doesn't mean going out and buying all new green-colored computer equipment.) Here, we also help you start thinking about simple ideas that you can put into action right away to begin making your computing — and your life — a little greener.

Knowing What Green Computing Means

You've probably noticed that people and corporations — *big* corporations — are suddenly all over the green. Perhaps that's happening because environmentalists' ideas about conserving energy and reducing waste are catching on and people want to begin making changes. Of course, it's also possible that businesses have discovered that green sells. And many people are discovering that real green technology is more efficient and can save them some real cash.

The result is that more and more people are becoming aware that they need to make good choices about the way they use the earth's resources — water, energy, land, and air. That's where green computing fits in.

The overall goal of green home computing is to use our systems efficiently and effectively, being smart about the energy we're consuming and responsible about the way we dispose of the components we no longer need.

Green home computing asks you to interrupt your day-to-day habits and consider these five simple ways you can reduce your consumption, make the most of what you have, and be more conscious of your earth-impacting computing choices:

1. Reuse what you can.
2. Rebuild or restore systems and peripheral devices.
3. Share resources.
4. Replace energy hogs with energy-efficient equipment.
5. Recycle safely.

Setting a green standard

A number of standards-setting organizations have been focused on greening technology for a while, and in this book, you find out how the resources each provides can guide you toward greener home computing.

✔ **Energy Star:** One organization you may already be familiar with is Energy Star. Created in 1992 by the U.S. Environmental Protection Agency (EPA), Energy Star offers consumers a way to know whether the manufactured item that they're purchasing meets energy-efficient standards. You see the Energy Star logo on any electrical appliance or computer that meets the EPA's standards. Other countries have adopted similar standards to encourage conscientious use of energy.

To find out more about the Energy Star rating, go to www.energystar.gov.

✔ **EPEAT:** EPEAT is a program sponsored by the Green Electronics Council, which focuses on issues of electronics and sustainability. EPEAT is a green electronics "certification" program that helps consumers learn more about the energy use of laptops, monitors, and desktop computers they are considering purchasing.

✔ **Greenpeace Guide to Green Electronics:** In the summer of 2006, the international environmental group Greenpeace began rating technology companies to gauge their progress in promises to reduce emissions, increase energy efficiency, and discontinue using toxic chemicals in their product manufacturing processes. In Figure 1-1, the Guide to Green Electronics chart from Version 11 shows the results of the March 2009 rating. As you can see, by this rating, Nokia and Samsung lead the earth-friendly tech companies, and Nintendo and HP pull up the rear.

Figure 1-1: Greenpeace connects the dots in the November 2008 Guide to Greener Electronics.

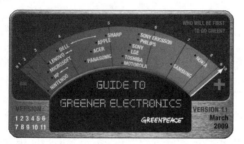

To see more of Greenpeace's Guide to Greener Electronics, go to

```
www.greenpeace.org/international/campaigns/
       toxics/electronics/how-the-companies-line-up
```

Finding good green info

Searching online is always a good place to start when you want to find out more about any aspect of anything. But *green* is a popular topic, and it's growing by leaps and bounds. In fact, if you just enter the word *green* in a search engine and press Enter, you'll get more than one billion (yes, with a "b") results! How can you narrow your search and find good information on the topics you want to research? Here are a few ideas to get you started:

✔ **Keep an eye out for greenwashing.** *Greenwashing* is the phrase used to describe companies that are using earth-friendly language to describe products that really aren't. In other words, their environmental consciousness is more marketing ploy than green effort. Throughout this book, you'll learn ways you can determine that a company is truly offering a green product or service, but in short, green companies who deliver on their promises care about energy efficiency, use materials and manufacturing processes that minimize the use of resources and the production of waste, and make it easy for consumers to dispose of equipment or devices they no longer use.

✔ **Stick with objective sources.** Computer manufacturers and vendors may give you the straight scoop on the green capabilities of the items they're selling, but when you're doing your homework to see how systems compare and what really matters in terms of energy efficiency, look for media sources (like `www.treehugger.com/buygreen`), university sites, or third-party research organizations that can supply data based on research.

✔ **Use wikis wisely.** Wikiagreen, at `http://green.wikia.com`, has a great green wiki that brings together all kinds of resources in one handy-dandy reference. As always, remember that open posting and editing of wiki entries means that not everything there is vetted; look for other sources to back up the information you find before you write a big check or otherwise wager something important.

✔ **Whenever possible, go straight to the source.** When you hear about a new study on global warming (released, for instance, by the Intergovernmental Panel on Climate Change), go directly to that organization's official site and see what they have to say. No need to search through blogs or articles when you can get the original document and see the charts and data yourself.

✔ **Know the names in the business**. If you're interested in one area more than another — say computer recycling is a big hot button for you — know who the experts are in that area and subscribe to their blogs, read their books, and follow the publications that their comments appear in.

As you dig deeper into green computing topics later in this book, you find help for researching specific topics and products, too.

Getting Started with Green Computing

Throughout this book, you build on the simple ideas of green computing in a variety of ways. Here you find an overview of how home computing can be greener and also how technology can improve efficiency and help you consume fewer resources.

What we cover in this section is just the tip of the rapidly melting iceberg. For details about how to get started with any of these topics, flip to the chapter we cross reference.

Assessing your impact

So now that you know a bit more about what's behind the need to green, you're probably wondering what you can do about it. Awareness is a good place to start. Take a moment and look around. Wherever you're reading — in the living room or your home office — notice the energy that's being used around you. What kind of lights are shining, and how many are there? Is the room (if you're in one) hot or cool? What's fueling that? Notice devices, computers, fans, and MP3 players. Anything that gleams, notice it. As I write this, I can see eight different devices that are drawing electric current (plus the furnace, which I can hear and feel but not see).

In Chapter 2, you can explore in detail the impact you make on your environment every day. You find steps for using a carbon footprint calculator to find out where you can conserve energy and see how your habits and practices contribute to increased carbon in the atmosphere.

In Chapter 4, you find tips and steps for assessing your home and home computing setup, including all the points where you're consuming power. Make tuning in to the power use in your surroundings part of your normal coming-and-going routine. Noticing your surroundings when you first enter a room, and again as you're ready to leave, will help you stay awake to the energy you can conserve. For example, when you leave an average 150-watt computer running for a year, it uses an amount of energy equal to half a ton of coal (that's 1,000 pounds) or more than 100 gallons of oil.

According to the Consumer Electronics Association's April 2008 *Market Research Report: Trends in CE Use, Recycle and Removal*, the average U.S. household includes approximately 24 electronic products.

If you're in your own home, of course, you can control the lights, the systems drawing power, the temperature, and the number of peripherals you leave on all day.

Exercising your purchasing power

People are voting green with their dollars more than ever before. The public reaction to earth-friendly products may be occurring, in part, because *An Inconvenient Truth,* the popular movie about the problem of global warming, struck a chord. Perhaps the public is tired and suspicious of potentially hazardous chemicals, or craves a simpler, more pure life. Whatever the reasons, green marketing is at an all-time high, and you can be sure that green initiatives are growing.

When you purchase a new computer or mobile device, do the legwork to find out the science behind the manufacturer's promises. Find information from objective sources to help you evaluate the best and most environmentally responsible choice for your home and family. Read user ratings and reviews; talk to other users if possible; and put time into weighing out the right choice. Your new computer or device will be part of your life for a while — maybe several years — using energy you'll be paying for. Some manufacturers offer trade-in programs when you purchase new computers; they'll dispose of your old computer safely for you.

In Chapter 6, you find tips for cutting through the greenwashing and finding a truly green new computer. In Chapter 10, you can check out a few green gadgets to go with your new computer and other devices.

Thinking efficiency

We don't think people set out to be deliberately wasteful. But in the world in which we live, efficiency takes a little work, at least up front. It doesn't help that technology changes so rapidly that keeping up can be a part-time job. That's why we show you ways technology can help you achieve efficiency and then forget about it, or least achieve efficiency with as little maintenance as possible.

Chapter 4 helps you take stock and begin thinking about the systems in your house, whether it's your computer system or your method for recharging devices or plugging in all your electronics. You find out how to

✔ Become aware of your own energy use.

✔ Take steps to increase energy efficiency at home.

✔ Begin to look for alternatives to energy use or spending.

✔ Discover how much power your computer needs.

You can also improve efficiency by doing the following:

✔ Rebuild, purchase, or streamline systems and peripherals to green them up. (See Chapters 5 and 6.)

✔ Share resources to coordinate systems and peripheral use. (See Chapter 7.)

✔ Improve your system and manage its power. (Check out Chapter 9, which helps you set the power management features that come with your operating system.)

Being efficient with your computer use means powering up when you need it, consolidating tasks, and powering down when you're through. It means using only what you need and coordinating your peripheral use. With a little reorganizing and changing the way you work with your computer, you can get a little greener.

Reducing consumption

Consumers come in all stripes. Chances are, if you're looking for ways to be more efficient in the way you use your computer and other technologies, you can also trim back the way you consume collateral products and resources. For example:

✔ **Paper recycling and conservation** can make a huge difference not only in the volume of paper you go through in your office, but also in the way you feel about your green efforts and your overall impact on important, big-picture issues like reforestation and sustainable resources. You can reduce your paper consumption by as much as 50 percent when you adopt a simple plan to use only recycled paper for in-office documents; print on both sides of the page; and use electronic documents whenever possible. And that's not small potatoes, in terms of good care of the earth. In Chapter 11, we discuss greener printing in more depth.

✔ **Virtualization and telecommuting** can make the most of your time and resources. Working in a virtual environment and telecommuting enables you to complete your work without traveling to the office, which saves gas, travel time, and CO_2 emissions. You learn all about telecommuting — including making the case to your boss — in Part IV.

Reducing waste (and watching where you throw it)

Waste of all kinds is a huge problem. Landfills are brimming; communities are sprawling; wildlife has less room to roam and do what wildlife does. The problem of computer dumping has become a mountain of an issue for developing countries. Because most computers — even those sold today — are manufactured with a number of toxic chemicals, they're a hazard when they're dumped without thought about proper disposal. Although it's illegal to do so, much of the toxic e-waste that we generate when we mindlessly toss out our computers, cellphones, televisions, and other devices is packaged and shipped to China and Africa, where families burn the materials to retrieve the precious metals and earn a small wage. The result is that children are growing up in villages where the streets are mounded with huge hills of discarded tech equipment, and the air has a sickening smog of burning chemicals.

For a disturbing look at the illegal practice of computer dumping, see this video report from *60 Minutes* at www.engadget.com/2008/11/10/video-chinas-toxic-wastelands-of-consumer-electronics-revealed.

To avoid these problems, you can make sure you get the most out of the computing equipment you have (see Chapter 5) and recycle your computers and devices safely. A number of computer manufacturers and vendors offer reuse and recycling programs that enable you to donate or recycle your electronics. Getting rid of your equipment safely is such a big issue that we devote all of Chapter 8 to this topic.

Speaking Green Jargon

Even though the word *green* can mean you're anything from financially flush to jealous to inexperienced to seasick, when you're talking about earth-friendly phrases, there's a whole new language developing. Here are a few green (as in, environment-friendly) words and phrases you can throw around at your next dinner party:

- **Biofuel** is energy created from renewable, biological sources, like plants, and used for heat, electricity, or fuel.

- **Biomimicry** uses designs based on patterns and processes in nature to solve human problems (for example, studying a leaf to design solar cells).

- **Brown power/energy** is the type of energy that results from the combustion of nonrenewable fuels (oil, gas, coal) and contributes to greenhouse gases.

- **Carbon footprint** refers to the human contribution to the emission of greenhouse gases in the atmosphere.

- **Closed-loop recycling** uses a recycled product to manufacturer a new product.

✓ **Closed-loop supply chain** is a supply process in which all wastes created during the production of a product are reused, recycled, or composted.

✓ **Ecological footprint** is the overall human use of natural resources compared to the capability of the earth to replenish or renew them.

✓ **Fair trade** is an international trading partnership that focuses on equitable trade, especially among producers who have often been exploited in the traditional market system.

✓ **Geothermal energy** is a natural form of heat energy from steam and hot water sources below the earth's surface.

✓ **Global warming** is the increasing temperature of the earth's surface and atmosphere as a result of greenhouse gases.

✓ **Green design** is used to create products, buildings, services, and processes that are in tune with environmental needs, create greater efficiency, and reduce consumption.

✓ **Greenhouse effect** is the trapping of heat within the earth's atmosphere; this effect is caused by greenhouse gases such as carbon dioxide.

✓ **Renewable energy** is energy that comes from non-fossil fuel sources, and it renews naturally. It can include wind, hydro, geothermal, or solar energy.

✓ **Sustainability** refers to the ability to meet environmental, social, and economic needs effectively over time.

✓ **Zero waste** is a system of production that seeks to eliminate waste and toxic materials through conservation and recovery of resources.

Chapter 2

Checking Out Your Carbon Footprint

• •

• •

*T*he phrase *carbon footprint* caught on because it offers a simple way to share an important message: We all share in the responsibility to do something about global warming.

A footprint is a personal thing — nobody else has a footprint quite like yours. In the same way, your carbon footprint is unique. It's the total of all the CO_2 (carbon dioxide) that your activities directly and indirectly contribute to the environment.

We can't change the sizes of our real, physical footprints; however, we can change the sizes of the carbon footprints we currently make. By discovering where you're currently using outdated technologies or accidentally or unconsciously burning fuel that you don't need to burn, you can reduce your footprint's size and be a little kinder to the earth. Taking a closer look helps you learn more about ways you can shrink your footprint — by making simple choices about things like lightbulbs and power supplies. And the best thing about that is that if we all make small, simple changes to the way we use energy, it translates to a whopping reduction to carbon emissions all over the earth.

In this chapter, you find out a little bit about the science so you can see clearly what contributes to the CO_2 pumping into the atmosphere. You also discover online resources to help you calculate your footprint, and the sections in this chapter walk you through a couple of especially helpful calculators.

Knowing Your Carbon Footprint ABCs

Focusing on carbon emissions is important because carbon dioxide is a greenhouse gas.

You've probably heard about the *greenhouse effect* and know that it has something to do with global warming. It doesn't mean you should avoid greenhouses or that the earth will soon become a kind of hothouse in which only the most exotic among us can thrive. In the most basic terms, the *greenhouse effect* is the warming that happens when solar radiation is trapped by the atmosphere.

Here's how it works: In the natural course of events, sunlight shines down on the earth, and most of that light is absorbed and warms the surface of the planet; some of that warmth is then radiated back out into space. Not all of it reaches space, because *greenhouse gases,* which are made up of carbon dioxide (CO_2), methane, nitrous oxide, and fluorocarbons, trap a percentage of the warmth in the lower part of the atmosphere. The more greenhouse gases there are, the hotter the earth and air gets. And as the earth's temperature rises, the polar ice caps melt (you've seen the heartbreaking commercials showing the polar bears in trouble, no doubt); the seas rise; farming cycles are disrupted; and new strains of viruses and who-knows-what-else appear. And that may be just the *good* news.

Some of the components of greenhouse gases occur because of natural processes; in fact, simple water vapor is the single biggest contributor. But the second biggest contributor is CO_2, which can range from 9 to 26 percent of all greenhouse gases. The amount of CO_2 is one factor we can do something about — and that's what you're affecting when you reduce your carbon footprint.

The carbon cycle: Don't hold your breath!

Yes, when you exhale, you add carbon dioxide to the atmosphere. But that doesn't mean you have to breathe less — or hold your breath! Some carbon dioxide is part of the natural carbon cycle. Green landscapes, including trees, grass, plants, and shrubs, all absorb the carbon dioxide we exhale and convert it to oxygen during *photosynthesis,* which is the process plants use to turn sunlight, water, and carbon dioxide into oxygen and energy. Photosynthesis also helps reduce other chemicals — such as nitrogen oxides, ozone, and more — that contribute to greenhouse gases.

Even indoors, plants can refresh your air supply by converting the air you've already breathed to oxygen. But here's a lesson I learned the hard way — don't hang a plant directly above your workspace. One false move with the watering can, and that monitor is history!

The emission and reduction of gases is all part of a natural cycle, but this cycle can handle only so much carbon. Many things people do contribute to excess carbon in the atmosphere.

Connecting fossil fuels to carbon emissions

Fossil fuels that we burn for energy are the largest contributors of the type of CO_2 that we need to reduce. Materials we use for transportation, heating, cooking, and manufacturing burn some kind of fossil fuel. Fossil fuel consumption has skyrocketed over the last 50 years, and you're sure to recognize these fossil fuels:

- ✔ Oil
- ✔ Coal
- ✔ Natural gas

Figure 2-1 shows two charts based on data from the nonprofit group Institute for Energy Research; these charts break down of the ways that we produce and use energy in the U.S. As you can see, fossil fuels are the most abundantly produced resources, and electricity gets the lion's share of use. That's a great reason to get serious about reducing your carbon footprint!

Half of all the electricity used in the U.S. comes from burning coal. And even though coal is a *nonrenewable energy source* (meaning, when it's gone, it's *gone),* there's no chance that scientists can turn that boat around any time soon. Coal is dirty (if you've ever poured charcoal briquettes into the grill, you know that), and when it burns, it pumps bad stuff into the air, adding to global warming, creating acid rain, and polluting water.

When you use online calculators discussed later in this chapter, these calculators help you assess how your everyday activities use fossil fuels and make up your individual carbon footprint.

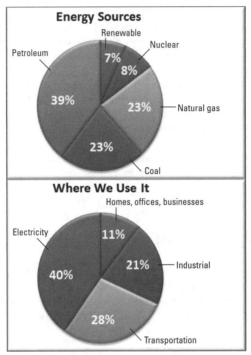

Figure 2-1:
Where
energy
comes from,
and where it
goes.

A lump of clean coal in your stocking

Have you heard the buzz about clean coal? If so, you might wonder how can coal be clean — and what turns it into a viable idea for green energy. Because coal is so cheap and handy (for now), it's relatively easy to get and easy to use. *Clean coal technology* puts the same dirty coal through a process that purifies it before it burns. Through techniques like coal washing and carbon storage, the damaging effects of coal can be dramatically limited (less acid rain) while other true green technologies develop.

As good as it sounds, clean coal is still a bit of a pipe dream. Right now, we don't have a practical way to contain carbon dioxide, but that could change. For instance, the World Resources Institute (WRI), an environmental think tank with a mission of working to protect the earth's environment, encourages a practice called *carbon capture and storage* (CCS). Using this approach, we can capture, transport, and lock away carbon in secure storage deep in the bowels of the earth (or, in scientist's lingo, "deep subsurface geological formations"), keeping the carbon separated from the planet's greenhouse gas layer, which is where it contributes to global warming.

As you can imagine, people passionately argue both sides of this possibility! Even the idea's supporters suggest that it's a temporary fix that would manage CO_2 production and release only until our green technologies develop enough to balance the release. Rachel Carson, where are you when we need you?

Facing the Facts: Calculate Your Carbon Footprint

It's a bit mind-blowing when you think about it: Everything really does matter, even small, seemingly inconsequential choices. Your choice to leave the computer on all day or turn it off before you leave for the office has an impact. Leaving your cell phone plugged in overnight when it's already fully charged really does matter. Using regular incandescent bulbs instead of energy-saving bulbs, forgetting to change your furnace filters, and buying lots of packaged foods has an effect — on your personal health, the health of your home, and the overall health of the planet.

So where can you start? Begin by finding out how much you're already doing, and how much more you can do, to shrink your carbon footprint. A number of environmental groups have developed carbon footprint calculators to help you discover how much of an impact you already make on the environment. The following sections walk you through using a few popular calculators.

Different calculators use different means to evaluate your carbon footprint, so don't be surprised if you receive unique numbers on various sites. Use the results to learn more about ways you can further reduce your carbon output instead of focusing on the numbers.

The Nature Conservancy's carbon footprint calculator

The Nature Conservancy site publishes a variety of resources that promote respectful care of nature and all life. The Nature Conservancy's carbon footprint calculator, which is available at http://nature.org/initiatives/climatechange/calculator, is all about choice. By thinking through the simple little choices you make on a daily basis as you drive around town taking the kids to school and soccer practice, as you print the draft of the report for this afternoon's meeting, as you consider whether to fix pasta or pot roast for supper, you can reduce the greenhouse gases that your actions contribute to the environment.

The Nature Conservancy's calculator helps you think through four key areas in your life: home energy, driving and flying, food and diet, and recycling and waste — and it gives you the option to calculate your whole family's footprint. Although the Nature Conservancy is a U.S. carbon calculator, Table 2-1 offers some carbon calculators used in the European Union.

Table 2-1	EU Carbon Calculators
UK Act On COs	`http://actonco2.direct.gov.uk/carboncalc/html`
Carbon Calculator	`www.mycarbonfootprint.eu/index.cfm?language=en`
Click 4 Carbon Calculator	`www.click4carbon.com/CarbonCalculator.php`
Global Action Plan	`www.carboncalculator.com`
Simple Carbon Calculator	`www.nef.org.uk/greencompany/co2calculator.htm`

When using these calculators, choose the family option whenever possible — it will give you a more accurate assessment of the total impact of your household. And that means you and your family members can share in the glory as you watch your totals drop.

Doing the carbon math

Ready to find out where you stand? Follow these steps to discover the size of your carbon footprint at Nature Conservancy:

1. **Open your Web browser and go to `http://nature.org/initiatives/climatechange/calculator`.**

   The Carbon Footprint Calculator: What's My Carbon Footprint? page opens with the Get Started tab displayed.

2. **Click the drop-down menu arrow and choose the number of people in your household.**

3. **Click the Calculate for Me Only button if you want to calculate your own carbon footprint, or click the Calculate for My Household button if you want to calculate the footprint for your entire household.**

   As Figure 2-2 shows, on the Home Energy tab, you answer a series of questions about the type of home you have and the efforts you've already taken to reduce your energy use.

After you answer the first two questions, the calculator figures your estimated household impact. Don't panic! The number seems huge (especially if you've already done a little homework and know what a good range is supposed to be), but as you go through the other questions, the calculator subtracts from the total when you give green answers. (And it sometimes adds to the total when you give not-so-green responses.)

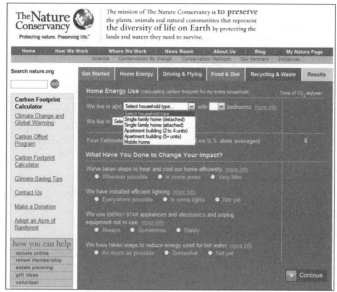

Figure 2-2:
Calculating carbon contributions at home.

4. **Answer the remaining questions on the Home Energy tab.**

   The two indicators at the bottom of the page (see Figure 2-3) show you how well (or how poorly) you're doing, compared to the national averages for home energy use and greenhouse gas emissions.

Figure 2-3:
Keep an eye on your progress.

   Notice that the state you live in has a big impact on the totals because some states have technologies in place to generate cleaner electricity than others. If you're not sure whether your electricity provider offers a green energy program, ask!

5. **Click Continue to move on to the Driving & Flying tab.**

   If you have a house full of teenagers, multiple cars, or a big family Hummer, take a deep breath before answering the next set of questions. It's not going to be pretty.

If you want to learn more about how these transportation choices make an impact, hover your mouse over the More Info link located to the right of any question. It's not necessary to click the link; the additional information pops up in a tip box. To close the box, simply move the mouse pointer to another location on the page.

6. **Answer the questions in the Driving & Flying tab.**

   Here you get the chance to enter the number of cars you have and the number of miles you drive, and you can choose the time period you're measuring. You're asked how well you do (or don't) service your car. Let the calculator know how often you fly.

   Are you a homebody? The environment thanks you. You still need to change your car's air filter and keep the tires inflated, though.

7. **Click Continue to move to the Food & Diet tab.**

   These questions relate to your eating habits, whether you cook and eat at home or dine out. Food preparation and consumption is a big part of CO_2 emissions because of the interrelated nature of growing, preparing, and consuming food.

   In general, eating locally produced foods — both produce and meat — is better for the environment. On average, food offered in restaurants travels across three states to get to your plate!

8. **Click Continue to move to the Recycling & Waste tab.**

   Chances are that you're already tuned in to recycling cans, bottles, and plastics. Most U.S. cities offer recycling programs that enable residents to recycle almost as easily as they put out the trash. On this tab, let the calculator know how much you recycle and whether you're currently composting.

9. **Click Continue and read your results!**

Want to see how your state ranks in terms of carbon emissions? Visit the Interactive United States Energy Use Comparison Chart at www.eredux.com/states.

Deciphering your results

So how did you do? It's possible that your carbon footprint shocks you — especially if you live in a U.S. state where green technologies haven't quite caught on yet. The final page of the Nature Conservancy's carbon footprint calculator shows you the total greenhouse gas emissions for the grouping you selected (individual or household) and ranks your results against national and world averages. (See Figure 2-4.) At the bottom of the page, you can see clearly how your behaviors in the various areas contribute to CO_2 emissions, and you can compare that against national averages.

Quick calculations

If you have only a few minutes of your lunch break left and want to do a quick calculation, go straight to the horse's mouth (www.climate crisis.net/takeaction/carbon calculator) and click Take Action. Click the Calculate Your Personal Impact link and use the Calculate Your Impact page to enter your totals quickly and get a fast estimate of your footprint size. It's not as detailed as the Nature Conservancy's calculator, but it gives you the big picture — and that's a start.

If you're motivated to do more, click the Native Energy link at the bottom of the calculator and find out how you can contribute to CO_2 offsetting programs, purchase green products, and more.

The point of calculating your carbon footprint is to give you a starting point of action, to find out where you can reduce and where you can conserve. The Nature Conservancy offers links to get you started on the road to increasingly earth-friendly choices.

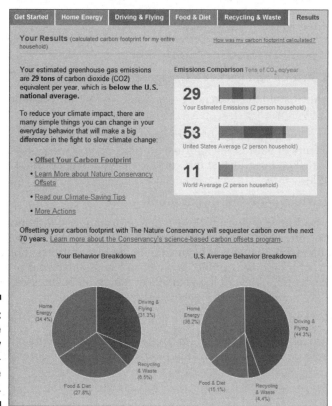

Figure 2-4: Home energy comparisons can be sobering.

Moving toward personal sustainability

Getting a quick picture of your carbon emissions with the Nature Conservancy's calculator is a great place to start, but what if you look at the greening of your efforts as a long-term relationship? Like any other big thing we try to change about our lives, changing our thinking about our impact on the environment is an ongoing project.

The site MakeMeSustainable.com helps you think through that kind of paradigm shift in your life, getting you in touch with how you feel about the environment. It provides you with fun and effective tools to help you manage it. A strong part of Make Me Sustainable is the community component, which helps you reinforce your dedication to green efforts by connecting with friends, family members, and like-minded people in your state, nation, or around the globe.

Make Me Sustainable calls its carbon footprint calculator the Carbon and Energy Portfolio Manager (CEPM). The online tool tracks your energy use and options over time, calculates your savings, and provides you with a range of sustainable actions that you can add to your routine.

To get started with the CEPM, follow these steps:

1. **Go to www.makemesustainable.com.**

2. **Click Sign Up and answer a few questions about yourself.**

   MakeMeSustainable.com is free, so don't worry that you'll be asked to subscribe for a fee.

   When you sign up, a profile is created for you, which you use to track the effects of your green efforts over time. As you work on your profile, you're asked questions about your home, your transportation, and your lifestyle.

3. **Review and personalize your profile.**

   Your profile page doesn't show much information at first, but this is where your sustainable efforts begin. On the profile page, you can invite friends to join you, join the community, and track green choices that you want to add to your life. You can also customize your profile by adding a photo, describing yourself, and inviting businesses to join you and "grow your tree," as Figure 2-5 shows.

4. **Click Take Action.**

   The Home Office tab of the Take Action page lists a number of ways you can reduce your energy consumption at home. (See Figure 2-6.)

Figure 2-5:
MakeMe
Sustainable.
com tracks
your energy
savings over
time in the
community.

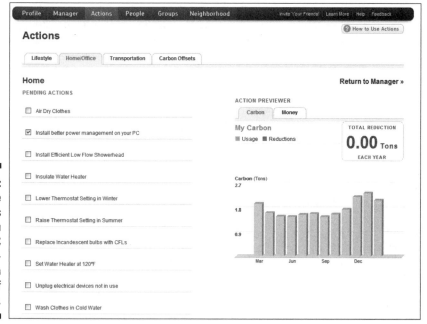

Figure 2-6:
The site
suggests
that you
reduce PC
power con-
sumption
right off
the bat.

5. Click Install Better Power Management on Your PC.

Three steps appear, enabling you to preview, pledge, and perform the step that MakeMeSustainable.com suggests for reducing PC power use.

- *Preview:* Gives you more information about the task.

- *Pledge or Already Do:* Enables you to either commit to taking the step or let the manager know that you already practice this technique in your everyday life.

- *Performed:* Marks the task as completed and grays it out in the list.

On MakeMeSustainable.com, beginning with a huge carbon footprint isn't such a bad thing because it can show the greater amount of improvement over time. Think positive!

Depending on the type of computer you use, you can reduce power consumption several different ways. Windows 7 includes great new power management tools; Windows Vista enables you to customize your PC power plan; Windows XP enables you to create power saving schemes; and the Mac OS X Energy Saver pane lets you choose the power management settings that work for you. For more about managing power for your computer, see Chapter 9.

6. Select additional actions and choose Preview, Pledge or Already Do, or Performed for each one.

As you add action items, the chart on the right side of the page shows the carbon reductions that are adding up. (See Figure 2-7.)

Figure 2-7: Make Me Sustainable shows the effects of the actions you take.

7. **Click the Money tab to see how much your green actions are saving on your utility costs.**

All this green initiative has a bottom-line value for you as well.

Tallying your ecological footprint

With just a little bit of searching, you'll discover another kind of calculator, one that measures your *ecological footprint.* The ecological footprint is different from a carbon footprint in that it measures the full range of human consumption of resources and compares that against the Earth's capacity to generate those resources. According to the Global Footprint Network, an international organization working to influence decision makers toward sustainability, the ecological footprint of the earth's human population is now 23 percent over capacity.

You can take the Ecological Footprint Quiz (at www.myfootprint.org) to find out how much of a demand your lifestyle makes on the natural world around you.

You may find that some calculators figure carbon footprints based on a life-cycle assessment (LCA) model, which takes ecological impact into account. When you look at carbon emissions from a life-cycle perspective, you take into account all energy and resources used (for example, the metals, energy, plastic, and more used to create your computer) from the time the item is created until the time you responsibly dispose of it.

Reducing Your Footprint

Once you know the size of your carbon footprint, you can begin to look for ways to reduce the impact you're having on the world around you. Whether you're way over the national or world averages or biking along in a pretty green space, you can make improvements to economize the energy you use and reduce the bills you pay.

Basically, we're talking about making chances in three key areas:

- **The way you run your home:** In this arena, technology can help in many ways. Check out Chapter 3, which shows you how technology and your energy use intersect. Parts II and III of this book help you keep your home or home office greener with PC power management, greener technology purchases, and more.

Other green home features, such as insulation, landscaping, and building materials, are beyond the scope of a computing book. If you want to explore ways to further green your home, check out *Green Building & Remodeling For Dummies* by Eric Corey Freed (also published by Wiley).

✔ **The way you use transportation:** Part IV of this book focuses on telecommuting and teleconferencing because they provide great ways to reduce your travel and thus your carbon footprint.

✔ **The way you feed yourself and your family:** Okay, the primary way your computer can help you here is with research. We include several online resources for green information in Chapter 19 of this book. On Dummies.com, you can find great green living how-to's. Also, check out *Green Living For Dummies* by Yvonne Jeffery, Liz Barclay, and Michael Grosvenor.

Are you a to-do lists and reminders kind of person? If so, set up a recurring appointment in your calendaring software on your computer, phone, or other electronic gadget. Getting a gentle reminder to "Drop off recycling today" or attend the "Farmer's market, 10-12" can help with your commitment to a greener environment.

Offsetting your carbon habit

Finding out about the size of your family's carbon footprint is a great place to start, and taking active steps toward reducing the way you contribute to greenhouse gas emissions is even better. Some folks take the effort a step further in an attempt to get to a point of carbon neutrality, by paying carbon offsets.

Carbon offsets offer you one way to lessen the impact of your carbon footprint — by supporting projects that reduce CO_2 emissions in a variety of ways. Your carbon offset, for example, might support a program that plants trees, refits power plants for green energy, improves energy efficiency in public transportation, or supports the development of new renewable energy sources.

Programs that encourage carbon offsetting do provide a reasonable response to a challenging problem, but they also take a lot of heat (metaphorically speaking). One concern is that people and businesses will throw money at the problem of greenhouse gas emissions instead of working actively to reduce their use of natural and energy resources. To find out more about carbon offsetting and gauge your own reaction, open your favorite Web search engine, type **carbon offsets**, and have at it!

Chapter 3

The Straight Scoop on Power

*H*ave you had a power outage lately? If you live in an area where storms roll through regularly, you may be accustomed to those surprising moments when everything goes black in the house — from power up to power down — in a split second. Lightning flashes give you enough power to find the candles, and then you sit and wait . . . and wait and sit . . . making plans for what you'll do when the power comes back on and you can resume your life.

If this sounds familiar, you're not alone. The average U.S. household consumes 10,656 kilowatt-hours (kWh) per year, which is 1.22 kWh per hour (or .02 kWh per minute!). The refrigerator, the computer, and the DVD player use energy while you sleep. Your house operates around you, in many ways, thanks to the lifeline of power on demand 24 hours a day, seven days a week.

This chapter takes a deep dive into the power issue — what it is, where it comes from, and where it goes. You discover which appliances and gadgets in your house are using power right now and how you can better manage your power consumption — through your choices and actions — so that the power you consume is more in line with your hopes for the earth (and your utility budget!).

Checking Out Sources of Electricity

Chances are that you remember the stories of Benjamin Franklin and the key and Thomas Edison and the light bulb. But do you know what electricity is, where it comes from, and why knowing that is an important part of energy conservation?

The electricity that supports your lifestyle right this very minute is a manu-factured product and not a *natural renewable resource* (one that we can con-tinue to use and that replenishes itself naturally, such as wind). An electrical generator somewhere in your area uses a technology based on magnetics and copper wire to create the spark of life that keeps your technology going: the light shining on this page, the charge in your cellphone, the current keep-ing your laptop charged, and the electricity running the ceiling fan.

When you flip the switch or plug in the cord, you open the gate for the electric-ity to flow to the device, appliance, or computer hardware. For the end user, it's pretty simple. But when you take a look at where energy for electricity comes from (which we do in the following sections), you may find you have a lot more to consider than simply paying your electric bill on time. You also find tips to help you consider whether solar energy for your home could be worthwhile.

Creating electricity

Electricity is a *secondary power source* — meaning that other primary energy sources are used to generate it. In the United States, electricity generated in 2008 came from multiple sources:

- ✔ 48.4 percent came from coal
- ✔ 21.4 percent from natural gas
- ✔ 19.4 percent from nuclear energy
- ✔ 1.5 percent from oil
- ✔ 9.3 percent from other sources, including wind, geothermal, and solar

Want the numbers? At www.eia.doe.gov/cneaf/electricity/epm/table1_2.html, you'll find a table published by the Energy Information Administration, the statistical agency of the U.S. Department of Energy, show-ing the sources used to generate electricity, state by state.

AC/DC: More than a band

Have you ever been curious about the difference between AC and DC power? It's not as complicated as it sounds. AC stands for *alternating current* and refers to the wave created as the current oscillates between –170 and 170 volts. AC is the type of power you draw from the wall outlet when you plug an appliance or a computer into the socket. DC, the type of power used in batteries, stands for *direct current,* which is the power that flows, for example, from the negative to the positive terminal on a battery.

We can generate electricity from many different sources, but all those sources, except solar technologies (which use photovoltaic cells to store energy), use a process in which a turbine spins and converts movement energy into electric energy. Steam, gas, and diesel turbine generators all use this process, as do nuclear power plants and alternate energy systems. When power plants create electricity by burning fossil fuels such as coal, oil, and natural gas, they boil water to produce high-pressure steam, which turns the turbines in the generator that creates the electricity. Nuclear reactors (which use nuclear fission to split atoms, releasing a great amount of energy) and hydroelectric power plants (which use moving water to generate electricity) use similar turbine-based procedures without burning fossil fuels.

When you look at how green these methods of generating electricity are, the differences among these energy sources become apparent:

✓ **Renewable versus nonrenewable energy:** Today, you see the terms *renewable* and *nonrenewable energy* everywhere. The difference between the two (not surprisingly) is that one type of energy continually replenishes naturally (like wind and water) and the other doesn't — when it's gone, it's gone (for example, oil, natural gas, and coal). Figure 3-1 shows you all the different types of mining operations that are going on to, among other things, keep Windows gleaming on your monitor.

Scientists tell us that available oil and natural gas supplies are limited and dwindling, although coal promises a longer supply, with experts estimating that the earth's coal supply will last well into the next century. You find large amounts of coal in the United States, Europe, Russia, China, and South Africa — anyplace that was covered with swampland a couple hundred million years ago. But just because today coal is handy and readily available — and cheap — still doesn't mean it will always be around. It's still a nonrenewable resource. Also, mining coal is difficult and dangerous, as headlines often attest.

✔ **By-products of different energy sources:** Most of the technologies that we use to generate electricity pump CO_2 into the atmosphere, including any technology that burns fossil fuels. (Chapter 2 covers the problems with greenhouse gases such as CO_2.)

The largest energy source in the United States — coal — has incredibly high costs: CO_2 production, carbon monoxide, and soot (which is really just unburned carbon that's released into the air we breathe). Remember acid rain? Thank coal. Smog in your city in the summer? Another coal contribution. And coal isn't smart consumption, either; yet another downside is that it takes an enormous amount of coal to create the same amount of energy using other technologies, which means that it carries a heftier CO_2 price tag than other fossil fuel–burning energy sources. Although you may have heard talk of clean coal (see the nearby sidebar), the viability of this option is debatable. Not a pretty picture (nor a good, long-term option) if what you want is a sustainable, green, healthy world.

The challenge you face in greening your computing practices is that creating and using electricity does impact the environment, not only by using up nonrenewable fuel sources but also by releasing harmful by-products. The good news is that renewable energy sources can be replenished and have less hazardous by-products. The bad news is that renewable energy isn't widely available as a primary energy source — although in some places solar panels may be a worthwhile expense. In the next sections, you find steps that walk you through various incentives and tools to help you assess whether solar is an option for you. If reducing your energy use is the best way to make a big difference, be sure to read the tips throughout the rest of this chapter for monitoring and reducing your energy use and find out how your home computer and Internet connection can help you in these efforts.

Thinking about renewable energy

As the green movement began to blossom in the U.S., the phrase *renewable energy* became popular. Today, we have options for the ways in which we generate electricity, many of which are considered renewable methods. But development is fairly slow, and the technologies still aren't widely adopted. Burning fossil fuel is still considered the easiest and cheapest way to power our homes and PCs, if you think in terms of short-term cost and not long-term environmental damage. But in 2008, 9.3 percent of the electricity used in the U.S. was generated with renewable energy technologies (hydroelectric, wind, solar, geothermal, and biomass). That's an encouraging sign, but we're just getting started exploring the long-term ramifications of the various renewable technologies. Be sure to research the different options available in your area, ask questions of your utility service providers, and think about the big-picture impact of the energy source you choose.

Today, the earth *does* ask us to consider the long-term effects of our choices, and renewable energy sources come from clean, nonpolluting sources that never run out. What's more, renewable energy is safe and can be produced domestically. Sounds good, right?

Table 3-1 introduces you to the various types of renewable energy now in development. The sections that follow describe a little more about each technology and the possibilities each offers for eventually powering our homes, PCs, and mobile devices.

Table 3-1	Types of Renewable Energy
Type	*Description*
Biomass	Organic matter, such as plant and animal waste, is burned or changed into gases to produce electricity.
Fuel cell	Chemical reactions combine hydrogen and oxygen to create electricity.
Geothermal	Pipes bring to the earth's surface dry steam or hot water, which powers a turbine that drives a generator to produce electricity.
Hydroelectric	Water flowing through dams turns turbines and generates electricity.
Solar	Photovoltaic cells gather sunlight and generate electricity.
Wind	Wind power turns two- or three-blade propellers mounted on rotors, which turn wind turbines that generate electricity.

A reality check on clean coal

The term *clean coal* might seem like an oxymoron, and some experts and advocacy groups agree that the terms definitely contradict. Check out the public service announcements that ThisIsReality.org, a site maintained by the Reality Coalition, posts at `http://action.this isreality.org/index/?source= reality&subsource=action`. Then follow it up with more information on what is required, long and short term, to get coal to clean up its act. The Reality Coalition is a collaborative project launched by the Alliance for Climate Protection, the Sierra Club, the National Wildlife Federation, the Natural Resources Defense Council, and the League of Conservation Voters. The following link gives you a good place to start if you want to find out more: `http:// action.thisisreality.org/about`.

In Chapter 2, we tell you about *carbon offsets*, which are programs that let you contribute financially to green energy programs and pay down the cost of your CO_2 impact on the environment. Supporting carbon offsets funds the development and deployment of these green technologies.

Ready, set, sun!

Solar electricity has been around for a long time, but it's been slow to catch on, particularly because it's incredibly expensive. (And also because solar panels used to be incredibly ugly. Did you see those solar homes in the 1970s?)

Solar energy is harnessed mainly through photovoltaic (PV) cells, which collect and control the energy, converting it through the use of a charge converter and distributing sunlight-generated electricity (both AC current produced by an inverter and battery DC power) to electrical appliances, lights, and more. (See Figure 3-2.) In recent years, solar batteries have become popular for use in landscape lighting — no wires needed, no fossil fuels burned, and they're not too bad looking! But what happens when you have four or five rainy days in a row? Yeah, your landscape is pretty dim at night.

On the upside, solar energy is a clean technology and contributes no greenhouse gases to the atmosphere. The solar cells have no moving parts (think of yourself stretched out on a blanket by the ocean) and require little maintenance and upkeep.

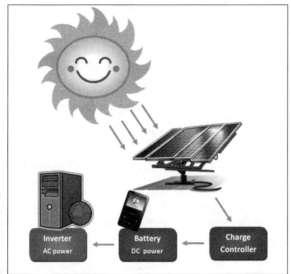

Figure 3-2:
You want
solar fries
with that?

One of the challenges of solar power is that it's still fairly expensive to produce. Although concern over burning fossil fuels is making solar energy power plants more appealing as a long-term sustainable energy source, estimated costs per kilowatt-hour are still higher than most consumers are prepared to pay.

Another type of solar energy, called *active solar heating,* involves heating and storing water or air in a collector and then transferring the stored heat directly into the space or storage system. Commercial systems are available in some areas and may help offset your other utility costs. It's worth a search on the Web, anyway.

If you're a PC owner, you can create your own solar-powered computer, if your pockets are deep enough (do you have an extra $5,000 sitting around?), and you have the technical expertise to pull it off. To find out more, check out the DIY Solar-Powered PC article at `www.tomshardware.com/reviews/technical-foundations-diy-solar-powered-pc,1693.html`.

Winds of change

Wind power is another contestant in Renewable Energy of the Stars. Like solar power, this technology is a familiar one that's taking on new purpose and life. Farmers have long used windmills to generate power on farms all across the globe, enabling them to pump water, grind grain, and accomplish other power-dependent tasks by harnessing a readily available natural resource. Today's wind turbines are mounted on tall towers 100 feet (30 meters) or more above ground so that they can catch the less turbulent, faster wind. The air currents move the propeller-like blades (usually two or three), which turn on a rotor.

Debunking wind myths

Although wind power is an affordable type of renewable energy that offers big benefits (no greenhouse gas emissions, few parts that require maintenance, and no fossil fuel burning), some people have concerns about wind power:

✔ **Wind turbines ruin the landscape.** What? You're not happy about seeing fields of green turn into fields of propellers? It's not as bad as all that. Wind farms — those slick fields of rotating-blade giants you've seen in green energy ads — are more the exception than the rule, but that may be changing. Yes, you'll likely see more wind farms in the future, both onshore and offshore, powering homes and businesses and schools. Wind turbines are available for personal use, but the turbines are small, with some mounting on a tower or a roof.

✔ **Wind turbines are dangerous for birds.** As earth-friendly authors, we care about the safety of all living creatures on the planet, but it does seem that birds are accustomed to flying around things: buildings, flag poles, fire towers, antennae. Although the swirling blades on wind turbines may look like, say, airplane engines (props to Captain Sully!), monitoring of wind farms in bird-happy areas has shown no negative effect on bird populations so far. If something comes up, though, we'll let you know.

✔ **Wind turbines are noisy.** Like anything else in the cycle of product development, early prototypes are often less elegant than final release versions. (Did you see Windows Vista?) Thankfully, we're a species that lives and learns, though, because today's modern wind turbines are much quieter (think *swoosh* instead of *urn-urn-urn*). If the turbine is seated properly (meaning that nothing's out of whack and it can turn unobstructed), it shouldn't make enough sound to disturb even the lightest sleeper. In fact, any sound is probably lost on the wind itself.

✔ **Wind power isn't reliable.** This is a common concern. So what happens when there's no wind? In some portions of the U.S., it's not unusual during the hottest period of the year to have a time that feels like a wind drought. If wind power is tied to wind and the wind doesn't blow, what happens? Do all our lights go out? One of the things we're learning right now with current conditions in energy consumption is that relying too heavily on any one resource — such as foreign oil or burning coal — creates an imbalance somewhere else. So although changes in the amount of wind are, yes, beyond our control and do vary, the chances that wind power will be the only resource supplying electricity generation is nil. A balanced, working energy system will use natural resources wisely and in complement, drawing what we need when we need it without pumping bad stuff into the atmosphere or creating a dependency we don't need. Plus, when wind power is widely used, wind turbines will be part of a larger grid — and the wind never stops blowing everywhere at once! (If it does, you know the world has stopped turning.)

One full-sized wind turbine generates more than 4.7 million watts of electricity each year. That's enough to run a PC for 1,620 years!

Wind-powered technology in the classroom is already a reality. One interesting project is the WindPC project in the United Kingdom. WindPC awards wind turbines and all that's needed to build, track, and report on the energy savings to schools that apply to the foundation and write about their green efforts. It's a great way to help kids participate in earth-friendly energy initiatives. You can read more about this project by visiting `www.rm.com/secondary/inthenews/article.asp?cref=mnews840348`.

Water your world

If you've ever held your hand under water as it runs out of the tap, you already know the basics of hydro power. Moving water generates force, and of course, the more water, the greater the force. Hydroelectricity technology harnesses the power of moving water (not necessarily *falling water*, by the way, although that really gets it moving!) and converts the energy into electricity.

Case in point: Niagara Falls. Although people have been going over the Falls in barrels since seemingly the dawn of crazy human tricks, Niagara Falls is a nothing-short-of-miraculous energy source for the state of New York. In fact, the Falls are New York State's biggest electricity provider, supporting homes, businesses, and government offices with more than 2.4 million kilowatts of electricity in a year. That in turn saves millions of dollars for everyone in that area of the country and keeps tons of CO_2 out of the atmosphere, which helps us all. See how great that works?

Hydro power works with the turbine system that we tell you about earlier in this chapter — the water moves the enormous turbines, which spin and feed the electrical generators, which pump out the electricity for you and me.

Okay, okay. Anyone who has ever spilled a glass of water on a keyboard knows that water and electronics don't mix. But they do have a common cousin — electricity. If you can convert water to electricity, you can use it to power your PC. Some people are already doing it. If you have running water near your home in the form of a lake or small stream, you may be able to install a home water power system (which may include a submersible propeller unit or a small water generator) and provide your whole home with power. Do a Web search for *home hydro power* and see what comes up!

Fitting solar panels on your roof

One of the criticisms — no, two — of solar energy is that it's expensive and ugly. Back in the days when people wore platform shoes and fringe jackets (oh, *those* were the days), people who really cared about the earth put solar panels on top of their houses. Although the panels in the '70s were oversized and unwieldy (well, what *wasn't* back then?), today's solar panels are sleek and much more affordable. Plus, depending on how progressive your utility company is, they may have an even better perk: payback.

Some utility companies today let you use your solar panels to generate electricity and sell it back to the company, which lowers your monthly bill. This process is often called *net metering*. The solar energy system you add needs to be in compliance with your utilities regulations to qualify. Visit the Database of State Incentives for Renewables & Efficiency (www.dsireusa.org), shown in Figure 3-3, to find out whether your state has a policy about net metering.

Figure 3-3: Help provide electricity for your utility company and get a break on your bill.

Here's a neat gadget you can try to see whether your home would be a good candidate for solar energy. Roofray.com uses Google Maps to locate your house and help you determine the right solar panel layout for your home. It's fun! Here's how to do it:

1. **Go to www.roofray.com.**

2. **In the Address field, type your house number, street, city, state, and zip code. Click Go.**

   The search process may take a minute or two because it uses Google Maps to locate your exact house. (See Figure 3-4.) Eerie, huh?

Figure 3-4:
Roofray.com
uses Google
Maps.

3. **Click one corner of the roof segment where you're thinking of putting solar panels.**

   A little marker appears at the spot you clicked.

4. **Continue clicking the roof corners.**

   A shaded section highlights the area that you select.

5. **Tell RoofRay.com the orientation (or *slope*) of your roof by dragging the handle of the red line toward the bottom of the roof.**

6. **Use the slider to indicate the *pitch* (or angle) of the roof.**

   If you're unsure of your roof's pitch, leave the slider set to 20, which is the average setting.

7. **Click Next.**

   For the next step, you need your utility bills. (You can estimate if you like, but taking the time to be accurate helps you better gauge your potential savings.)

8. **Enter your monthly electric bills (or estimate, if you'd like). Click Use This.**

   Calculations at the bottom of the window show you the percentage of savings, the power per square foot, the area of the panel section, the orientation of your roof, and the total power that you can collect at peak times.

9. **Click Next**

   The gadget calculates your savings and displays the estimated costs of your electric bills for the various months of the year. (See Figure 3-5.)

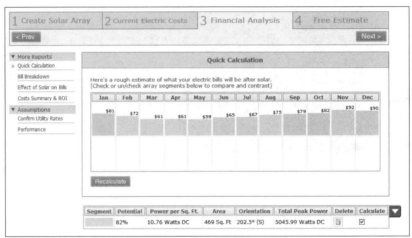

Figure 3-5: Roofray.com shows you an estimate of your monthly electric costs after you install solar panels.

10. **Click Next one final time.**

    The last step gives you the option of letting RoofRay.com know you'd like a free estimate. Whether you decide to go ahead with solar panels, you've got to admit that this is one slick online tool.

How Much Energy Are You Using, Anyway?

If you're like many people, learning the size of your carbon footprint can be a bit of a shock. (Find the steps for sizing up your own footprint in Chapter 2.) Literally everything we do consumes energy and outputs some kind of waste. Sitting there right now, your eyes are focusing and you're breathing and burning calories. (We won't go into discussing your output at this point, but we hope you're converting this idea energy into things you can do around your house to cut down on your energy use.)

The carbon footprint is different from an overall estimation of your energy consumption, however, because the calculations are designed to figure how much of an impact you're making on the environment in terms of greenhouse gas emissions. (So that's more about output; get it?)

Thinking through what you consume, and looking for ways to reduce what you can and manage the rest, is the focus of this section. You start by taking a look at the data you already have, consider the ways in which your existing applications (computers included) use energy, and then find out about several ways to use smart meters, your computer, and even your cellphone to monitor and manage your power use.

Tracking your bills in a spreadsheet

You can use some of the information from monthly bills and receipts to determine the amount of energy you use on a monthly, weekly, daily, even hourly basis. Follow these steps to set up a system for tracking your usage and monitoring your progress:

1. **Gather a few month's worth of the following:**

   • Electric bills

   • Natural gas bills

   • Water bills

   • Gasoline receipts

   • Pizza coupons (No, wait; that's a different book.)

2. **In a spreadsheet program, such as Excel, set up a grid like the one shown in Figure 3-6, with rows for each utility you want to track and columns for each month.**

   We like to chart our use in months because it's less pressure than hour-by-hour, and it gives you a sense of how things change over a longer period of time.

   Typically, residential electricity is billed in kilowatt hours (kWh). That's the number you want to track. If you have trouble finding the number of kilowatt hours on your electric bill, go to your electric company's Web site, where you can probably find a tip sheet to help you read your bill.

	A	B	C	D	E
1	How much power do we use?				
2					
3					
4		January	February	March	April
5	THIS YEAR				
6	Electricity (kWh)	3620	4017	3712	2693
7	Water (gals)	3900	3400	3520	3340
8	Gas (therms)	NA	NA	NA	NA
9					
10	GOAL				
11	Electricity (kWh)	3200	3500	3200	3000
12	Water (gals)	3000	3000	3000	3000
13	Gas (therms)	NA	NA	NA	NA
14					
15	LAST YEAR				
16	Electricity (kWh)	4140	4500	4250	4150
17	Water (gals)	4200	4350	4100	3000
18	Gas (therms)	NA	NA	NA	NA
19					

Figure 3-6: Every little bit helps, and tracking what you use is a good first step toward cutting back.

3. **To get a better look at where you're at and where you'd like to be, set up one table on the same spreadsheet that displays last year's energy use and another table that displays your goals.**

   As you can see in Figure 3-6, you can use this same table to track your water and gas usage. Your water utility may charge by the gallon, cubic foot, or some other unit. Natural gas is often billed in therms.

4. **Compare the three tables each month.**

Want to make the most of your competitive nature? Set a goal for yourself by creating a chart of your real and projected usage. Draw a line (make it a big green line) to mark your consumption goal and try to stay under it. When you achieve the goal one month, celebrate! Go out and hug a tree. (If you've never tried it, you might be surprised to discover how much fun it actually is.)

The worksheet in Figure 3-6 doesn't include gasoline consumption, but tracking the number of gallons of gas you use in a week — or in a month — is a good way to remind yourself to consider the real costs and long-range effects of burning fossil fuel. The amount of gas you buy is typically listed on your receipt.

Calculating costs and savings with a home energy audit

As you find out in this chapter, the secret of making good choices about the power you consume begins with identifying which items in your home use power, how much power they use, and how you can monitor and manage the energy consumption of those items.

Another way to get a detailed look at your power consumption options involves getting a home energy audit. Certified professionals in your state are glad to do this for a fee. See the Residential Energy Services Network at www. natresnet.org/directory/raters.aspx to find auditors in your state, or you can use a free online tool, such as Home Energy Saver, which is available at http://hes.lbl.gov. (See Figure 3-7.)

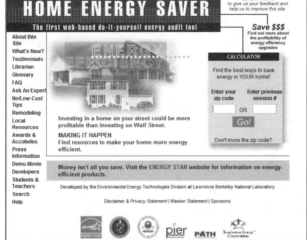

Figure 3-7:
Home
Energy
Saver
enables
you to do a
home audit
online.

To do a home energy audit, follow these steps:

1. **Go to the Home Energy Saver site at http://hes.lbl.gov.**

2. **Type your zip code in the box provided and click Go.**

3. **Enter information to help fine-tune the cost calculation for energy use in your home.**

   The calculations are based at first on averages for your area, but you can customize the detail about your home so that the calculations reflect your situation more accurately. You can continue to make changes even after you click Calculate.

4. **Click Calculate to see the results.**

   The results of the calculation show you the energy costs that you'll run up during a year in your particular area with a house that has the features you selected. The Web site compares these results to estimated costs after you make energy-efficient upgrades to the property.

5. **Click View Upgrade Report.**

The tool displays a list of all energy upgrades that you can consider based on the types of features you selected for your home (see Figure 3-8). The report shows you not only the amount of money you'll save but also your return on investment, how long the upgrades will take to pay for themselves, and the amount of CO_2 you'll save the environment.

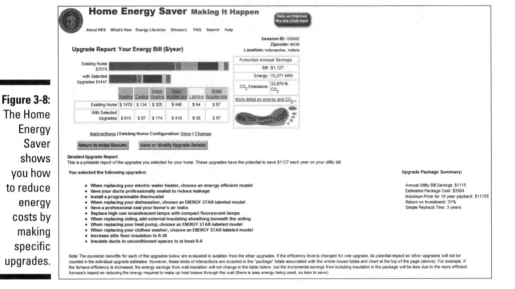

Figure 3-8:
The Home Energy Saver shows you how to reduce energy costs by making specific upgrades.

Monitoring usage with ploggs and smart meters

Becoming aware of something is the first step toward changing it, but without awareness, how do you know what you don't know? That's where power plugs and meters come in. A number of manufacturers (and some really big companies) are realizing that most people aren't laughing gleefully as they mindlessly gobble energy that they could share with the rest of the world. They simply don't realize the cost of their normal day-to-day operations.

So in an effort to empower consumers to make their own responsible energy choices, smart meters and ploggs were born. These smart devices plug into your electrical outlet and enable you to see easily how much power various devices in your home are drawing. This section introduces you to a few popular meters available today.

Considering the cost

This book tells you about wattage quite a bit, and you may wonder what wattage is actually all about. A watt is an instantaneous value. All this value tells you is the amount of power that a device uses at any given moment. However, power companies can't charge for power unless they quantify it. When you turn on a 100 watt device and leave it one for 1 hour, you've used 100 watt/hours. Power companies charge by the kilowatt/hour (a kilowatt is 1,000 watts). Let's say your power company charges $0.35 per kilowatt/hour. Turning on a 100 watt device for 1 hour costs you 100/1000 * 0.35 or $0.035. Three and a half cents doesn't sound like much, but it does add up.

Kill A Watt power meter

With the Kill A Watt power meter from P3 International, you can check your appliances to find out how much electricity they use. Plug Kill A Watt into an outlet and plug the appliance into the device; the meter tracks the electricity consumption and displays the result in kilowatt-hours (kWh). Kill A Watt is a low-cost option, available for as little as $40 in some online stores.

The Energy Detective

The Energy Detective (TED) from Energy, Inc. is a power meter that uses a transmitter and an LCD to track your energy use in real time and report it on the digital device. This product does require installation and involves electricity, so consider hiring an electrician to install the transmitter.

Energy, Inc. also offers TED Footprints, which is PC software that works with TED as you monitor your power use. It produces various reports and graphs, and you can even export the data to CSV (comma-separated values) format so that you can use it in other applications. The TED unit, including the transmitter and display, is available on the meter's Web site (www.theenergy detective.com) for $144.95; the TED Footprints software is $44.95.

Plogging along

A *plogg* is a combination power meter and data logger that measures the electricity you're using and sends the data wirelessly anywhere in the world to a mobile PC, laptop, or desktop computer.

Plogg is actually a small computer in its own right, with an 8051-compatible microprocessor, RAM, flash memory, a real-time clock, and Plogg Manager software that tracks instant and cumulative energy consumption.

PloggZgb acts as a ZigBee end device, router, or coordinator and is available on the Plogg site (www.plogginternational.com) for $80. The PloggBlu version offers Bluetooth connectivity and is available for $95.

The ZigBee alliance is an association of companies working together to incorporate wireless technology in remote monitoring and power-control applications. Partnering utilities and third-party applications can use ZigBee technology to send energy use reports via wireless communications to end-user devices like the PloggZgb.

Connecting power education to action

Power meters help give you the information you need to make educated choices about your power consumption. Various companies are working to solve different parts of the puzzle and enable you to take what you learn about your power usage to the next level — by managing your consumption effectively, in real-time. Following are some pieces that have yet to be resolved before that capability will be available in all its glory.

Utility companies don't give consumers a lot of information to work with. Whether this is by design, when you look at your electric bill, you see a few numbers. A typical electric bill includes your meter reading from last month, your meter reading this month, the difference in kWh from one month to the next, and how much that's gonna cost you. Companies jumping into the energy empowerment arena want to see consumers who can monitor, track, and adjust their power consumption in real time.

In early 2009, the Google Foundation announced a new green initiative designed to empower consumers by giving them real-time access to their power-use data, but instead of building a device like Plogg or TED, Google is creating an iGoogle gadget, Google PowerMeter, to do the tracking. Imagine being able to log in to your Google account and check the energy consumption going on at home while you're at the office. Now take it a step further and imagine that you can click the mouse and turn off the lights you left on in the morning! This technology isn't so far away!

Google is testing the PowerMeter now in Northern California, in conjunction with Pacific Gas and Electric Company. Google plans to work with utility companies nationwide and make it easy for consumers to access their own power use information. For those consumers who can't get real-time access from their utility companies, Google plans to work with third-party designers who will create display devices that will do the trick. To find out more about Google PowerMeter, check out www.google.org/powermeter.

Checking for Efficiency with the Energy Star

If you've purchased anything that draws electric current within the last 10 years or so, chances are that you've seen the Energy Star label on the box. Figure 3-9 shows you what that label looks like today.

Figure 3-9:
Life feels
better with
an Energy
Star.

The Energy Star program started in 1992 as a collaborative venture between the U.S. Environmental Protection Agency and the U.S. Department of Energy. The purpose of the Energy Star is to create a standard for energy consumption and let consumers know which appliances and devices meet this standard. (The Energy Star can let you know that the refrigerator that you're thinking of buying isn't going to cost a year's college tuition to run and won't reduce a glacier to mush anytime soon.)

Here are a few stats from the Energy Star site that are sure to wow you:

✔ More than 2.5 million Energy Star products have sold since the program began.

✔ 2007 numbers show that the Energy Star helped save U.S. consumers more than $16 billion in energy costs.

The Energy Star site at www.energystar.gov offers a whole world full of information for consumers, businesses, manufacturing plants, parents, kids, and your favorite pets. (Okay, maybe not your pets.) You can listen to energy podcasts, find out about tax credits for energy savings, find out how to fix common household problems, and much more. Figure 3-10 shows the site; be careful, you can follow a single link in there and not come out until dinnertime.

Energy Star's Web site can help you identify energy-efficient products. Say, for example, that you're thinking about purchasing a new dehumidifier for your house. How can you find out which model is best? Which ones last longest, make the smallest amount of noise, and produce the healthiest environments? You might call your favorite aunt to ask her advice, or you could consult the Energy Star site (and, of course, look for the star on the box of the dehumidifier you eventually buy). Energy Star gives you the basics on products and offers user reviews and ratings, but best of all, it tells you how much energy each appliance consumes while it's doing its thing every day.

In Chapter 6, we tell you all about finding, purchasing, and setting up a new green computer, so we thought we'd choose an example here that your favorite aunt is more likely to be an expert on.

To use Energy Star to do your due diligence before you buy, follow these steps:

1. **Go to the Energy Star site at `www.energystar.gov`.**

2. **Click the Explore Products link near the top-left side of the page.**

   The Energy Star Qualified Products page provides a series of links with many kinds of appliances and home devices organized by category.

3. **In the Appliances area near the top of the page, click Dehumidifiers**.

   The next page presents you with a collection of information about dehumidifiers. (See Figure 3-11.) The Web site helps you determine if you really need a dehumidifier. It tells you how to know a good dehumidifier from a bad one, how they work, and how much energy they consume.

   Ah, so now you know where your aunt was getting her info all along.

4. **To see a list of dehumidifiers that measure up to the Energy Star standard, look at the Find a Product link on the right side of the page and click the link that provides the information in the format you want (Excel or PDF).**

   If you don't have Excel installed on your computer, you should choose the PDF option. You can look at PDF files in Adobe Reader, which is available for free at `http://get.adobe.com/reader`.

Figure 3-11: Energy Star helps you make educated, energy-aware choices.

Don't miss the bargains! While you're on the Energy Star site researching a new purchase, click the Special Offers button, enter your zip code in the Special Offer/Rebate Finder field, and select the check box next to the type of product you're looking for. Click the Locate Special Offers/Rebates button at the bottom of the page to display a list of stores in your area that are offering special deals on the product you want. Saving money *while* saving energy is a nice add-on to increasing your good earth karma.

EnergyGuide — What's the difference?

When they first begin to shop for new appliances and equipment, some people confuse the EnergyGuide (the big yellow sticker shown in the figure) with Energy Star. These are two different programs, designed with different purposes. The EnergyGuide sticker is a little like the ingredients label on the cookies you buy. The manufacturer is required by the U.S. Food and Drug Administration (FDA) to tell you what's in those cookies, along with how many calories and what percentage of daily cookie calories they represent. The EnergyGuide gives basic information about the item you're looking at (manufacturer name, model number, capacity, and so on) and lets you know how the energy efficiency of this particular item compares with other appliances in the same general category. The U.S. Department of Energy sets the standards and regulates how manufacturers display this information on the EnergyGuide.

EnergyGuide displays efficiency measurements differently for different devices. Fridges and dishwashers show an annual energy consumption (for example, kWh per year). The EnergyGuide also shows you an estimate of what it will cost you to run the appliance for a year, based on a national average of energy prices.

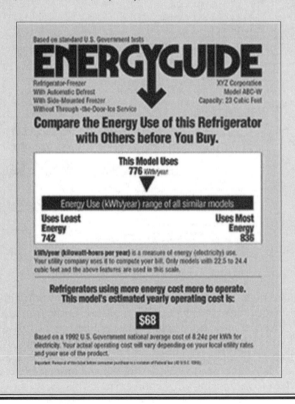

Based on standard U.S. Government tests

ENERGYGUIDE

Refrigerator-Freezer
With Automatic Defrost
With Side-Mounted Freezer
Without Through-the-Door Ice Service

XYZ Corporation
Model ABC-W
Capacity: 23 Cubic Feet

Compare the Energy Use of this Refrigerator with Others before You Buy.

This Model Uses
776 kWh/year
▼

Energy Use (kWh/year) range of all similar models

Uses Least
Energy
742

Uses Most
Energy
836

kWh/year (kilowatt-hours per year) is a measure of energy (electricity) use. Your utility company uses it to compute your bill. Only models with 22.5 to 24.4 cubic feet and the above features are used in this scale.

Refrigerators using more energy cost more to operate. This model's estimated yearly operating cost is:

$68

Based on a 1992 U.S. Government national average cost of 8.24¢ per kWh for electricity. Your actual operating cost will vary depending on your local utility rates and your use of the product.

Important: Removal of this label before consumer purchase is a violation of Federal law (42 U.S.C. 6296).

Here's a little more detail on energy factors: Because different devices use energy differently, the way in which energy is used needs to be taken into account. The energy efficiency of a dehumidifier is measured in the amount of water removed from the air per kilowatt-hour (kWh).

Penning Up Energy Hogs in Your House

Conserving energy is often one of the easier and cheaper things you can do to lower your energy use. This section takes you on a quick tour of your home to help you pinpoint ways you can conserve energy throughout.

In Part II, you learn more about the ways in which the individual parts of your computer — and the other devices that are its friends — conspire to jack up your electric bill.

This section merely scratches the surface of greening your home. For a more in-depth look at creating a green home, check out *Green Building & Remodeling For Dummies,* by Eric Corey Freed (Wiley).

Controlling power flow to electronics: Managing your media

Do you have the TV on all day when you're home? Is the clock still flashing 12:00 on your DVD player? Is your cellphone plugged in (even though it's charged), your printer light gleaming, your monitor feigning sleep with an empty, blank face?

All these items draw current, whether they're turned off or on. Different devices draw various amounts of current. (Visualize hoses of different widths draining water out of a pool; the wider the hose, the more water goes through.) The following paragraphs tell you how power consumption can vary, just among the types of items you already have around your house (or may be considering purchasing):

- ✔ **Televisions:** An average LCD TV uses 213 watts of power when it is turned on. By comparison, a plasma uses 339 watts, and a rear-projection TV uses 211 watts.

- ✔ **Gaming consoles:** Adding an Xbox 360 heaps on another 187 watts. Playstation 3? Even worse — that's an additional 197 watts, please.

- ✔ **Computers:** Oh, and how many computers do you have in the house? Three? That's another 234 watts (78 watts per PC).

A new Energy Star shines for TV standards

The new Energy Star 3.0 TV specification was unveiled in February 2009, offering consumers new standards to raise the bar for the way TVs consume power. TVs that have the new Energy Star rating are as much as 30 percent more energy efficient than other televisions. The criteria are based on power use in both active and standby states, the way in which power is used for brightness, and the power consumption for various screen sizes. Energy Star also asks manufacturers to provide consumers with information on how to adjust a television's settings to get the most use from the smallest amount of energy.

With two LCD TVs, an Xbox 360, and three PCs, you're pulling almost 900 watts without even trying. With the average cost of electricity (based on 2007 figures) at $10.06 per kWh, those numbers can add up pretty quickly. And that's only the cost you see in your checkbook. It doesn't count the CO_2 emissions produced to make the energy that those devices mindlessly drink.

If you're in the market for a new television, check out CNET's energy-use comparisons of high-definition TV makes and models. The study gathered energy use on dozens of TV models and compared them based on a watts-per-screen-inch ratio. You can see at a glance which models are guzzlers and which aren't. Here's the link: `http://tiny.cc/IB4bM`.

Squealing over heat and air conditioning costs

Ah, here's a nice word: *saving*. Saving your hard-earned dollars. Saving greenhouse gas emissions. Saving the planet.

It's possible that, depending on where you live in the country, half of your energy consumption comes from heating and cooling your home. The average heating and cooling expense for a mid-sized house in the U.S. is close to $1,000 a year. That's a lot of pizza. A huge list of things contributes to this use factor, of course, including the following:

- Whether you live in a warm, cool, or moderate area
- The size of your home
- Location and landscaping (big trees keep houses cooler)

✔ Your home's age and construction

✔ The number of doors and windows you have (and how tightly they're sealed)

This list could go on and on, but you get the picture.

Whether you have a new, sparkling, energy-efficient heating and cooling system, you can perform some simple, low-cost tasks to make a big difference in the amount of power you use to keep your home comfortable. The sections that follow give you more details.

Two words: Programmable thermostat

Programming a thermostat isn't nearly as geeky as it sounds. You need to have someone who understands electric current install it for you (hopefully your HVAC contractor), but then it's all yours for the programming. Chances are, your heating-and-cooling contractor will help you get started with this as well.

A programmable thermostat enables you to set temperatures for different times of the day, which regulates the amount of energy you use to maintain the temperature. For example, if you go to work every day, and you're gone from 7:30 a.m. to 5:30 p.m., you can set the thermostat to automatically drop the temperature when you leave in the morning and raise it to your favorite degree when you return at night. And yes, programmable thermostats are smart, so you can set different schedules for weekdays and weekends.

Programmable thermostats that have the Energy Star come preprogrammed with the temperature settings shown in Table 3-2. Even if you think these look a little cool (or warm) to you, try them out for a day or two to see whether your internal thermostat adjusts.

Table 3-2	Keeping It Cool with Energy Star		
Action Setting	Time of Day	Temperature for Heat	Temperature for Cool
Wake up	6 a.m.	< 70 degrees	> 78 degrees
Daytime	8 a.m.	Drop at least 8 degrees	Increase at least 7 degrees
Evening	6 p.m.	< 70 degrees	> 78 degrees
Sleep	10 p.m.	Drop at least 8 degrees	Increase at least 4 degrees

Some thermostats go all out — the electric cars of the heating and cooling world — and include bells and whistles such as warning lights that display when it's time to change the filter, voice activation features (so you can say, "Honey, I'm home!" and change the house temperature), and a variety of settings for customizing your schedule.

No programmable thermostat? No worries. Just adjust the thermostat a few degrees before you leave the house and when you come back and put on a sweater (or take one off, depending on the season). Many people are surprised by the savings they discover when they change their thermostat setting by just three or four degrees.

The 411 on filters

Ah, can't you just hear you father's voice? *How often do you change those furnace filters?* Back in the day, furnace filters were big, clunky things designed to protect your furnace equipment. Today, they still keep the detritus in your air out of the inner cogs of the furnace, but they may also strip out evil allergens, improve air quality, and help — or hinder — air flow.

Changing a furnace filter is a simple task, and it can make a big difference in the way your furnace, air conditioning, or heat pump circulate the air in your house. If the filter is clogged and messy, the fan has to work considerably harder to try to pull air through it. For a happy fan, cleaner air flow, and lower electric use, replace your furnace filter (or clean it, if you have the reusable kind) more often than the standard manufacturer requirements say. (If the package says "Lasts up to three months," change the filter early in month two, for example.)

If changing the furnace filter is something you forget — like changing the oil in your car or letting the cat in — put yourself on a regular schedule. Pay the mortgage, change the filter. It's that simple. (It worked for us, anyway.)

What kind of culprit is your air conditioner?

Many people don't know how air conditioners work (do they just pump cool air into your house?) or how to improve their efficiency. Your air conditioner *is* circulating cooler air throughout your home, but the air that it circulates is actually the same warmer air that you were sweating in before the AC kicked on.

The first air conditioner was a fan placed over an ice block (designed to cool sick patients in southern Florida). As the invention evolved, it used toxic or flammable gases to do its temperature-altering work. Soon, someone invented a gas called Freon, which was safer for humans, but unfortunately, it punched a hole in the ozone layer. Today, air conditioners (both the one you use for your house and the one in your car) use a slightly less-effective version of Freon, but at least it's not hurting the planet.

You can do several things right away to reduce the amount of energy your air conditioner uses:

- ✔ **Turn it off.** Consider other types of cooling efforts first. And then, if the heat is really unbearable, go ahead and use your air conditioner.

- ✔ **Raise the thermostat.** You may *think* you need the temperature set to 72 degrees when it's 95 degrees outside, but will a couple of degrees really matter that much? Won't 78 degrees still feel cooler than 95 degrees? It could reduce your electric consumption by as much as 3 to 5 percent.

- ✔ **Close the curtains.** Sure, it's beautiful to see the sun streaming in your windows on a gorgeous summer day. But if it raises the house's temperature 6 degrees, maybe opening the curtains in the evening is a better idea.

- ✔ **Use ceiling fans.** A ceiling fan uses a supply of electricity, but it's a smaller amount than an AC unit. Plus, a ceiling fan can reduce the temperature in a room by 5 to 8 degrees.

- ✔ **Seal the ducts and sills.** You're paying for every bit of the cool air your AC generates, so make sure you get the benefit of it all. Make sure your windows are caulked. (You may want to get newer energy-efficient windows if yours are outdated, but that's a bit of an expense.) Also, have the ductwork cleaned and patched, if necessary.

- ✔ **Double-check your insulation.** Insulation helps you maintain the temperature you want in your home no matter what the season, so check it. And add insulation in the attic, garage, and other areas as needed.

What's a heat pump and why does it have such a dumb name?

A *heat pump,* perhaps not surprisingly, changes the temperature of your house by moving heat around instead of actually generating the heat, like a furnace. Air-source heat pumps are the most common type, and they use outdoor air temperatures and indoor air temperatures to change the temperature in your house. According to the U.S Department of Energy, heat pumps can save homeowners 30 to 40 percent on their electric bills during the winter months. (Okay, maybe it's not such a dumb name after all.)

Heat pumps work like air conditioners, but they have the ability to work in reverse. They are efficient only in certain climates or at certain temperatures. If you live in a temperate climate, heat pumps may work well for you. If your location offers extreme cold or extreme heat, a traditional furnace and air conditioner is likely to be the more energy-efficient option.

Geothermal heat pumps use this same kind of exchange system, but they use hot water from deep within the ground instead of the air to draw the hot or cool energy. Geothermal heat pumps also often include components that draw hot water. These pumps are more expensive than air-source units, but they're more efficient than traditional heat pumps. To find out more about geothermal heat pumps, visit `http://www.geoexchange.org/`.

In Tokyo, Japan, a 2001 city ordinance mandated that buildings over a certain height include rooftop gardens to counteract what some are calling the *heat island phenomenon*, in which rooftops of tall buildings in the city exceed 50 degrees Celsius (122 degrees Fahrenheit) during the day in the summer. Planting lush gardens with trees and flowers lowers the rooftop temperatures to 30 degrees Celsius (86 degrees Fahrenheit), reducing the need for air conditioning and creating a nicer place to be.

Improve your air circulation

Have you ever had anyone out to clean your ducts? No, it's not off-color at all; it's about maximizing air flow, which means that the blower motor in your fan has to work less hard to move more air — and that means a savings in power (not to mention a squeaky clean feeling). Depending on the type of heating and cooling you have in your house, the ductwork that circulates the air can (and does) get gummed up with fuzz, gunk, pet hair, and dust bunnies.

The process is usually painless and relatively low cost. You can do some of the work yourself and help keep the dust to a minimum by replacing your furnace filters regularly and vacuuming the vents if they show signs of dusty buildup.

Cutting the pork from appliances

Okay, now that we've focused on the big power picture, we zero in on some quick ways to drop those power bills a bit further. You may be surprised to see how much you can do with a small investment.

First things first — if your appliances have energy-saver settings, use them! Dishwashers, refrigerators, washers, dryers, and standalone freezers may all have energy-saver settings. These are the no-brainer fixes that may cause you to wait a little longer for dry dishes, but if you can reduce greenhouse gases and save a buck or two, it's worth the trade.

If you feel in the dark about a piece of electronic equipment or appliance you already own, you can use the Energy Star product list to see whether an item makes the cut. That basic info gives you a little more insight into how serious a suckler that particular item is, and then you can make better choices about when and how to use it. See "Checking for Efficiency with the Energy Star" earlier in this chapter for details.

Is your refrigerator running?

Your fridge may look innocent enough, but it's actually one of the biggest energy hogs in your house. The amount of power required to regulate the interior temperature, with the opening and closing of the doors, is a steady stream of consumed wattage. In general, newer refrigerators are more energy efficient than older ones. (Here's where we sing the Energy Star refrain again.) The most energy-efficient fridges are the ones with the freezer on the bottom. (There's not much you can do to change that if you have one of the other kinds, but we just thought you'd like to know.)

Here are some ways you can reduce the energy drain your fridge is throwing into deep freeze:

- ✔ Cool foods before placing them in the fridge. This means that the fridge doesn't have to work as hard to cool the food.

- ✔ Stop using the ice maker and drink dispenser. (And for heaven's sake, turn off the LCD television screen on the freezer door!)

- ✔ Defrost foods in the refrigerator rather than on the counter. This helps boost the cool factor in the fridge (which means that the electric current doesn't have to do it).

- ✔ Make sure the door of the fridge seals tightly. Coolness could be seeping out without you knowing it.

- ✔ Clean the back of the refrigerator periodically. This helps keep the air flowing freely inside the appliance, which helps increase efficiency.

- ✔ Sure, it's kind of hip to have a fridge in the garage, where you can store beverages for party guests. But it's more earth-friendly to trade in two smaller fridges for one large, energy-efficient one.

Heat food on the stovetop

You may not think about the amount of energy you use when you cook, but heat is heat is heat. (Plus, you probably have the stovetop light on and, if you cook like we do, the fan!) Whether you cook with gas or electric heat, here are some ways that you can conserve the power you use to prepare meals for yourself and your family:

- ✔ On an electric stove, choose the burner size that fits the pot you're using. Putting a small pot on a big burner just heats a lot of space (and the surrounding air) for no reason.

- ✔ Check the seal on the oven door because heat can leak out.

- ✔ Use lids on pots to keep the heat in. (There's that *escaping* theme again.)

If you're considering purchasing a new, energy-efficient stove, keep these ideas in mind:

- ✔ Electric stoves are more efficient than gas.

- ✔ Self-cleaning ovens are most efficient because they're well insulated and retain heat best.

- ✔ Magnetic surface stovetops are becoming more popular as an affordable green option. They never wear out, they don't use electricity or gas, and they don't burn little fingers! (Yes, magnets really can cook. Weird.)

This is the way we wash the clothes

Okay, nobody is a fan of dirty, smelly clothes. Especially if you've lived in a house with a teenage boy, you know that laundry just *needs* to be washed. That being said, however, you can adopt the following practices to reduce your consumption as you do your regular laundry loads:

- ✔ Keep an eye on your washer's water settings. The average load uses 40 gallons of water. Control the load selection based on what you really need and reduce the amount of water when possible.

- ✔ Insulate your hot water heater to help retain the heat.

- ✔ Reduce the temperature on your hot water heater to 120 degrees.

- ✔ Keep the dryer's lint trap clean.

- ✔ Dry loads one after another. Stopping and starting actually uses more energy.

- ✔ Choose the Permanent Press dryer cycle because it air dries the last few minutes of the cycle.

If you're in the market for a new dryer, consider buying one with an automatic sensor that ends the load when the clothes are dry (and of course — think Energy Star!)

Leave the light on, Mother

Please make sure you're using energy-efficient light bulbs! This is the year to make the choice to replace all those 60-watt incandescent light bulbs that burn out every eight months with 60- to 100-watt CFLs (compact fluorescent lights) that last 10 years or more. CFLs light your house with the same warm light — and in a variety of styles and output levels — but use only about one-fifth the energy.

You can now buy the new energy efficient bulbs in department stores, hardware stores, and probably even grocery stores nationwide. Consider it an investment in sustainability over disposability.

Governments all over the world are introducing measures designed to curtail incandescent bulb use. Venezuela and Brazil already made the change; Ireland and Switzerland phase their bulbs out this year; and Argentina, Italy, and the United Kingdom set a deadline of 2011. Canada and the United States bring up the rear with 2012 and 2012–2014 switchover dates, respectively.

Upgrading to green batteries, anyone?

Continuing with the theme of sustainability over disposability, do you have a gamer in the house? If so, you know what it's like to pay $8.99 for an 8-pack of AA batteries . . . every other week. Similarly, if you have a GPS system in your car, an attachable flash for your high-end camera, remote controls for your television, or any number of other portable battery-driven devices (don't get us started on remote-control cars), you may be an easy audience for a presentation on the benefits of green batteries.

Green batteries, which you'll see labeled as nickel metal hydride (NiMH) and lithium ion (Li-ion), can save you money, time, and consternation if you get in the habit of recharging and monitoring their use.

If you've had your rechargeable batteries for a while and they don't seem to be charging properly, clean the tops with rubbing alcohol and they should work just fine!

Don't want to be disloyal to the Energizer Bunny? Don't worry! Energizer makes its own line of rechargeable batteries. Prices range from $25 to $40 for chargers and $8 to $12 for small packs of rechargeable batteries. It's a good way to cut down on expense and hassle and do something good for the earth at the same time.

Trimming fuel consumption

Conserving fuel is another way to conserve energy and resources. Here are a few ways to reduce the number of gallons of gas that your ride guzzles:

✔ Think through your trips and combine errands.

✔ Take shorter routes wherever possible.

- ✔ Plan your route so you won't sit in traffic.
- ✔ Use public transportation wherever possible.
- ✔ Share a ride with a friend.
- ✔ Ride your bike or walk when you can.
- ✔ Work from home a few days a week (or every day).

For great ideas on how to convince your boss of the earth-friendliness and practicality of working at home (perks all around!), see Part IV.

Part II
Choosing Your Green PC Path

"Good news — we found PCs that consume less energy."

In this part . . .

So it's no secret that little choices can bring big results. Watch any weight-loss reality show and you know that over time, leaving that bagel on the plate, skipping the extra cookie, and doing a few extra sit-ups really do make a difference. Greening your home computing practices is just like that. A bit at a time, you can work from the general to the granular, looking more and more closely at the subtle but important ways your computing choices can help the earth. This part of the book focuses on your technology options — from powering up your hardware to making the call about a new green PC — you find out about all the opportunities you have to make a green difference with technology.

Chapter 4

Assessing What You've Got

*I*f you've read the previous chapters, now you know the lay of the land in relation to your household energy use, and you're ready to zero in on the amount of energy that your hardware and peripherals are sipping. In the scheme of things, dialing back your energy use for a single PC might not seem like a huge energy savings or take much of a bite out of the greenhouse gases pumping into the air right now. But every watt you save makes a difference. And by multiplying your energy savings by all the people in your office, school, city, or state, you begin to see what a big change just a few watts can make.

So. It's time to take a closer look at that hardware. Grab a cup of organic, fair-trade coffee, scoot on up to the computer, and take a closer look.

Starting an Inventory of Your Computing Equipment

When you begin to look at energy use and computers, you realize there are a few givens:

✔ Every computer uses some sort of power to do what it does.

✔ There is little uniformity about energy use — different computer systems use different amounts of power for different things.

✔ When you add peripherals — such as mobile devices, printers, and cameras — you increase the amount involved to run it all.

Pretty simple, don't you think? The challenge comes in determining how much energy this all adds up to for your home (chances are that you've got more than one computer and at least a couple of digital devices) and finding ways to scale back or upgrade to a higher efficiency, as the case may be.

As you start on your green computing path, you'll find it helpful to know what you have exactly. For example, how many computers, printers, sets of speakers, game consoles, and more are in your house? Also, take a closer look at when you bought those items and whether they're Energy Star certified. You can use Table 4-1 to get started.

Table 4-1		Assessing What You've Got			
Component	*Manufacturer*	*Model*	*Year Purchased*	*Energy Star?*	*How Many Do You Have?*
Desktop CPU					
Monitor					
Router					
Mouse					
Printer					
Scanner					
Laptop					
Digital camera					
Digital camcorder					
MP3 player					
Game console					
Computer speakers					

Spotting an energy hog

What you gain from completing Table 4-1 is a picture of not only what you have but also how old and thus how energy-efficient your equipment is. In general, older computers don't have the same green consciousness of newer computers. That's understandable, really. In the early days, developers were just trying to get the things to work. The working *well* comes with age and refinement (which is true for some computers and programs, anyway).

If you have a PC that shipped with Windows XP or a Mac that came with OS 9, chances are that energy efficiency wasn't foremost in the designer's mind when that system was on the drawing board. More often than not, however, you can't just look at a list of what you have and determine how green your current home computing environment is. Case in point: The Greenpeace *Guide to Greener Electronics* considers a company (in this case, a computer manufacturer) green if it has a plan for three areas of greening:

- ✔ **Toxin-free manufacturing**
- ✔ **Energy efficiency**
- ✔ **Responsible recycling programs**

In the 2008 version of the *Guide,* Sony, Toshiba, Dell, and HP were somewhere between *trying to be green* and *just don't give a damn*. And some of the other players — including two huge manufacturers of popular game systems — fell on the lowest end of the scale.

However, the way the companies are rated on that scale may be different from what you see drawing current through your house. Based on laboratory tests (no PCs or Macs were mistreated during the application of these tests), the following manufacturers' systems did pretty well when it came to energy efficiency when using basic desktop applications:

- ✔ **Apple**
- ✔ **Dell**
- ✔ **Lenovo**

If you want to take a look at the ratings yourself, you can download the *Guide to Greener Electronics* at this site:

```
www.greenpeace.org/raw/content/usa/
           press-center/reports4/
           guide-to-greener-electronics-9.pdf
```

To take a look at the detailed grid (maintained by the University of Pennsylvania) of energy use of various computer models, point your browser to this site:

```
www.upenn.edu/computing/provider/docs/hardware/
           powerusage.html
```

A more holistic inventory of your home computing environment gives you a clearer picture of your energy use and helps you pinpoint realistic ways to green your home computing based on your needs and activities. In later sections of this chapter, you discover how to assess your equipment as well as your habits.

How much juice is it, really?

Whether you have a desktop or laptop computer from one of the manufacturers listed in the preceding section, you may wonder just how much energy your computer consumes.

Laptops understandably require less power than desktops because they have fewer pieces (no standalone monitor, at least). With that big watt difference out of the way, Table 4-2 outlines generally what your computer and accompanying components may use, energy-wise.

Table 4-2	Average Power Consumption: Computer and Peripherals
	Energy Use
Desktop computer CPU	100 watts
LCD monitor (15–17 inches)	50–150 watts
Laser printer	100 watts
Inkjet printer	12 watts
Multifunction printer/copier	15 watts
Laptop	22 watts
Wireless router	6 watts
Computer speakers	7 watts
USB hub	3 watts

These are general estimates, but bear in mind that your computer uses different amounts of energy depending on what it's doing. If your computer or peripheral device is in Sleep mode or sitting idle, for example, if consumes less power than a printer pumping out a 20-page report. For more information on specific energy measurements in different computer operating states, see Chapter 9.

Your computer equipment may not break the bank for you in terms of energy expense, but when you add up all your tech equipment (that's right, desktops, laptops, digital cameras, printers, MP3 players, game consoles, and more) and then add your neighbor's tech items, and their neighbor's, and your whole city, state, region . . . you get the idea. A little savings can mean a lot, if those little savings are made to scale.

You really are cutting back on CO_2 when you conserve power. You can reduce carbon emissions by as much as 67 kg per desktop per year when you just shut it down when it's not in use. If 5,000 people decide to do this regularly, that keeps 288 tons of CO_2 out of the atmosphere! (See Chapter 2 for an introduction to energy and CO_2.)

Understanding How You Use Devices

How you use your devices is as important as your inventory. In the following sections, we take a look at common habits in the way people use their computers, printers, and more. As you read through the following sections, consider how you and others in your household use your equipment. Having this information can help you find ways to green your home computing.

When is your computer on? Generally, people power their computers in one of the following ways. Read through the following scenarios and consider your typical powering method.

- ✔ **All the time:** Not long ago, repeated power-down and power-up cycles could shorten computers' lives, and the conventional wisdom was to leave your computer on all the time. Today, it really is okay to power down your computer. You won't hurt its feelings by letting it know you're putting it away.

- ✔ **When you step away:** Studies show that the majority of the time that most business and school computers are on and drawing current, they are idle or in a low state of active use. For example, as you write a report in Word, you might write a paragraph, stop, look something up, get a cup of coffee, go back to the computer. . . . How much of that is work-intensive processing time?

The general green rule of thumb is that if you will be away from the computer for more than two hours, it's worth the power you're going to conserve if you go ahead and shut down the system completely. (Turn off the power strip, too, while you're at it.)

✔ **Just when you need it:** Okay, so you know you don't leave the computer on all the time. If you just turn on your computer now and then when you need it, you're already conserving resources. To create a clearer picture, consider making a conscious effort to note when you tend to use your computer over the period of a week or a month.

Knowing how much energy your computing tasks need

Different computing tasks use different amounts of power. Some activities, such as watching a movie on your computer, playing a game with high-end animation, or working with a processing-heavy illustration and modeling program, really do make the computer work for its power.

A clear understanding of how you use your computer can be helpful as you decide whether to work with equipment you have or to upgrade an old computer. For example, if you use your computer to watch movies one or two times a week, you'll maximize the benefit of upgrading to Energy Star equipment. However, if you use your computer mostly for reading newspapers on the Web and writing e-mails to your friends and family, sprucing up what you have may be the greener (and money-saving) way to go.

Thinking about your printing habits

Printing is a key area in which you can green your home computing. To get started, assess how you use the printer and what your current printing habits and needs are. The following points can help you get started in your assessment; to save paper, feel free to make notes in the margins:

✔ **When is your printer turned on?**

✔ **Is the printer always plugged in?** If the printer is plugged into a power strip, note whether the strip is always turned on.

✔ **How many printers do you have in your house?** If you have multiple printers, you can set up a home network and share one printer, which cuts down on the amount of toner or ink you use, along with the amount of energy consumed.

✔ **What do you print and what happens to those printouts?**

✔ **What print settings do you use?** For example, many printers offer quality settings, such as Draft or Best, that use less or more ink. You may also have the option of printing on both sides of the page (a setting sometimes called Duplex). And most software offers a Print Preview option so that you can check whether your printout will look right and change your document if needed before you print.

✔ **What kind of paper do you use?** This may include blank white paper as well as photo paper and more.

Chapter 11 is dedicated to green printing. You discover ways to change the way you use your printer to save energy. And you can consider reducing the number of pages you print or eliminating printing altogether by reading and sharing electronic files instead.

Get rid of those catalogs

Do you feel bad when your mailbox is stuffed with catalogs you'll never use? CatalogChoice. org is a free service that helps you ask companies to remove your address from their catalog lists. You can also opt-in for catalogs you really *do* want to receive, as well. The following steps walk you through the process:

1. **Open your browser and go to www. catalogchoice.org.**

   You can explore the links on the left or move right to the process by clicking Get Started.

2. **Enter your information to sign up for a free account.**

   The steps are simple — just the basics. At the bottom of the page, read the terms of service, let the site know you're over 18 (you *are*, aren't you?), and indicate whether it's okay for Catalog Choice to give you a cookie and send you an e-mail once in a while.

3. **Click Sign Up.**

   The site sends you a confirmation e-mail message. Click the link in the message to confirm your new account and go to the How to Use This Site page.

4. **Click Find Your Catalog.**

   The Find Catalogs page appears so that you can enter the name of the catalog you receive.

5. **Type the name of the catalog you want to discontinue and click Search.**

   Catalogs affiliated with the name you entered appear in the lower part of the screen.

6. **Click Set Mail Preferences for the catalog you want to stop.**

   On the Set Preferences page, you can customize your response, find out more about the sender, and indicate why you no longer want to receive the catalog.

Doing the peripheral math

If your house is like many U.S. households today, you have a number of devices that connect to your computer at various times. Your added devices might include any or all of the following:

✔ Digital camera

✔ Digital camcorder

✔ Cellphone

✔ Computer speaker system

✔ Xbox 360

✔ Nintendo Wii

✔ Playstation 3

✔ MP3 player, such as an iPod or a Zune

Add to this the electronic equipment that might not be considered computer equipment but can be used alongside your favorite PC — your HDTV, a DVD player, and more — and you've got quite a bit of power in use. And perhaps much of that is in Standby mode. For now, take an inventory of all the peripherals in use in your house as well as how you use them and how they need to be charged.

Later in this chapter, you find details about smart power strips for plugging in stationary peripherals. In Chapter 10, you find out how to choose power-saving settings for gadgets you use on the go as well as how to charge these devices using green power.

Working Better with What You Have

The growing use of computers — in homes, businesses, schools, and elsewhere around the world — has a big impact on energy consumption, adding a load to household and office budgets everywhere. Basic good practices for computing — backing up data and programs, securing networks, managing user accounts, and planning and paying for services — is something every computer user, not just corporate IT departments, needs to deal with.

When you think about it, you realize that even though businesses and schools have a huge number of computers — one college campus, for example, has 18,000 computers that contribute to half a million dollars a year in university expenses — homes far outnumber businesses and universities. Each person who works in a business goes home and likely turns on the computer at night, as well. Students at the university level may use computers in the library and then go home to check their Facebook pages, play Call of Duty on their Xbox 360s, and listen to the Shins on their MP3 players.

The hits go on and on.

So you can see that you've got an important role here. Whether you use a desktop or laptop system, whether you have a make and model from a green-leaning manufacturer or one who hasn't really caught on yet, you can reduce your consumption and begin to manage your energy use more efficiently. In the sections that follow, you take a look at habits, upgrades, tools, and services that can help you get the most out of any home computing setup.

Developing computer habits that save energy

Here are a few guidelines you can use to cut back on the power you pump into a dozing system:

- ✔ **Turn on only what you use.** (Leave the printer off if you don't need it.)

- ✔ **Unplug devices you aren't using.** If you have more than one system on the power strip, unplug the one you don't need before flipping the switch.

- ✔ **Consolidate the tasks you do at the computer.** With a good plan in mind, you can power up, do what you need to do, and power down all in one session.

- ✔ **Put yourself on a schedule.** (Yes, it's more fun to check e-mail every so often in the evening, but is it really that much different than once after work and once a few hours later, before bed?)

- ✔ **Find an enjoyable way to spend the brief period of time it takes for your computer to power up after you turn it on.** (That delay is what causes many folks to leave the computer running.) What can you do in two minutes? Meditate? Jog in place? Sing? (Your family will love that.)

- ✔ **Know what you're saving.** Use a power meter or keep track of the watts you're consuming when you turn off the computer. Over time, it adds up — and that inspires you to look for other ways you can green your computing practices. Chapter 3 covers devices that can monitor your power consumption.

You can reduce the amount of energy your computer uses while it's active by optimizing your computer's power management settings. It's easier than you might think! See Chapter 9 for details.

Do you have lots of electronic equipment on all at the same time? Think heat waves. Your technology is raising the temperature in your house — perhaps ever so slightly — if you leave the current running all day while you're at work. Why waste the watts? Turn your electronic devices off; unplug; shut them down when they don't have your undivided attention. The earth thanks you (and the rest of us breathe easier).

Using your monitor with efficiency in mind

It's not hard to imagine the amount of power your monitor must drink in. Early monitors — those old cathode-ray tube (CRT) displays that took up half of your desktop — slurped up a huge percentage of the total wattage your computer needed.

Today's monitors are considerably more energy-efficient, smaller, lighter, and better in just about every sense of the word (including the display technology and screen resolution). Monitor manufacturers take the Energy Star seriously and live up to its standards.

But one misconception is that any monitor that is Energy Star approved comes configured with energy-saving features already in place. In fact, the opposite is true — your Energy Star monitor has energy-saving features, but you'll need to consult the manual (sorry) either in the box or on the CD with the monitor's drivers to find out how to make the display as energy-efficient as possible.

Here are a few ideas for saving energy that might otherwise shine out through the monitor's face:

- ✔ **Turn it off.** If you're going down the hall, to a meeting, or to the store and don't want to turn the computer off or put it to sleep, turn off the monitor.

- ✔ **Don't use a screen saver.** It wastes energy and can mess up fast recovery from Sleep mode.

- ✔ **Consider upgrading your monitor.** Depending on the monitor you choose, your purchase might quickly pay for itself in saved energy. Chapter 5 covers monitor upgrades in more detail.

Monitors are the stuff that toxic dreams are made of, and they aren't meant to end up in landfills or burn piles. Be sure to dispose of an old monitor appropriately. Chapter 8 explains how.

Souping up your current computer

Although the new greenest-laptop-on-the-planet ads look great (don't they?), it may be a lot greener to consider ways you can make your own computer more energy-efficient. By keeping the system you already have and making some small changes to increase its energy efficiency, you may be able to keep the system out of a potential landfill, get a few more years of use from a perfectly good system, and save money.

You don't have to buy fancy items and enhancements to make your computer greener. You may be able to improve the earth-friendly qualities of what you already have and save valuable power — and reduce CO_2 emissions — at the same time. Here are a few ways you can enhance your current computer's energy efficiency:

- **Increase your RAM.** A faster computer processes information more quickly, with less churning and chunking for disk access — and that's good for energy flow. (Of course, with a faster computer, you also run the risk of enjoying being at your computer more, which could increase the number of hours you're staring at the monitor.)

- **Upgrade your operating system.** The latest operating systems — Windows Vista, Windows 7, and Mac OS X — include power management and energy-saving features.

- **Use your operating system's power management features.** Windows XP, Vista, and Windows 7 enable you to choose a preset power management theme or create one of your own. Be sure to use the power management features to reduce your power use as much as possible. See Chapter 9 for details.

- **Upgrade some hardware.** New graphics cards, printers, and monitors have been designed in the energy-aware era. As always, look for the Energy Star, and be sure to do the due diligence to find out what energy-saving features the manufacturer has included.

Upgrading can be a complicated but cost-effective and green endeavor. If you're considering this path to greening your computer, flip to Chapter 5, where we cover upgrades in more detail.

Control your fans, control your fate

Now consider yourself warned right up front: This isn't for the faint-hearted or the technophobe. But if you're handy with a few computer tools and know your way around the inside of a PC, consider replacing your computer fan, changing your power supply, or reorganizing the cables on the motherboard to allow for better air flow through the case.

Better air flow equals less resistance, which results in more air and less power to push it. Nice. And better air flow equals PC cooling, which means a longer life for your PC. *Really nice.*

One other easy-to-forget-but-oh-so-important reminder: Clean your fan vent regularly to remove grime, dust, and stray boll weevils that just happen to wander by.

Behold the power of power strips

You can reduce and control the amount of power leaching away when your many devices are in Standby mode by getting a smart power strip. This type of surge protector knows when your various peripherals are idle so that it can stop the draw of current automatically. Slick, eh?

The Isole IDP-3050 Plug Load Control, shown in Figure 4-1, has a total of eight outlets. Two are traditional outlets like you'd find on any regular power strip. The remaining six are controlled in the sense that when energy is being drawn, the outlets recognize that; when power is not being drawn, the device turns off the outlet so that the inactive peripheral does not leach unnecessary energy. Another feature, called the Personal Sensor, turns on all power for connected items at one time, based on settings you control. The company site (www.wattstopper.com/products/details.html?id=74) offers the strip for $90.

Figure 4-1:
This strip automatically senses when peripherals are on or off.

The Smart Strip has a similar goal but monitors when computers and other devices are turned on or off. The Smart Strip is available in a number of different models (and price ranges), and refurbished Smart Strips are also offered on the company's Web site, at `http://bitsltd.net/ ConsumerProducts/index.htm`.

Considering your mouse's environmental impact

Although real four-footed furry mice may abound in landfills (let's not think about that, okay?), the mouse on your desktop isn't contributing to global warming in any major way. In fact, a regular wired mouse, connected to your desktop computer, isn't using any power. Of course, it's possible that your wired mouse is made from not-very-earth-friendly chemicals, so don't throw it in the fireplace when you're done with it.

A wireless mouse draws a little current from its battery, and you'll need to replace the battery from time to time.

At the time of this writing, there isn't a preponderance of green mice scampering around. Google sells a mini wireless mouse made from recycled plastic. It's colorful and hip and available at the Google Store (`http://tinyurl.com/ gmouse`).

So how can you reduce the appetite of your favorite navigating rodents? Here are a few pointers:

✔ Trade the wireless mouse for an old-fashioned wired one. We know, it's not as cool to have a wired mouse. But it's the planet we're talking about here.

✔ If you must use the wireless mouse, go green in the battery department. Flip to Chapter 2 for tips on green batteries.

✔ Use your laptop's touchpad instead of the wireless mouse just to save a tiny bit of DC power.

Researchers at Delft University of Technology in the Netherlands were developing and testing a solar mouse, complete with mini solar panels inside. The problem? Usually a hand was covering the surface of the mouse, blocking the solar rays needed to charge the device. Not sure we'll be seeing that green tech product in the big-box stores anytime soon.

Speed up your Internet access

Most people spend quite a bit of time online every day. At first you might think, well, that doesn't really cost anything. I'm just surfing the Web. But think again — your computer, monitor, and other components are still pulling current. The ISP (Internet service provider) that provides you with access to the Internet pulls a *lot* of current. And as you click from link to link, site to site, bouncing all over the world, your actions move through dozens or hundreds or thousands of servers, through miles and unfathomable miles of cable (or transmitted via wireless transmission) that was created and is maintained by goods, services, employees, utilities, and . . . the list goes on and on.

So that little act of browsing can have a big footprint, when you consider all the touches along the way.

How can you green your Internet access? There are a couple of things you can do. First, you can check out the access speed you're getting from your service. Find out if the access is as fast as they promise. The faster the access, the quicker you'll find what you need and the faster you can turn the computer off, go outside, and work in the garden.

CNET offers the Bandwidth Meter Online Speed Test that enables you to clock your Internet speed. Want to take a test drive? Here are the steps:

1. **Go to http://reviews.cnet.com/internet-speed-test. (See Figure 4-2).**

2. **Enter your area code in the box.**

3. **Click the appropriate radio button to indicate the type of connection you currently have.**

4. **From the drop-down menu, choose your ISP.**

   If you don't see your provider in the list, click the Other box and type the name of the service provider you use.

5. **Click Go.**

   The results of the access speed test show you where your access speed rates in comparison to the range of possibility.

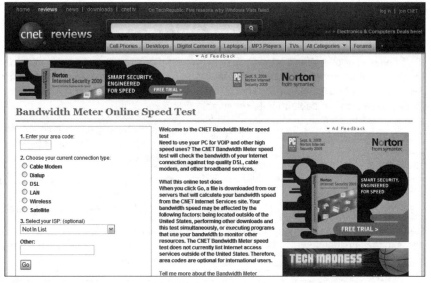

Figure 4-2:
Use the
CNET
Bandwidth
tool to
see how
fast your
access is.

You also can download a widget to your desktop (for both PC and Mac systems) that enables you to check your access times no matter where you connect. To get the tool, go to Yahoo! Widgets at `http://download.cnet.com/Yahoo-Widgets/3000-12565_4-10335368.html?tag=bandwidth_sponsorship`.

Choosing an ISP who cares

If you have the option in your area, you can choose a service provider that offers at least some kind of green policy and action plan. (We were surprised to find that some providers lack any kind of green language.)

A few ISPs use renewable energy sources to power their Web hosting and access services, but it's still early in the green tech industry for total sustainability and green offerings. Some companies purchase a percentage of energy from renewable sources. (AT&T buys 10 percent of its energy from green sources, for example.) One company, Green ISP (`www.greenisp.net`), operates out of the U.K. but draws on renewable power sources in the U.S. The idea has merit, but ISPs are still in the infancy of providing truly green, workable, sustainable options for Web access and hosting.

What about Web hosting?

If you have your own Web site and pay to host it, check out green Web hosting services as well as green ISPs. Although ISPs are still slow to demonstrate their dedication to renewable energy, Web hosting companies are a little further down the road. Some groups buy renewable energy credits (RECs), which are available in a kind of carbon offset program, to counter the amount of carbon emission their services kick into the atmosphere.

Here are some Web hosting companies that currently use renewable energy to provide services to their customers:

✔ **Dreamhost** (www.dreamhost.com/aboutus-green.html) is a completely carbon-neutral Web host.

✔ **AISO** (www.aiso.net) has a tagline of "Web hosting as nature intended" and generates 100 percent of its power using solar energy.

✔ **ecoSky** (www.ecosky.com/faq/powered-by-renewable-energy.html) is powered by renewable energy.

✔ **Planetmind** (www.planetmind.net) uses both solar and wind energy to power its services.

One of the best things you can do at this point is find out more about your current Internet provider's green policies. If the company doesn't have green policies, ask them why not! Table 4-3 provides a quick look at who among the top 10 ISPs is thinking green.

Table 4-3	Top 10 ISPs in the U.S.	
ISP	*Subscribers*	*Green Policy?*
SBC	14.8 million	Yes
Comcast	14.7 million	No
Road Runner	8.6 million	Yes
Verizon	8.5 million	Yes
AOL	7.5 million	Yes
EarthLink	3.0 million	No
Charter	2.9 million	No
Qwest	2.8 million	No
Cablevision	2.4 million	No
United Online	1.5 million	No

Making the Case for a New Purchase

In the reuse, reduce, recycle approach, purchasing a brand-spanking-new computer comes in way last:

- ✔ **Reusing what you can is important.** If you can extend the life of your current computer, you're making the most of the energy and resources that were already used in manufacturing the equipment. You also delay the disposal issue (you find out more about that in Chapter 8). By evaluating your computer's age, performance, components, and energy consumption (for the system as well as all peripherals that tag along), and doing what you can to reduce the power you may be wasting, you can reduce your consumption and reuse what you have, which helps the planet.

- ✔ **Reducing the power and other resources you use is the next natural step.** Manage what you can by controlling where, when, and why electronics draw power.

- ✔ **Recycling the devices you replace is an essential part of the process.** If your system is an old energy hog, buying a new green PC becomes an earth-friendly act *if* you make sure to recycle your system responsibly. (You find out more about recycling electronics in Chapter 8.)

Are you on the fence about whether to upgrade what you have or move into something new (with a good plan for recycling)? No worries — Chapter 5 walks you through the process of giving your computer a green makeover, and Chapter 6 shows you the green-light specials.

A prop for not-so-green laptops

A *carbon offset* is a way of paying for the size of your CO_2 footprint to help offset its negative effects. The Powered Green laptop initiative is a program that lets laptop buyers offset their machine's effect on the environment by investing in wind energy. Powered Green sells stickers for $16 each. Participating users can display their stickers proudly (on the laptop lids) and know that their contributions support wind turbines that more than make up the cost of the sticker and the CO_2 they're contributing by using their laptop. To get your own Powered Green sticker or check out the rest of the gear, visit www.poweredgreen.com.

Chapter 5

Giving Your Computer a Green Makeover

*G*iving your computer a green makeover is a little like renovating your favorite room. In most cases, the basic structure is fine. Chances are that you won't want to bust down walls and add new doorways, but changing the lighting, wall decoration and color, furniture, and arrangement are all part of the fun.

Similarly, you can pinpoint a few things in your computer to update or change so that your existing computer can continue pumping out the bits and bytes needed to keep up with current technology. Choosing this path may be the best way to green your computer, because it offers the following advantages:

✔ **You get more use out of the energy used to build your current computer.** With the average lifespan of the typical U.S. home computer estimated at only three years, a lot of computers wind up in landfills or shipped across the sea!

The most earth-friendly thing you can do is take a close look at what you already have and determine whether you can work with what you've got.

> ✔ **Upgrading certain computer parts can yield high energy savings,** as we explain later in this chapter
>
> ✔ **You may get more bang for your buck with an upgrade over a new purchase.** Memory is cheap, folks!

In this chapter, you find an introduction to several high-impact green upgrades. Even if you're not one to tinker with your PC, you can still reap these advantages by hiring a pro to do it for you.

Consider both options: making over your existing computer or springing for a new one. If you decide to go the purchase route, you'll know you've done your due diligence and made the best choice for the environment, your family, and your wallet.

Weighing Your Makeover Possibilities

Although some of the techniques in this chapter require a little technical know-how — as well as the willingness to pop the hood on your computer and take a look inside (or have your favorite tech guru do it) — most of the sections in this chapter are simple enough to do without training wheels.

The three biggest energy hogs in your computer system include the system's CPU (the microprocessor that is the brain of the whole machine), your graphics card, and your monitor. Chances are that you're not going to swap out the CPU (unless you want to rebuild the system from the ground up, which is beyond the scope of this chapter). You can renovate your system and save *beaucoup* watts (and dollars, too) by making the following changes:

> ✔ **Replacing energy-draining components with more efficient models:** If you're still using an old CRT monitor, trading it for an LCD monitor is a good bet. Your graphics card can also use a lot of energy if you're a gamer, use graphics-intensive programs like Photoshop or Photoshop Elements, or watch a lot of movies on your computer. Many graphics card manufacturers have stepped up the efficiency of their products in recent years, so you'll find it worthwhile to take a look.
>
> Or if you're using a high-power card for low-power tasks, you might benefit from right-sizing your card to the tasks you typically do on your computer. That is, make sure the card you're using doesn't consume more power than you really need. You're not benefitting from a gaming card if you mostly surf the Internet and do word processing, for example.

✔ **Increasing RAM and storage capacity:** RAM (Random Access Memory) stores the programs and files you open and work with during a single work session. When you turn the computer off, whatever is stored in RAM goes away (the actual program and your saved data file remain in storage on your hard disk, however). Computers that don't have enough RAM run slowly and spend a substantial amount of time retrieving information and updating memory; this causes more processing and increases wear and tear on the system. If your computer is running slowly, redrawing the screen at an agonizing rate, and chewing on even simple changes for a long period of time, adding RAM to your computer can help speed up things and reduce the processing power your computer is using.

If your computer is pretty quick with programs and files, but turns sluggish when you hop online, your Internet connection (not your RAM) may be the culprit. Flip to Chapter 4 for help on testing and upgrading your Internet connection.

Storage memory, on the other hand, reflects your computer's capacity to store files such as photos, documents, home movies, software, and more. If you're considering replacing your computer because you're running out of room, check out the section "What's a Terabyte among Friends?" later in this chapter, which explains just how easy replacing your hard drive or adding an external hard drive can be.

✔ **Choosing an earth-friendly laptop battery:** The first step, of course, is to use the one you've got as long as you can and then dispose of it properly when it begins to bow out. When you're ready to shop for a new battery, look for green batteries like the Boston Power Enviro battery available for 18 different HP laptops. The Enviro can be charged 1,000 times (average laptop batteries begin to show a drop in quality after 100 to 150 charges) and is made from earth-healthy materials.

✔ **Swapping your old power supply for a greener model:** Most power supplies pump out one steady rate of power whether your system uses the whole amount or not. You can check out the 80 Plus program (www.80plus.org) to find a power supply that delivers only the amount of power the computer and peripherals are drawing. All power supplies certified for the 80 Plus program are also lead free, making them environmentally friendly, too.

VIA Technologies, a manufacturer of energy-efficient processors, has a well-developed green strategy. To find out more about VIA and their processors' power efficiency, visit www.via.com.tw/en/initiatives/greencomputing. Although you probably won't be doing anything as drastic as swapping out the motherboard and processor in your PC in order to improve your green factor, it's not a bad idea to keep in mind — or refer to your favorite IT person — if you ever need to make a big change.

Spicing up your Mac

Before you make any upgrades for your Mac, it's a good idea to check your warranty before you pop the hood and decide to add RAM as a do-it-yourself project. You can make an easy and safe upgrade that doesn't risk your warranty coverage by adding a bigger, faster hard drive, which gives you much more space for storage.

You may also want to upgrade RAM or add a faster graphics card. Before you do either of these things, though, talk to your Apple representative to find out what is permitted under warranty and what isn't.

You look at wattage quite a bit in this chapter — really throughout this book. When you turn on a 100 watt device and leave it one for 1 hour, you've used 100 watt/hours. Power companies charge by the kilowatt/hour (a kilowatt is 1,000 watts). Let's say your power company charges $0.35 per kilowatt/hour. Turning on a 100 watt device for 1 hour costs you 100/1000 * 0.35 or $0.035. Three and a half cents doesn't sound like much, but it does add up.

Shrinking the Elephant (Er, Monitor) on Your Desktop

Now admit it. If you've still got a huge CRT monitor sitting on your desktop at home, you hide it when friends come to dinner. You put a tablecloth over it and position a plant on top and pretend it doesn't exist. Or you close the doors to the computer cabinet or make sure your guests never walk down the hall past your office.

Early CRT monitors were large radiating machines that poured light out the front and heat from the tops and sides. They took up the entire surface of the system unit, or at least half your computer desk. You needed to take a deep breath before you hoisted it off the desktop.

CRT (which stands for cathode ray tube) monitors are still sold today, and although they consume a lot of energy and pump out a lot of heat, they still have their advocates. CRT monitors offer high quality and a level of flexibility — you get good, clear resolution whether you look at the monitor from the side or spot on. Some CRTs are also lower cost than LCDs, at least initially; but LCDs live longer, use less energy, and radiate a lot less heat — all of which add up to some extra green.

LCD (which stands for liquid crystal display) monitors are smaller and more compact, use considerably less energy, and don't ramp up the heat in your office. Monitors for home use have, on average, 15- to 20-inch screens. Some popular LCD manufacturers include Acer, Asus, HP, Samsung, and Sony.

Trading in the CRT for the LCD is an easy place to start when you want to make a big impact on your power bottom line. Be sure to go to a store to do some shopping before you buy (even if you purchase online), because being able to see the variety of sizes and styles gives you a sense of the best monitor for your space.

Your CRT may slurp down 100 watts of power all by itself, but the threat to the environment doesn't stop there. CRT monitors may contain up to five different toxic substances: lead, mercury, barium, cadmium, and phosphorous. Dumped in a landfill or burned in a village, these elements can leach into groundwater or be released into the air. Earn good karma by retiring your CRT monitor in an earth-friendly way.

Finding a green monitor

Want to know which monitors measure up to green standards? Use the EPEAT (Environmental Product Environment Assessment Tool) to find out. EPEAT is designed to help you evaluate whether tech products live up to their green promises. Follow these steps to find a green replacement monitor on the EPEAT site:

1. **Check a site such as CNET for reviews on the latest green monitors.**

   The EPEAT registry lists more monitors than most people want to research, so it helps to have a few models in mind before you begin. Alternatively, you can randomly select a few monitors from the list and compare them, which we cover in a moment.

2. **Visit the EPEAT Registry at `http://www.epeat.net`.**

3. **On the main page, scroll down to see the EPEAT Quick Search Tool.**

4. **Find Monitors in the Product column on the left. Then on the right click the number for the grade of monitor you'd like or the total number of monitors (on the right) if you want to see all monitors in the registry.**

   The grade indicates the EPEAT rating for a monitor's efficiency. As in the Olympic Games, gold is for the best, or most efficient, products.

5. **Select the check boxes of any monitors that interest you. Then click the Compare button.**

   You can then see how the monitors compare based on the specific EPEAT criteria. Hover your mouse pointer over the criterion and a ToolTip explaining it appears.

Hopefully, you have narrowed down your selections to two or three different monitors. If you want to do a little price comparison, write down the model numbers for each monitor that interests you and point your browser to www. nextag.com. Enter each model into the search box to find out who's offering the best deal on each one.

Understanding Energy Star standards for monitors

Before a monitor is approved as Energy Star–compliant, it must meet stringent requirements for On, Sleep, and Off modes:

- ✔ The amount of power used in the On state varies depending on the monitor's screen resolution. For example, a 17" monitor may qualify when using 28 watts (such as the Acer V173 q), while a 19" monitor may qualify when using 35 watts (such as the Acer P193W t). It's interesting to note that a search of the Web site at http://www. energystar.gov/index.cfm?fuseaction=find_a_product. ShowProductGroup&pgw_code=MO shows all kinds of LCD monitors making the grade, but not a single CRT monitor.

- ✔ In Sleep mode, the monitor must consume 2 watts or less.

- ✔ In Off mode, the monitor must consume 1 watt or less.

Be sure to set the power management features for the monitor you buy; not all monitors ship with energy-saving features in effect.

Gaming and More with a Greener Video Card

The graphics card in your system is a big power draw — in some cases requiring up to a 750-watt power supply to keep things moving. The graphics card has a lot of work to do, turning bits of information into the image you see and interact with on the screen. The graphics card displays everything visible — text, images, buttons, game characters, animations; but it's all just moving dots on a screen. (That's hard to believe, isn't it?)

Your graphics card works hand-in-hand with your monitor, converting the data into information that's displayed on the screen. Different graphics cards have different capabilities. The processing power and cooling system of the card have a big impact on the card's energy efficiency and life. Although the specifics of upgrading your card vary from computer to computer, the following steps walk you through the basic process of researching a new card:

1. **Check what your current graphics card is.**

   If you completed the inventory of your system in Chapter 4, then you already have this information. Flip to that chapter for help identifying what hardware you have.

   One popular graphics card in PCs is the ATI Radeon HD 3870 (`http://ati.amd.com/products/Radeonhd3800/index.html`). The steps in this section use this graphics card as an example. The specifications for your card will vary (unless you own the same card).

2. **Check the energy specs for your current card.**

   One of the reasons to chose the ATI Radeon HD 3870 is that it has a number of different specifications as described at `http://ati.amd.com/products/Radeonhd3800/requirements.html`. This graphics card starts by needing a 450-watt minimum power supply. The graphics card requires Peripheral Component Interconnect (PCI) Express power connector that supplies 75-watts, so you need to check your power supply to ensure it can supply that much power. The PCI connector is the most popular graphics card connection today.

   Some motherboards actually supply two PCI connectors so you can connect two graphics cards together in a Scalable Link Interface (SLI) configuration. More graphics cards always means more power — twice as much, in fact, and you don't even get twice the graphics processing power for your investment. It's better to buy a higher powered single card solution, rather than invest in a dual card technology unless you actually need the processing power.

   Older motherboards may also support an Accelerated Graphics Port (AGP), but AGP isn't a popular solution any longer. Even so, AGP tends to require far less power than PCI Express does. For example, look at the specifications for the ATI Radeon X800 at `http://ati.amd.com/products/radeonx800/radeonx800series/index.html` and you see that this graphics card only requires a 300-watt power supply. Of course, you also get far less graphics processing power when using AGP than you do using PCI Express.

It's important to look for hidden energy costs when working with graphics cards. For example, ATI recommends 1 GB of system memory for the ATI Radeon HD 3870, but the ATI Radeon X800 only requires 128 MB. More memory always translates into more power. Vendors tend to tell you about many of these special requirements in an "oh by the way" section of the specifications.

Knowing the minimum system requirements for a graphics card is helpful because the system requirements indicate how much peak power the graphics card will use. However, it's also helpful to look for hardware reviews that tell you more details. For example, Tom's Hardware provides a review of the ATI Radeon HD 3870 at `http://www.toms hardware.com/reviews/ati-r680-rage-fury-maxx-2, 1764-17.html`. This Web site shows you precise power requirements for both peak and idle states. Unfortunately, it isn't always easy to find an independent review with numbers you can believe.

 3. **In addition, determine how much graphics processing power you need.**

The MHz specification tells you how quickly your current card can process graphics. For example, the ATI Radeon HD 3870 specifications at `http://ati.amd.com/products/Radeonhd3800/specs.html` tell you that the card runs at 400 MHz. However, processing speed isn't the entire story. A graphics card with more onboard, dedicated, memory is likely to run faster than one that has to rely on sharing motherboard memory. Using dedicated Synchronous Dynamic Random Access Memory (SDRAM) is always faster than the standard RAM on the motherboard, plus the graphics card doesn't have to fetch data from motherboard memory using the slower system bus. Features also make a difference. If the operating system doesn't have to simulate a feature, such as anti-aliasing, the graphics processor can deliver data to the screen faster. Finally, having drivers from the vendor specifically for your operating system will reduce power requirements and enhance processing speed. When you have to use generic operating system drivers, the graphics card can't operate at maximum efficiency and won't use all of the functionality it can provide.

  • *If you find the graphics on your computer okay,* then just stick with a number similar to the one you already have.

  • *If you'd like to improve graphics processing speed,* then you'll want a more powerful card. Avoid older AGP cards because they're truly only worthwhile for simple word processing, a bit of work with a spreadsheet, or extremely simple games. If you do standard business activities, then a slower, non-SLI, PCI graphics card that relies on shared memory should work for you. Business users who perform graphics intensive activities such as drawing or creating charts should look for a faster (350 MHz or above), non-SLI, PCI graphics card with 1 GB of onboard SDRAM. If your computer habits are more graphics intensive, such as gaming, then you may want to obtain one of those SLI PCI graphics cards with a fast bus. Avoid getting a two-card setup because they really aren't a good value from a power consumption perspective.

4. **Use sites such as Tom's Hardware (`http://www.tomshardware.com/`) to research greener graphics cards.**

Read the specifications carefully. Look for evidence of energy efficiency (even if only by comparison) as you investigate the power consumption of the cards you consider. Make sure you compare cards equally. Some vendors will try to make their cards sound more efficient by quoting the idle power requirements, rather than the peak power requirements. Sites such as Tom's Hardware often report both specifications so that you can make a good comparison.

Figure 5-1 shows the ATI Radeon X1650 XT graphics adapter, which the manufacturer touts as great for gaming and home theatre enthusiasts. AMD, the makers of the card, offer Cool 'n' Quiet technology that focuses on reducing power consumption and costs and increasing the green factor for all the company's processors.

Figure 5-1:
Read the specs, when you're considering a new video card, to find out about its energy-consumption habits.

After you have your new graphics card in hand, you need to perform the following steps to replace the card:

1. **Make sure your machine is shut off.**

2. **Open the case and discharge any static electricity by touching the power supply case.**

Static electricity can damage your system and will definitely damage your new card. If you move, then you must discharge any static electricity generated by the move.

3. **Locate the current graphics card.**

   You can determine which card is the graphics card by looking for the monitor connector.

4. **Disconnect any monitor cables from the card.**

5. **Unscrew the case screw that holds the graphics card in place.**

   Some cases don't have screws — they may use a lever or other hold down method. The point is to make sure you can remove the card without damaging anything.

6. **Pull the old card straight out of the case.**

   You may need to wiggle the card just a bit to get it to move. At no time should you need to exert more than a little force to remove the card. If you're wrestling with the machine, stop now! Look for a screw or other hold down and remove it.

7. **Carefully line up the new card and gently press it in place.**

   Pushing the card hard can damage the gossamer pins used to connect the graphics card to the motherboard. These pins are very tiny and easy to damage. Gentle handling prevents damage to the motherboard or your card.

8. **Make sure the new graphics card is fully seated in the slot and replace any screws used to hold the old card in place.**

   If you encounter any difficulties, make sure you double-check the placement of the graphics card. It should seat fully in the slot without any coercion.

9. **Reconnect the monitor cables.**

10. **Turn on your system and verify that you can see the system boot.**

    There isn't any need to log into the operating system — in fact, it's better if you don't at this point. Simply verify that the system will boot and that you can see something onscreen.

11. **Shut the system down.**

    Make sure you perform a normal shutdown and don't simply turn off the power switch. You don't want to damage your operating system setup.

12. **Replace the case cover.**

    You're ready to begin using that new card.

13. **Follow any vendor software instructions for your operating system.**

The custom drivers provided by the vendor will always outperform generic drivers supplied by the operating system vendor. You don't necessarily need to install all the add-on software, however. The add-on software adds nice functionality, but often consumes power by keeping your computer churning away whenever you stop typing.

Adding Memory without Ginseng

You may or may not realize it, but your computer is constantly working, processing, chewing, and running data to and from various components and peripheral devices every nanosecond it's in use. Whether you press a key on the keyboard, adjust the brightness on your monitor, or build a complicated Excel spreadsheet, your computer's RAM (random access memory) stores the programs and data you need to keep things moving forward.

If you've ever worked on a system that didn't have enough RAM, you probably remember what happened. You pressed Page Down to move through your spreadsheet — and waited while your monitor repainted the screen. Or you opened a demanding program like Photoshop and tried to be patient while the program window appeared, one toolbar, one panel at a time.

Back in the personal computer stone age, people flipped out if they were able to get their hands on a system that had 256K (that's *kilobytes*) of random access memory for programs and data. Today, the RAM recommendation for Windows Vista and Windows 7 is 1GB, and it's not unusual to find 4GB of RAM already installed on a new computer. (That's gigabytes, or 1,600 times the RAM of yesteryear.)

Adding more RAM to your machine enables it to keep up with the increasing demands that software programs place on a computer, enabling you to continue using the computer. Adding RAM also reduces the amount of energy your computer consumes because it won't be forever churning away, paging through programs and data, trying to swap important things in and out of the available memory space. You'll have less time to wait (which means shorter time spans at the computer — while you get more done!) and overall a smoother PC experience. Harmony for both you and your PC. Nice.

Finding out how much memory you have

All you have to do is look around your local coffee shop and you know: Not all computers are created equal. When your computer was made, the type of model it is, and the types of applications you run on it all have something to do with how much memory came with the system and how much you need to run it well now.

You can find out how much memory is already in your Windows Vista system by following these steps:

1. **Click Start and right-click Computer.**

   A menu appears. (See Figure 5-2.)

Figure 5-2:
Checking
out your
computer's
short-term
memory.

2. **Select Properties.**

   The System Properties window appears. (See Figure 5-3.) The System area shows you your computer's system rating (this is a Windows Vista thing) and then lists your processor, the amount of memory installed in your system, and the system type (whether you're running a 32-bit or 64-bit version of the operating system).

   Obviously, the memory number is what you need most here (although the processor information is important, too). Write down anything you don't think you'll be able to store in your own internal memory (that is, your head), and take a look online to see what upgrade options are available for your system. Find out the amount of RAM on your Mac by clicking the Apple Menu and choosing About This Computer.

Figure 5-3:
503MB? No *wonder* this system is so slow!

Still got the manual that came with your computer? This is one of those situations when having the manual can actually help. Chances are, it provides a diagram of the mysterious inner workings of your system (which can come in handy later), and it may also give you a clue about the kind of memory modules to look for when you begin to search online.

32-bit, 64-bit, six bits, a dollar

What do these numbers mean, why do they matter, and should you try to change them? Yes, these phrases sound like cryptic codes that people in the know whisper to each other when James Bond walks in the room. The simple answer is in raw data processing power.

A *bit* of information, in computer-speak, is a binary digit. And in binary, there are only two possible digits: 0 and 1. (You've probably heard this before, in the Annals of Computing History course you took in middle school.) Early, on, computer microprocessors were capable of chewing up and spitting out information using 32-bit processing (with numbers representing values from 0 to 4,294,967,295), but today, 64-bit microprocessors and operating systems can double the processing power, which means faster processing and bigger talent for calculations, databases, design, and more.

Finding your computer's memory type

Here's an important point about adding memory: You need to get the RAM that's right for your system and processor. The motherboard manual that comes with your system will tell you what kind of memory to get and the size memory (in MB) that your system will accept. If you don't have a motherboard manual, try to locate one on the vendor Web site. Some third party Web sites, such as Technibble (http://www.technibble.com/types-of-ram-how-to-identify-and-their-specifications/), tell you about memory types as well. To make sure you're ordering the right module, follow these general steps:

1. **Write down the make and model number or name of the system to which you want to add memory. If there's a user account ID or item number label on the system, write that down, too.**

   In fact, write these items down in a notebook you keep with your computer, if you're not doing that already. They will come in handy when you begin shopping for the upgrades you need.

2. **Start by searching your manufacturer's Web site. Enter something obvious, like *memory upgrade.***

   Depending on who made your computer system, you may have the option to log in and let the site's database tell you what your system is capable of and how much room you have to add memory. Dell offers a nice feature that lets you do a system scan live on the site, or enter a service code. (It's somewhere on the side or bottom of your computer.) The site tells you what kinds of upgrades are possible for that system. (See Figure 5-4.)

Note that your laptop looks a little different inside — and of course, it's more compact — but the general process still applies. In any case, find out about any specific instructions your computer manufacturer offers on adding memory before you begin dismantling things and plugging new stuff in.

If your computer doesn't have an available slot for a new memory card, you'll need to replace one of the memory cards you already have with an increased amount of memory. For the best energy savings, use one memory module with more memory instead of two modules with smaller amounts of memory.

Figure 5-4:
See what
you can
upgrade on
your system.

Adding memory

The actual process of adding memory to your computer is easier than it sounds. Be sure to check your system documentation (or search online) for any techniques that are related specifically to your own computer model. But here's the general process:

1. **Turn off and unplug your computer, and remove any attached cables.**

   It's important to remove all cables from the unit and move it out where you can open the cover easily.

2. **Open the case so you can see the inside of the computer.**

   Your computer cover may have small thumbscrews holding the cover on at the corners or back; you may also need a small Phillips screwdriver or be required to push or slide a small plastic button to release the cover. Check the manual if you aren't sure.

3. **Ground yourself by touching a metal part of the cover or back of the system.**

   This discharges any static electricity safely.

4. **Locate the memory slots on the motherboard.**

   You'll see several slots together, with a small white clips on each end. Depending on your system's capabilities, you may see memory modules already in the slots.

5. **(Optional) To remove a memory card, gently press down on the plastic clips.**

   Remember, you need to remove an existing memory card only if you're replacing it with a card with more memory.

   The clips open outward and you can lift the memory module out.

6. **Insert the new memory module by turning it to align with the connectors on the bottom of the card.**

   A small divider shows you how to align the module before you press the memory into place.

7. **Press the module gently into the slot.**

   When seated properly, the module snaps into place, and the clips close.

8. **Put the case cover back on, connect the power cable, and reconnect the peripherals — monitor, keyboard, mouse, router, and printer.**

9. **Turn the power on and check your system properties.**

   Did it take? Congratulations! (If not, take everything apart and do it all again. Chances are that the memory module isn't seated properly.)

As you can imagine, there's a lot more to say about RAM than we can go into here, but for more information, check out this basic introduction to all things RAM: http://tinyurl.com/pq992p.

What's a Terabyte among Friends?

Adding a hard drive or replacing the one you've got can be considered a green upgrade if you find a unit, made with non-toxic materials, that offers a low-energy solution. The list of vendors providing such a thing is still pretty short, but there are a few contenders. We expect the list to continue to grow.

Western Digital's Caviar GP hard drive fits this bill, providing a 3.5-inch hard disk available in capacities up to a terabyte (TB). (Doesn't that just blow your mind? That means 12 zeros.) To take a closer look, you can visit Western

Digital's site at www.wdc.com/en. And you can find a detailed review with access speed and power consumption data available on the Tech Report site at http://techreport.com/articles.x/13379.

Computers are generally tolerant of hard drives when it comes to size. Replacing a 100 GB drive with a 200 GB drive of the same type usually won't cause problems. In addition, the computer doesn't care how fast the disk spins. A disk that spins at 7,500-RPM works just as well as a drive that spins at 10,000-RPM, but the 10,000-RPM drive will access data faster. However, you do need to consider the kind of interface the hard drive supports. Your motherboard manual should tell you what kinds of interface it provides. The most popular interfaces are:

- ✔ Integrated Drive Electronics (IDE)

- ✔ Extended Integrated Drive Electronics (EIDE)

- ✔ Serial Advanced Technology Attachment (SATA)

- ✔ Small Computer System Interface (SCSI)

In some cases, a motherboard will support multiple interfaces. For example, ASUS makes some motherboards that support both EIDE and SATA drives. The EIDE drives provide average performance and low cost. You generally add these drives one at a time. The SATA drives offer higher performance and redundancy that enhances system reliability. However, you normally add SATA drives in groups, so they consume more power and cost more.

You can also add an external hard drive and share it among different computers — in your house or wherever you go. It can serve as a backup unit or as an easy way to add storage capacity. The SimpleTech [re]drive (see Figure 5-5) is a beautiful, energy-efficient external hard drive that's made with a potentially earth-friendly material: bamboo! The drive is designed to turn off automatically when your computer isn't in use. It works via Turbo USB 2.0 with both Macs and PCs, and it comes with 2GB of free online backup. Find out more at www.simpletech.com.

Figure 5-5:
The
SimpleTech
[re]drive
is earth
friendly and
energy
conscious.

You can recycle an existing hard drive you don't want any more by using Gazelle (`www.gazelle.com`). This site pays cash for all kinds of gadgets — not just hard drives — which you can then donate to green causes, put into carbon offsets, or put back into your own checking account.

Improving Your Laptop Battery

Rechargeable batteries for your MP3 player, game controllers, and various other devices have been around for years, but green batteries for laptops are something new. I know what you're thinking — my laptop has always had a battery, so it must be green. Older laptop batteries can have hazardous chemicals in them such as lead, so they aren't green. A green laptop battery often relies on lithium-ion technology. It holds a charge longer and fades less over time so that you replace the battery far less often. *Fade* is a term that describes the gradual failure of the battery — you get four hours of computing time from it today, but by tomorrow you only get three hours. Eventually, the fade effect means the battery won't hold a charge and you must replace it. Longer charges mean you need fewer batteries for your business trip and less fade means fewer total batteries over the life of the laptop.

An environmentally friendly laptop battery has the following features:

- ✔ **It's made and packed with earth friendliness in mind.** Of course, the big thing is that the battery doesn't contain hazardous chemicals such as lead. Most green batteries today rely on lithium-ion technology, but look for new technologies to show up as science discovers them.

- ✔ **It needs to recharge at a rate that makes it practical for computing.** A green battery should provide you with at least four usable hours of work time.

- ✔ **It needs to have a lasting power that holds its own.** You don't have to replace the battery as often. A green battery will fade less over time — you should be able to use it twice as long (or more) as an old technology laptop battery.

The battery for your laptop is an extremely personal thing. Your laptop won't work well with a battery that isn't designed for it. In fact, your laptop may not work at all with the wrong battery — assuming that you can even connect the battery to the laptop. If you use the wrong battery with your laptop, you risk fire or other terrifying consequences as well. In short, always use batteries that the laptop vendor has approved for use with a particular laptop.

Boston-Power, a company started by Dr. Christina Lampe-Onnerud with a vision of a whole-system approach to portable power, has developed the Sonata battery that is now being offered as the HP Enviro Series batteries for the following laptop computer models:

✔ HP Pavilion (models dv4, dv5, and dv6)

✔ HP HDX 16

✔ HP G50, G60, G61, G70, and G71

✔ Compaq Presario (models CQ40, CQ45, CQ50, CQ60, CQ61, CQ70, and CQ71)

The new Sonata battery (called the HP Enviro) promises like-new functionality for three years. This means that even though traditional laptop batteries begin to lose capacity after only 100 to 150 charges, the Sonata continues charging fully like a new battery would for up to 1,000 charges (a promise HP covers by warranty). To find out more, go to `www.boston-power.com/enviro`.

Greening Your Power Supply

Your computer's power supply is normally a silver box that appears at the back of the case — usually near the top or left side of the case depending on your case configuration. The power supply accepts alternating current (AC) input from an outlet in your house and outputs the direct current (DC) that the computer components require. DC is the same kind of power that batteries output. Power supplies are rated by their wattage and special features they provide, such as connectors for an SLI graphics card. Not all power supplies are created equal. A cheap power supply won't last nearly as long or output steady power like a heavy duty one (such as those from PC Power and Cooling, `http://www.pcpower.com/index.html`). Steady power output is important because it helps your computer components work more efficiently, use less power, and last longer. If your power supply is inefficient, upgrading it can be a very green move and maximize your energy savings.

Changing out the power supply in your system requires a little more than a "How-do-I-plug-this-in?" kind of mindset, so unless you're technically inclined (or have a friend who runs a PC fixit shop), you may want to leave this one for the specialists. But power supplies do get right to the heart of the matter, and they can make a big impact on the amount of power your computer consumes.

Looking closer at your power supply

Most regular power supplies actually pump out more power than the computer needs, and the wasted energy adds up over time — both for your electric bills and for the CO_2 emissions in the atmosphere.

So how do you know whether your computer would benefit from a power supply upgrade? You need to check your power supply against your usage. If you have a 750-watt power supply, for example, but your computer uses only 200 watts to function, that's a bit of overkill, which means you have room for a healthy reduction. Here's how you find out these specs:

- ✔ **To find the wattage of your power supply:** Locate the label found on the top of the power supply. You must open the case to see this label.

- ✔ **To find out how many watts your computer uses:** Create a list of the components that your computer contains and their individual peak wattages. Add all the wattages together. Never use the idle power wattages for components in your computer or you could overload the power supply during peak power usage.

Finding an efficient power supply

One way you can find an environmentally friendly power supply is to reference the 80 PLUS program (find more information at www.80plus.org), which connects you with manufacturers who offer *smart power supplies* (those that deliver only the current needed by the system). For example, if you're surfing the Web on an 80 PLUS-certified computer and it needs only a little power, it draws only a little. If you're running a graphics-intensive game and the system needs a lot of power, it draws a lot. Knowing how to accommodate the system's different needs makes all the difference between blasting power at full force (and wasting it) and using it wisely, which is better for the planet and your checkbook.

All power supplies in the 80 PLUS program also are lead-free and manufactured without other toxic substances. You can read through the list of manufacturers and see how each model rates — Bronze, Silver, or Gold — for both individual use and data center applications. (See Figure 5-6.)

Figure 5-6:
The 80 PLUS
program
helps you
find just
the power
supply you
need — and
not a watt
more.

Here are a few additional resources to help you further investigate the greenness of the power supply you're considering:

✓ **Energy Star on power supplies and adapters:** www.energystar.gov/
index.cfm?c=ext_power_supplies.power_supplies_consumers

✓ **Research and global policies on power supplies:** www.efficient
powersupplies.org

Chapter 6

Buying a Green Computer

● ●

● ●

*T*his chapter helps you cover the essentials that lead up to that green purchase — and tells you what, exactly, a green computer is and how to know when you find one. We give you reliable information (*sans le* greenwashing, or deceptive marketing) that you can use to make choices. In addition, we highlight some specific new green computers and examine how the old standby manufacturers (Dell, Apple, and more) are focusing on developing greener systems.

Computer manufacturers today would have to be crazy to ignore the green opportunity rippling around the world. With green buzz, green jobs, green marketing, green initiatives, green advocacy, and yes, some major greenwashing jobs, you can be sure that focusing on the green (environmental issues) is foremost in manufacturer's minds. The challenges are manyfold: Creating energy-efficient, earth-friendly, affordable systems that are made from earth-friendly (non-toxic) materials, with sustainable lives of longer than three years.

Fortunately, some manufacturers are rising to the challenge. This chapter helps you take a look at what's out there right now so that you have a place to start as you research your own growing green initiative. Because green options are growing exponentially these days, this chapter is intended as only a starting point — use it as a springboard for your own research into manufacturers that pique your interest.

So You Decided to Make a Purchase, Hmmm?

Who doesn't like to buy something new? You're not alone, with your flushed cheeks and your accelerating heart rate. You keep glancing at ads. You want to show your friends. You play out different scenarios in your head, trying to come up with just the right argument that will help you get what you want.

It's a little like falling in love, isn't it?

We've all been there. And even though the big purchases are especially exciting, green computing would have you do your best to set aside the romance factor and get what you really need, and only what you really need, and make it last.

Understanding what makes a computer green

Your first question, as you begin to investigate all the different ways you can reduce your impact on the environment by revisiting the way you use your computer, might be "What makes a computer green, anyway?" You want to check out the manufacturer as well as the computer itself.

When you start to shop (and you will), look for the following clues to the manufacturer's dedication to earth-friendly initiatives (or lack of them):

- Search the manufacturer's Web site to see whether the company has any kind of green policy.
- Consult green buying guides to find out where the system or manufacturer rates. (We point you to a few of these later in this chapter.)

In terms of the computer itself, check for the following:

- **Look for the Energy Star logo.** We introduce Energy Star in Chapter 3.
- **Find out how much energy the computer uses.** Any peripherals, such as a printer, and the monitor, have their energy usage stamped in a panel on the back of the unit. The advertisements you read normally contain this information as well. The energy used by the computer itself is a little harder to determine. The power supply rating tells you the maximum the computer will use. If a computer has a 300 watt power supply,

it can't use more than 300 watts of power. However, most computers use only about half of the power that the power supply can provide. The exact amount of power that the computer uses depends on the components you place inside the box and what activities you perform (playing a game typically requires more power than writing a letter because the graphics card is working harder, as is the hard drive, during game play).

✔ **Look for information that tells you how the system is made (including the materials used in manufacturing).** In some cases, you see a label attached to the device that tells you about its manufacture. More commonly, you must ferret out the information by checking the vendor Web site. For example, Hewlett-Packard publishes its hazardous material use policy at `http://www.hp.com/hpinfo/globalcitizenship/ environment/productdesign/materialuse.html`. You want to avoid devices that include lead in them and most vendors are already addressing this problem metal. In addition, you want to avoid computers that contain mercury, Brominated Flame Retardants (BFR), Polyvinyl Chloride (PVC), cadmium, hexavalent chromium, Polybrominated Biphenyl (PBB), and Pentabromodiphenyl Ether (PBDE). Wow, what a nasty chemical soup! The European Union Restriction of Hazardous Substances (RoHS) directive (`http://www.rohs.gov.uk/`) is a good place to look for additional information.

✔ **See whether the system supports power management.** For in-depth look at power management, flip to Chapter 8.

Deciding what green means to you

We don't think a one-size-fits-all solution works for computer purchases, let alone green purchases. *Viva la difference!* Instead, we suggest you consider what green means to you and then make your purchase accordingly.

It's important to consider your skills when determining what approach to take for green computing. Many people have no idea what goes into the computer case and really don't want to know. Even if you dislike the very thought of working directly with hardware, you can still buy an Energy Star computer and obtain many benefits of green computing.

Some people really do like working with hardware, but lack detailed knowledge of how to put a computer together. In this case, buying a computer that is almost bare-bones (no, we don't mean you can see the motherboard) may be the greenest possible option. You can choose the individual components that you feel comfortable working with and ensure they all provide great power usage and lack harmful chemicals.

A few people know all about computer systems and don't even mind wielding a soldering iron should the need arise. If you fall into this category, you can buy custom components that not only meet green computing requirements, but also perform well. You can have a hotrod computer without hurting the environment.

No matter what your experience level, you do need to think about the purchases you make. The following list tells you a few of the things you should think about when making component purchases.

- ✔ Consider the power consumption of all the components (or even entire systems) that you're thinking about purchasing — and choose the most efficient.

- ✔ Buy all Energy Star-recommended equipment. (This is easy and makes a good minimum green effort.)

- ✔ Select a system with good power management features.

- ✔ Add a smart meter that remembers to turn off peripherals when you forget. (See Chapter 18 for details on working with smart meters.)

Matching a computer to your needs

Investigating what you really need in a computer, and then using that to guide your purchasing decision is another way to keep your new buy in the green zone. Sure, the temptation is to get the fastest, most powerful and innovative model on the showroom floor. But is that really what you need? How often do you play games that require a 750-watt power supply? Will a honking 30-inch monitor really make those Word documents you write any better?

 The following list helps you think through the types of things you actually do with your computer (granted, with room to grow) so that as you start shopping you have a general sense of what you need and what is enormous overkill. Write down how many minutes per day or per week you typically do the following activities with you computer:

- ✔ E-mail
- ✔ Shop online
- ✔ Browse Web sites
- ✔ Use social networking sites and blogs
- ✔ Create, edit, and format documents
- ✔ Work with spreadsheets

✔ Maintain a database

✔ Design Web sites

✔ Use photo editing software

✔ Listen to music

✔ Watch video

✔ Playing graphics-intensive video games

✔ Other _____

Many people don't actually know how long they perform various activities. If you fall into this group, create a log that lists the time you start the activity, the time you stop, the name of the activity, and the minutes you spend doing it. Track your activities during a typical week. At the end of the week, total the minutes spent performing each activity. With your list in hand, compare what you do most often or the activities that are most important to you with the specs outlined in Table 6-1.

Table 6-1	Thinking through Your Purchase		
What You Do with Your Computer	*Suggested RAM (Memory)*	*Suggested Processor Speed*	*Suggested Hard Drive Capacity*
E-mail	256 MB	500 MHz	1.5 GB
Shop online	128 MB	500 MHz	52 MB
Browse Web sites	64 MB	233 MHz	52 MB
Use social networking sites and blogs	64 MB	233 MHz	52 MB
Create, edit, and format documents	512 MB	500 MHz	1.5 GB
Work with spreadsheets	512 MB	500 MHz	1.5 GB
Maintain a database	512 MB	1 GHz	1.5 GB
Design Web sites	1 GB	2.2 GHz	2 GB
Use photo editing software	1 GB	1.8 GHz	1 GB
Listen to music	128 MB	500 MHz	300 MB
Watch video	512 MB	1 GHz	1 GB
Other	Check the vendor specifications	Check the vendor specifications	Check the vendor specifications

Table 6-1 provides guidelines, not absolutes. You need to review the specifications for the particular software you want to use. In some cases, the specifications for software vary by a number of factors, such as the operating system you use. Vendors usually make the information you need available to ensure you have a great computing experience. For example, you can see the specifications for Open Office at `http://www.openoffice.org/dev_docs/source/sys_reqs_30.html`. When you look at this Web site, you see that the specifications for Open Office vary by operating system, so you need to know which operating system your machine uses as part of determining how much memory and hard drive capacity you need.

So, how much of everything do you actually need? The following sections explain how to pull all this information together.

Memory

Memory is additive. Let's say you want to run your word processor, e-mail program, and Web browser at the same time. You need to add the amount of RAM for the word processor, e-mail program, and Web browser together. In addition, you need to add memory for the operating system and some additional memory (I usually add 50 percent more) for data. To make this example real, let's say we're using Windows XP Professional, which requires 128 MB RAM minimum according to the Web site at `http://www.microsoft.com/windowsxp/sysreqs/pro.mspx`. You end up with these memory requirements:

```
   Word processor:                     512 MB
 + E-mail program:                     256 MB
 + Web browser:                         64 MB
 + Operating system:                   128 MB
 = Minimum total:                      960 MB
 + 50% additional:                     480 MB
 = Safe total:           1,440 MB or 1.4 GB
```

Of course, you only need 1.4 GB if you plan to perform all the tasks at the same time. It's important to know what tasks you'll perform together and then use the maximum number when buying your computer.

Processor

Processor speed isn't additive. You need a processor that meets the minimum requirements for the most processor intensive software you use. Using the example of a word processor, e-mail program, and Web browser again, you'd need a 500 MHz minimum processor. Of course, the system will slow down as you add tasks and eventually slow to a crawl if you add too many. When selecting a processor, I normally choose one that is twice the speed of what I need or 1 GHz in this case.

Hard drive space

Hard drive space is tricky. The specifications you see for software don't include any space for the data you create. Realistically, vendors don't have any way to tell you that number. To obtain a ballpark number, add the values of all the software you intend to install (whether or not you plan to use it at the same time — applications and data use hard drive space even when you aren't using them) and then multiply by five. Using the previous example again, you get these numbers.

```
  Word processor:             1.5 GB
+ E-mail program:             1.5 GB
+ Web browser:                 52 MB
+ Operating system:          1.5 GB
= Minimum total:             4.6 GB
= Safe total:                 23 GB
```

Many vendors try to make their software look more attractive by providing minimum and recommended requirements. Always use the recommended requirements as your minimum value. The minimum values produce an environment where the software just barely works — it's unusable really. In addition, vendors often sneak all kinds of other requirements in. For example, check out the Nero (a product for creating and playing both music and video disks) system requirements at http://www.nero.com/eng/support-nero7-system-requirements.html. You immediately notice that you have to have Internet Explorer 6 or above (which means adding the requirements for running this software to your list), some special hardware, and operating system updates. In addition, you have to have 9 GB additional hard drive space to work with DVDs. Read all of the fine print before you decide on the hardware requirements for your system.

Researching Your Options

Now that companies know that green sells, you don't have to go very far to find manufacturers pitching their green computers. In fact, you can sit in your easy chair in the family room, and Apple will come through your television, telling you that it has the greenest family of laptops on the planet. If you open your e-mail inbox, you're likely to get a message from another computer company — maybe Dell — sharing its green vision and telling you that its committed to being the greenest computer manufacturer on the planet.

Okay, bring it on.

The great race for green isn't a bad thing. If you're voting with your dollars (and you are) and manufacturers know it, their development of ever-greener technologies (in competition for your business) will ultimately lead to better and better systems that have a smaller impact on the planet.

That is, of course, if their systems do what they say they will do.

In this section, you find out how to wade through all the promises and the hype and know you're getting a good green system. Here are a few guidelines to get you started, and we explore these in more detail in the sections that follow:

- ✔ **Do your homework.** Just because a company *says* it's green, prints a cleverly designed, natural-looking label, and goes to a couple of green conferences doesn't *make* it green. (In the next section, we show you how to do the due diligence to make sure you're not getting greenwashed by a manufacturer that has learned to walk, talk, and quack like it's green.)

- ✔ **Check for a seal of approval.** Any manufacturer or shopping site worth its carbon offset will show that its product has qualified as an energy-efficient offering by proudly displaying two standard achievements: an Energy Star qualification and Electronic Product Environmental Assessment Tool (EPEAT) rating. The Climate Counts rating is another one to check if you're looking to reduce your carbon footprint. (We discuss carbon footprints and tips to clean them up in Chapter 2.)

- ✔ **Go for the numbers.** Look for quantifiable evidence that the system does what the manufacturer promises. Look at things like wattage, battery life, cooling mechanisms, and power supply measurements. Compare the numbers with the same numbers on other systems — and families of systems. See "Matching a computer to your needs" earlier in this chapter for help sorting through the specs.

- ✔ **Ask around.** Search online for user reviews and ratings to give you a "real people" sense of how green the computer really is. Chances are, you'll find reviews for and against — and you'll need to wade through the opinions, flames, and blind loyalties people sometimes develop to one computer company or another.

Because so much of a purchase like this can be based on gut and sex appeal (come on; admit it), it helps to do all your homework, research various systems, and gather your info before you make a choice. The following sections guide you through the research process.

Cutting through the greenwashing

Greenwashing is representing a product as environmentally friendly when it really isn't. When a company greenwashes its products — whether it's marketing laundry detergent, automobiles, or power supplies — it attempts to appeal to your good intentions and sell you a product with a false promise. The company might lead you to believe that its product is made with earth-friendly materials, designed to consume less energy, or that it otherwise supports eco-responsible practices.

The majority of the companies you purchase green products from are doing what they say, thank goodness — doing their best to reduce and reuse, while creating products from safer materials that last a long time (and use less energy). But it's important to be able to sniff out the green paint fumes when the less reputable companies come along. If you catch a whiff of these kinds of things, steer clear:

- Green colors on the package, but no clear statement that the product benefits the planet, was produced from renewable or nontoxic resources, or uses less energy
- Claims of energy efficiency but no numbers to back them up
- No information available on specific tests related to energy consumption
- No Energy Star logo (on products that Energy Star reviews)
- No green policy or initiative

If you're unsure about the legitimate greenness of a company you're considering buying from, check out the company's partners, as well as its paper trail. Who does it donate to? Where do its employees volunteer? Does it have a green policy posted on its Web site?

Chances are, if you don't see evidence of green initiatives in the company's portfolio, there's a good reason: It's greenwashing its products.

Climate Counts for you and me

Want a quick way to see which companies really make green efforts? ClimateCounts.org is a non-profit organization that scores companies on a three-part scale, with a 0–100-point scale that provides additional detail.

- **Stuck:** Companies with this rating haven't gotten with the green program. (And Climate Counts suggests you avoid purchasing their products until they get moving.)
- **Starting:** These companies are making a green effort. (And the additional scores that the Web site provides show you how much progress they've made.)
- **Striding:** This rating identifies companies that are really making the grade and starting to pull away from the pack. (Use your purchasing dollars to reward their efforts and encourage their progress.)

ClimateCounts.org rates companies on a scale of 0–100 based on four key questions. Has the company

✔ **Measured its carbon footprint?**

✔ **Done anything to reduce its contribution to global warming?**

✔ **Made any effort to support climate legislation?**

✔ **Posted its climate actions clearly where others can find them?**

Based on 2008 numbers, Figure 6-1 shows the technology scorecard from Climate Counts. According to Climate Counts, IBM leads the pack and Apple still sits on the sidelines.

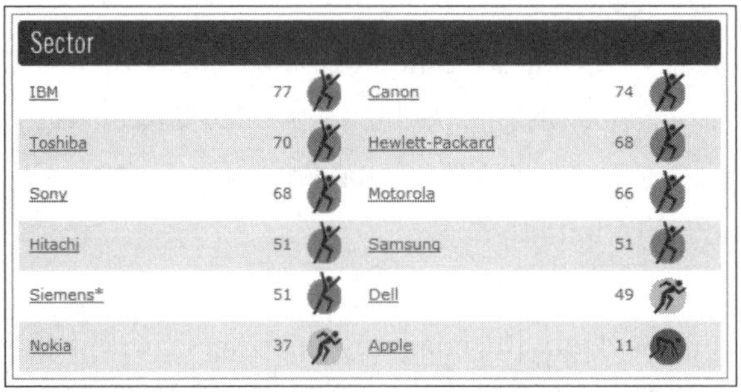

Figure 6-1:
Climate
Counts rates
companies
on a score
of 0–100.

Sector				
IBM	77		Canon	74
Toshiba	70		Hewlett-Packard	68
Sony	68		Motorola	66
Hitachi	51		Samsung	51
Siemens*	51		Dell	49
Nokia	37		Apple	11

An overview of Climate Counts

It pays to know about some of the organizations that can help you create a greener system and Climate Counts is one of them. This organization works with both companies and individuals to fight against global climate change. Climate Counts is a nonprofit organization funded by Stonyfield Farm, Inc. and launched in collaboration with Clean Air-Cool Planet.

If you think Climate Counts is just about computers, you're wrong. This organization is involved in just about every aspect of your daily life — from the tennis shoes you wear to the building in which you live. If you want to discover how a particular company fares when it comes to green, this is the place to look.

This is only a brief overview of Climate Counts. You want to know more about this organization because they do so much for the environment. The Web site at `http://www.climate counts.org/` tells you more about Climate Counts and enlightens you about what you can do to create a greener planet.

Let's hear it for Energy Star

We talk about Energy Star in other places in this book, but this section shows you how to use the Energy Star system (as well as other resources) to shed some light on your upcoming green computer purchase.

Not all computers live up to Energy Star standards. Computers that are energy-efficient enough to display the Energy Star on the label have to

- **Meet energy guidelines in three modes: Standby, Active, and Sleep.**

- **Have efficient internal power supplies.** We introduce power supplies in Chapter 5.

- **Offer power management features so that you can tailor the way energy is used on your system.** Power management features are the focus in Chapter 9.

In addition to looking for the actual Energy Star logo on the computer box, you can search the Energy Star site to see whether a computer you're interested in meets the power settings for the program. Here's how to do that:

1. **Go to the Energy Star site at `www.energystar.gov`.**

   The Energy Star home page offers basic information for parents, kids, and partnering businesses.

2. **In the Products area, click Office Equipment.**

   The Office Equipment page displays a list of equipment choices in the left side of the screen.

3. **Click Computers and scroll down to the bottom of the page.**

   The Computers page provides you with basic information on Energy Star guidelines for computers and offers a search tool you can use to see whether the computer you're considering buying is an Energy Star system. (See Figure 6-2).

4. **Click the Product Type arrow and choose Workstation, Notebook/ Tablet, or Desktop.**

   Chances are that for a home computer you want either Notebook/ Tablet or Desktop, but nobody's stopping you if you want to look for a Workstation.

5. **Enter the information you have on the computer.**

   It's not necessary to have it all — brand, processor, operating system, RAM, number of hard drives, storage, video card, and model name and number — but the more you can provide, the better.

6. **Choose the number of results you want to be displayed on the page and the way in which you want the results arranged.**

7. **Click Search.**

After the search, you're given the opportunity to refine the search criteria.

Take the ENERGY STAR Pledge today to join the fight against global warming!

Find ENERGY STAR Qualified Computers

climate savers
smart computing
Find out how you can participate with Climate Savers Computing Initiative EXIT

Product Type: Desktop

Brand: All Brands

Processor Brand:

Processor Name:

Operating System Name:

System Memory - RAM:

Number of Installed Hard Drives:

Total Hard Drive Storage in Product (GB):

Video Card Dedicated Non-Shared Memory (MB):

Model Name/Model Number:
All similar model numbers will be found. Enter only the first few digits for the best results.

Results per Page: 10

Order Results by: Brand

Search

* - This search will display products that are available in the US market. For a listing of ENERGY STAR qualified products available internationally, visit the full Qualified Product List for computers.

Figure 6-2:
You can use the Energy Star site to search for energy-efficient computers that meet the Energy Star standard.

EPEAT that, will you?

The EPEAT (Electronic Product Environmental Assessment Tool) registry is another consumer-protection tool you can use to make sure that computer manufacturers who promise green really deliver the goods.

When manufacturers state that their products live up to environmental standards, EPEAT evaluates products based on a set of 51 criteria; some are required and some are optional. After evaluating the products, each is rated with a Bronze, Silver, or Gold rating, determining how closely the products measure up to EPEAT standards.

To display the current list of products earning a Gold rating by EPEAT standards, follow these steps:

1. **Go to www.epeat.net.**

   The EPEAT home page provides the latest updates on the EPEAT registry and offers links to new items and industry announcements.

2. **Scroll down to the EPEAT Quick Search Tool and click the Gold column head.**

   A listing of all qualifying Gold products appears. (See Figure 6-3.) You can sort the list by product name, type, listing date, or status by clicking the appropriate column heading.

Want to save the list for later? You can export the list by clicking Export to Excel or Export to CSV. In the pop-up box that appears, navigate to the folder where you want to store the file and click OK.

Figure 6-3: The EPEAT registry lists all products that meet Bronze, Silver, and Gold standards for electronics equipment.

The EPEAT Registry is helpful for more than simply finding the computer models that measure up to environmental standards. You can also easily compare models so that you can see how each computer measures up toe-to-toe (metaphorically speaking). Here's how to do that:

1. **On the EPEAT site (www.epeat.net), click the icon of the standard you want to view (Bronze, Silver, or Gold).**

2. **On the product listing page, select the check box in the right column for any computer model you want to use in your comparison.**

   There are a couple of things to keep in mind:

   - *You can compare only three items at a time.*

   - *You must choose products within the same type (for example, all notebooks or all desktop computers).*

3. **After you choose the models you want to compare, scroll down to the bottom of the list and click Compare Products.**

   The resulting page lists the products you selected and shows their results for each of the optional criteria in the EPEAT standard. You can review the list and determine which model of those compared best fits your idea of a truly green computer.

 Export your product comparison to CSV or Excel format by clicking the appropriate link at the top of the results page. That way you can refer to the report later when you're doing some online shopping for that new green computer.

Using green buying guides

Lots of people want to make your computer shopping easier, especially if you're in the market for good green products. In addition to the standards designed to give consumers a reliable way to find dependable and truly green electronics, a number of sites offer green buying guides to help consumers (that's you) learn what they need to know before buying.

This section introduces you to a few of the buying guides that can help you find out more about the computer(s) you're considering bringing home to be part of the family.

Check out the Daily Green

The Daily Green (www.thedailygreen.com) isn't actually a downloadable, printable guide *per se.* (It's not the greenest thing in the world to print a bunch of pages anyway — unless you really need them.) The tagline on the site is "the consumer's guide to the green revolution," and the site offers you the latest information on product recalls, green living, do-it-yourself green projects, and more.

The section Green Products A to Z provides product profiles and reviews on lifestyle products. You'll find a few green tech items scattered in there, too.

TreeHugger Guides

TreeHugger.com is one of those green sites that will continue to pull you back in for more earth-friendly info on all kinds of things ranging from green science to cars to fashion to computing. It offers a number of buying guides for your gadgetry and provides a little background info (and links, as well). Here's how to get TreeHugger buying guidance:

1. **Go to www.treehugger.com.**

2. **In the Take Action column, click Green Buying Guides (or go directly to www.treehugger.com/buygreen).**

   A page of buying guides meets your eager gaze. Here, you'll find all the TreeHugger hand-picked favorites for green stuff you're considering.

3. **Scroll down to the guide you want to see, and click it.**

   You'll find buying guides for laptop computers and desktop computers, but you might want to take a look at the desks and chairs, too, while you're at it.

One caveat, though; some of the TreeHugger guides are in need of updating, so you may be looking at older reviews. Whatever you find there, be sure to check the numbers with EPEAT and look up the latest versions available by visiting the manufacturer's site.

Listening for the green buzz

Another way you can make sure you're getting the straight scoop on the green capabilities of the features you're considering is to read user ratings and reviews. The question-and-answer format abounds online. On many sites, you can post a question, respond to other peoples' questions and reviews, or just browse to see what others are saying. This section offers a smattering of sites where you can benefit from the shared knowledge of other earth-loving computer users.

- **Yahoo! Answers** (www.answers.yahoo.com) enables you to easily ask, answer, and gather points for sharing your expertise in greendom. This is kind of "mass consciousness meets gamerland," in a social networking environment that enables you to gather cred points and cash them in for new levels. We like it because you can get real opinions of real people — who, um, use avatars.

- **LinkedIn** (www.linkedin.com) is another social networking site used in large part for professional purposes. After you sign up and log in, you can ask other users questions in the Answers section (and respond to others' questions as well). To find the green topics, click Answers at the top of the screen, click the Sustainability category, and choose Green Products.

✔ **Epinions.com** is a site that collects and shares user reviews on a variety of topics, including green tech. Go to `www.epinions.com` and click the Computers & Software tab. In the Find and Compare area, click the type of computer you want to know more about (such as PC Desktop or Mac Laptop) and then click to see all reviews in the category you want to see.

You can also narrow the search to a specific computer model by typing the model name in the Search For box and selecting the category before clicking Search.

✔ **Amazon.com** is another source of great user reviews, and the computer comparisons enable you to view a variety of systems side by side, feature to feature. (The computer comparisons appear when you perform a search, such as all desktop computers or all computers from Apple.)

Checking Out Small, Green, Niche Computers

Although any computer manufacturer worth its salt currently offers (or is developing) greener systems, here are a few systems you might not find out about with all the Dell-Apple-HP-Lenovo-Sony messaging in the atmosphere. This section tells you the stories of a few computers you'll find off the more traveled paths.

Fujitsu's Esprimo Green PC

In March 2009, Fujitsu announced at CeBIT (the world's largest trade show for the digital IT and telecommunications industries) a new zero-watt series of PCs called ESPRIMO Green (`http://ts.fujitsu.com/products/deskbound/personal_computers/epa.html`). The new desktop computers will be available in three models (C, E, and Q) and will use earth-friendly materials and an environmentally sound production process.

In Standby mode, the zero-watt PC won't consume any energy at all, but you can still return it to normal operation in a snap. Expect to see more of this kind of wonder-working in the future. This computer meets the new Energy Star 4.0 requirements.

The CherryPal Bing

Imagine a world in which costs are low, systems are light, and everything's green. CherryPal develops Linux-based green computers (which are capable of running Windows XP, as well) that keep the footprint small, your budget manageable, and your power consumption minimal. This company is relatively new on the computing scene, having been established July 21, 2008. However, they have received more than a few accolades in the press. Read more about this company at `http://www.cherrypal.com/news.html`.

The CherryPal Bing is a netbook that offers all the features you want for Web browsing and connecting with friends and family around the globe. A *netbook* is a subnotebook computer in the $200 to $400 range and originally referred to Intel computers that used the Atom processor. However, many vendors now describe their small computers as netbooks.

CherryPal also builds in a *cloud computing* (performing computing tasks through the Internet, rather than through a local server) component so you can do more intensive processing tasks as well. Check out CherryPal at `www.cherrypal.com`. (See Figure 6-4.) The vendor doesn't tell whether this computer meets Energy Star or EPEAT Gold requirements.

Figure 6-4: CherryPal offers a 2-watt Linux-based system.

The *CherryPal*™ C114 desktop doesn't heat up, no noise, about double the size of a smart phone. What's inside? Not much actually, but more than enough. The Freescale power architecture triple-core 5121e processor provides a pleasant Internet browsing and multimedia user experience. Many free open-source based applications are pre-installed locally, as well as access to the CherryPal Cloud (optional):

Specifications:

Freescale's MPC5121e mobileGT processor, 800 MIPS (400 MHz) of processing
256 MB of DDR2 DRAM
8GB NAND Flash-based solid state drive (increased from 4GB C100)
WiFi 802.11b/g Wi-Fi
Two USB 2.0 ports

fit-PC: You've gotta see it to believe it

Okay, talk about your small footprint! The fit-PC (`www.fit-pc.com`) is a tiny hold-in-the-palm-of-your-hand computer that is available in both Windows and Linux versions. The manufacturers say the Windows XP version (called the fit-PC Slim XP) is good for e-mail and instant messaging, Web browsing, running Microsoft Office applications (we may have to get one just to test this), music storage and playback, and the good, old-fashioned family room PC used for movie downloads and the like. With a system unit barely bigger than your car keys, this is hard to believe! But with 4- to 6-watt power consumption and a retail of just over $300 (U.S., for the XP version), it might be worth a serious look. The vendor doesn't tell whether this computer meets Energy Star or EPEAT Gold requirements.

Making Your Purchase

If you do your computer-shopping research using a variety of tools, you'll probably discover the make and model of the computer that best meets your needs — and the environment's. You can purchase the computer through any traditional sales outlets — drive to stores like Best Buy, Comp USA, or the bricks-and-mortar Apple stores. Or you can order from any number of online retailers (including Amazon.com, of course, as well as the sites of all the physical stores we just listed).

To reduce the almost unlimited variety of online sales outlets you can choose from, you may want to go with one of two sales sites that are recommended by EPEAT: Buy.com and TechDepot.com. Both sites are in partnership with EPEAT and use the EPEAT ratings — Bronze, Silver, and Gold — to help you find the computer you want. Figure 6-5 shows the EPEAT page of Buy.com.

Figure 6-5: EPEAT Gold, Silver, and Bronze systems are identified on Buy.com.

Telling your green computing story

You can make another commitment to support the green movement in computer manufacturing: give companies your feedback. If manufacturers overpromise, tell them so. And don't just tell them: Post it on your blog; contribute to forums; post user reviews and ratings. We aren't asking you to flame anybody — that's just not nice, and it earns you some nasty e-mail karma — but we do want you to tell your story about the system you purchase. If it's green and you love it, terrific! Tell the world. If it falls short and the manufacturer could do a better job representing the green features it promises, your fellow environment-advocating computer users deserve to know that, too.

Or consider whether you can buy the computer you want as a refurbished system. This may not be the sexiest option, but it's probably the greenest. Many computer manufacturers and resellers offer refurbished systems or individual parts you can replace. (Dell is one example of a company that enables you to buy refurbished systems.)

Chapter 7

Choosing Earth-Friendly Peripherals

In This Chapter

▶ Planning an eco-friendly purchase

▶ Checking out gleaming green monitors

▶ Meeting printer superheroes

▶ Buying drives, storage, and other not-so-boring necessities

The microprocessor chewing away at the data inside your computer is a little like a caterpillar, eating hundreds of times its weight in energy in a single day. It continually devours electric current to fertilize your spreadsheets (sorry for *that* image) and help your productivity blossom. But what goes on inside your computer is only part of the story. In the bigger scheme of things, peripherals drink quite a carafe of juice on their own — especially the peripheral you look at all day. *Peripherals* are devices outside the main computer and include printers, mice, monitors, keyboards, cameras, and myriad other devices. A peripheral is always a device of some sort. For example, a DVD isn't a device, so it isn't a peripheral. Standalone devices (those that don't connect directly to your computer), such as routers, aren't considered peripherals, but you should consider them in your plans for a green computing environment.

This chapter gives you what you need to explore green components to add to your green computer. You find out about the green factor for monitors, printers, mice, and keyboards. You also find the answer to the age-old question, "Does the Hewlett-Packard I-can-do-everything-including-the-dishes-with-my-printer model really save any energy?"

Along the way, you pick up a few sources of green peripherals and come away with some good ideas you can try at home without a net. Ready to get started?

Planning Your Purchases of Green Peripherals

Consumers are interested in trying green versions of their favorite brands, as the green movement in computer manufacturing bears out. But manufacturers that produce green peripherals know that they're competing for market share with other manufacturers on important qualities including size, performance, and price. To get the right green peripherals, you have to consider all these qualities and weigh some trade-offs, including the following:

- **Price:** One challenge that peripheral makers face is offering products at competitive prices. The new technology used to create green devices costs more than the old polluting technologies commonly used in existing devices. Vendors pass the additional cost of the new technology onto buyers and then add a premium because they feel they can charge more for the new device. Buyers won't necessarily want to fork over an extra 10, 12, or even 20 percent just to get good green components. Over time — and as green awareness grows — we're betting that more people will.

- **Energy use:** Some peripherals use more energy than others because each type of peripheral uses different types of resources:

  - *Monitor:* The monitor you choose consumes quite a bit of energy compared with other peripherals. It has become more common to connect multiple monitors to a computer to help coordinate data activities (a word processor on one display and a browser on another, for example). When your computer has multiple monitors attached to it, the energy consumption is magnified. Use a single monitor whenever possible. For tips on choosing a green monitor, see Chapter 5.

  - *Printer:* Your printer uses less energy than your monitor but still consumes its share. Look on the vendor Web site for printer specifications. For example, you can see the specifications for the HP LaserJet 9050 series at `http://h10010.www1.hp.com/wwpc/uk/en/sm/WF06a/18972-18972-3328059-3328068-3328068-410000.html`.

  - *Mouse:* Your mouse doesn't eat much. Wired mice draw their energy directly from the system, which is kinder to the environment than wireless mice where you must supply batteries.

- *Keyboard:* Your keyboard, if it's the wired kind, draws the minimal amount of power it needs from your system unit, and that's a negligible amount. If you use a wireless keyboard, you've got some battery action going on — batteries can be problematic for the environment.

- *Other:* There are many other peripherals you can connect to your computer. For example, most people connect their digital camera to their computer to download and process pictures they take. Many people also use external storage devices for backup purposes. Every peripheral you connect to your computer uses energy and you must consider that energy use as part of your green computing plan. Normally, the vendor will tell you how much energy each device uses.

✔ **Performance:** Many people associate performance with speed; however, speed is only part of the equation. A green device performs well when it delivers a maximum number of tasks in a given amount of time for a limited amount of energy. A device that can deliver four tasks for 300 watts is better than a device that can only deliver three tasks for the same amount of energy. If the device can also perform the task faster than another device, meaning it draws energy for less time, it also saves energy and the environment.

✔ **Materials:** You should consider what kinds of materials were used to make any device you're considering buying. Keep away from harmful materials such as lead and mercury in any device you buy. See the device-specific sections later in the chapter for details on hazardous materials for particular device types.

All that guilt aside, you *do* need a monitor for a desktop system, and you probably need a printer too.

Part of the equation in green home computing is purchasing the type of peripheral you need to do the job you need it to do. This may mean purchasing a midrange monitor instead of a super-snazzy, power-hungry, oversize screen, or it may mean getting one printer that you share with other people in the house instead of buying one for each computer (a topic that we discuss in the next section).

Use Table 7-1 to get a sense of what — and how much — you need.

Table 7-1	Planning for Peripherals		
Equipment	*How Many Do You Have?*	*How Many Do You Need?*	*Replace or Recycle?*
Printers Inkjet Laser Other			
Scanners			
External storage			
Digital cameras			
Video cameras			
MP3 players			
Digital recorders			
Personal digital assistants (PDAs)			
Game systems			

Sharing Peripherals: A Friendly Way to Save the Earth

At one time, peripheral devices were extremely expensive, so people shared them. A printer might cost more than several terminals connected to a mainframe. However, as the PC revolution progressed and people embraced the personal in computing, peripheral devices became less expensive. Suddenly, everyone has to have their own printer.

There are more peripheral devices now than ever before, too. At one time the monitor, keyboard, mouse, and printer were the four peripherals that every computer owner wanted. Now, computers have all kinds of connections to scanners, digital cameras, external drives, and a host of other devices. The result is that single computers have scads of power hungry devices attached to them.

Why not share that equipment? Sharing is a friendly thing to do, and it's good for the earth too. At home, you probably already share many things — the refrigerator, the microwave, the washer and dryer (okay, maybe one person uses those more than another does) — so sharing technology isn't a completely foreign concept.

Breaking resource sharing to the kids

Introducing the idea of resource sharing in your household may be something that you have to do strategically. If your kids are still in that "Mom, he's breathing my air!" stage, getting them to share peripherals, such as digital cameras, may prove impossible. The amount of CO_2 you'd produce managing the stress of your household would probably offset any savings you might create. (Remember that you can always share a printer — just make sure you put it in a public place, rather than one child's room.)

If you want to introduce the idea of resource sharing — *á la* computer peripherals — to your family, here are a few ideas to keep in mind:

✔ Depending on your kids' ages, they may either grumble no matter what you say or take credit for the idea ("I've been telling you that for a year, Dad!").

✔ Give and take are required. If you're time-sharing a family PC, start with a schedule, and be prepared to renegotiate and revisit it for weeks, *ad nauseum.* Even if you aren't sharing a PC, make sure shared peripherals have a schedule. If one child is using the scanner, everyone else will suddenly decide they need it too.

✔ Be willing to give up some of your own time when someone has a need that's really urgent. Demonstrating kindness sends a good message (and reinforces your own good effort).

✔ If you expect great resistance in the computer-sharing department, start with peripherals only. Have one digital camera instead of four. Get a wireless router, and have everybody print to the same printer. Make it a point to look for energy-efficient devices as a family; read the numbers and do the research together.

✔ Give your family periodic energy updates by letting them know how much CO_2 they've reduced through family efforts. Have a carbon-offset party. Plant something to commemorate a milestone. If you reward everyone's efforts and keep them informed about the difference they're making, you give them incentive to do more. Everyone feels better when we're doing our part; it's part of our species DNA.

Want to add a little extra oomph to your argument? Have your kids check out Lose Your Excuse, from the U.S. Department of Energy (www.loseyourexcuse.gov/index.html#/index).

What can you share?

Depending on the number of people in your family, your ages, the type of work you do, and the ways in which you all use computers, your family members may be able to share computer time and resources easily — or not. Some peripherals are easy — you can always share a printer. Other devices are hard — only one person can process the pictures found on a digital camera at a time. A few devices may be impossible. For example, sharing a single PDA may prove impossible because the very definition of a PDA is something you use to store your personal information. Here are a few ideas to get you started thinking about what you can share and what you definitely can't:

- ✔ **Schedules:** Think of the overall schedule at home. Are some people home when others aren't? Schedule single use peripherals so that everyone can use the same device. For example, it's likely that not everyone will need the camera at the same time, so create a schedule for it that reflects the schedules of the people who need it.

- ✔ **Priorities:** What types of activities do people use the peripherals to do? Letting someone use the digital camera for a school project probably has a higher priority than taking snapshots of friends. Likewise, a scanner used to input data for your home business is probably a higher priority than scanning recipes into a database.

- ✔ **Usage:** Are some peripherals used only once in a while, and can all family members share them? Everyone can use the same printer at the same time — the printer will keep the print jobs straight. However, only one person can use a digital recorder at a time. Is it possible for everyone to share a single device?

In Chapter 12, you find out how to set up a home network to make sharing resources a simple reality.

Picking Printers

Okay, we've been a little hard on printers in this chapter. We're not telling you to recycle *all* the printers in your house, but you can make a significant contribution to the greenness of the planet by reducing your paper consumption and cutting down the amount of power that your printer soaks up.

You can green your printing by using a variety of methods that reduce, reuse, and recycle what you've already got. We share the how-to's on those techniques in Chapter 11. But what's important to consider when you're thinking of purchasing a new printer? What makes one printer greener than another? This section gives you some resources for answering those questions.

In Chapter 11, you see how to cut way back on printing resources. In that chapter, you also find out how to set up *duplex* (double-sided) printing and change other print options so that you're getting the most use out of every watt possible.

Operating costs (in energy and dollars)

Here are some ballpark figures that give you a general idea of the operating costs, in kilowatt-hours (kWh) and dollars, of various printers:

- A small inkjet printer uses about 156 kWh per year and costs $9.44.

- A medium inkjet printer uses 184 kWh annually and costs $11.10.

- A small laser printer jumps to 1,173 kWh per year, with a $70.82 price tag.

- A medium laser printer weighs in at 1,568 kWh per year, at a whopping $94.68 annual cost.

- A small multifunction printer (with scanning, copying, and faxing capabilities) uses only 119 kWh per year and costs $7.18. (Ding, ding, ding! Bruce, we have a winner!)

  Figure 7-1 shows one of the new multifunction printers from Hewlett-Packard (HP): a Photosmart C6380 multifunction printer, which sells for around $100. According to HP, this printer requires a maximum of 42 watts, 5.2 watts while sleeping, 6.6 watts while in the ready state (ready to print, but not printing), 0.6 watts when turned off, and 24 watts while active or printing.

- A medium multifunction printer uses 171 kWh per year and costs about $10.30. Yep, that's *per year.*

Figure 7-1:
Multi-
function
printers
save *beau-
coup* bucks
and CO_2
emissions.

As you can see based on these estimates, the printer you choose really does make a difference, both in the CO_2 you're pumping out and the dollars you're shelling out.

One easy green move is to trade your laser printer for an inkjet printer because inkjet printers generally require less power and fewer resources (such as ink). (The tradeoff is that the per page cost of inkjet printers is higher than laser printers.)

Printers that do it all

As you see in the preceding section, multifunction printers — devices that do printing, copying, scanning, and sometimes faxing — really save a whopping amount of wattage. For that reason, if you can pack two devices that you need into one (such as a scanner and printer), you reduce your power consumption dramatically, so we say, "Do it!"

Here are some questions to ask when you're considering a new green multifunction printer purchase:

✔ Is the printer Energy Star compliant?

✔ What functions does it offer?

✔ Does it offer duplex printing?

✔ How fast does it print?

✔ Does it use inkjet or toner cartridges? Inkjet cartridges are generally better because they require less oil. In fact, if you use soy-based products, inkjet cartridges don't require any oil at all.

✔ Does it work with a variety of papers?

Although looking for an all-in-one multifunction printer manufacturer is a good start, also be sure to look for the Energy Star logo before you buy. Table 7-2 shows some manufacturers you may recognize that meet Energy Star specifications for their all-in-one devices:

Table 7-2		Green All in One Manufacturers	
Canon	Dell	Epson America	Hewlett-Packard
Kodak	Konica	Kyocera	Lexmark International
NEC	Okidata	Olivetti	Panasonic
Pitney Bowes	Ricoh	Samsung	Sharp
Toshiba	Unisys	Xerox	

To qualify for the Energy Star certification, a printer needs to meet the following standards:

✔ It must demonstrate a 25 percent energy savings compared with conventional models.

✔ It must be able to print double-sided pages.

A printer all by its lonesome

If you need a stand-alone printer — no scanner or copier, thanks very much — go with the smallest and most energy-efficient offering you can find. One that also uses recycled ink cartridges (or even soy-based ink cartridges) is even better.

One new offering that's getting good reviews is the HP DeskJet D2545, which is made almost entirely of recycled plastic. Here are some of its green features:

✔ Made of 83 percent recycled plastic

✔ Print cartridges made of 75 percent recycled plastic

✔ Packaging made of 100 percent recycled material

✔ Fast printing

✔ Paper-saving Print Cancel button

✔ Compliant with Energy Star standards

Seeing Some Specialty Drives

We all need places to store the documents, programs, games, music, videos, and contacts we collect. If you're like us, you're collecting more every day! When you consider how to increase the amount of storage you have available, think green. This section introduces a few storage options — external hard drives as well as travel and flash memory — that can meet your storage needs in a planet-friendly way.

SimpleTech (re)drive

The SimpleTech [re]drive external hard drive is a small, low-power storage device that is made according to the European Union's Restriction of

Hazardous Substances (RoHS) standards. Packaging is reduced to a minimum, using recycled materials.

But the big surprise is what is used to make the [re]drive — bamboo (yes, you read that right) and recycled aluminum. (See Figure 7-2.) The lightweight, small-footprint device stays cool without a fan (which lessens its power consumption) and includes an Energy Star power adapter. The unit also comes with online backup for extra storage. You can find out more about the [re] drive by going to www.simpletech.com/products/storage/redrive.

Kanguru Eco Drive

The Kanguru Eco Drive is an external hard drive that the manufacturer touts as being the most environmentally friendly external hard drive on the market today. The drive has a smart power-saving mode with three settings — Power Down, Standby, and Idle — that tailors power consumption to the use of the drive, which conserves energy and extends the drive's life.

The drive uses a high-speed USB 2.0 connection and is compatible with both Windows and Mac computers. The unit is also European Union's Restriction of Hazardous Substances (RoHS)–compliant, which means that it's lead and mercury free, and that it can be sold in and exported from the European Union.

Earthy flash drives

You can green up your temporary storage by choosing flash drives made of earth-friendly materials such as corn-based or recycled plastics or bamboo. The ATP 8GB EarthDrive, shown in Figure 7-2, comes loaded with security software that ensures the privacy of your data and allows drive partitioning.

Figure 7-2:
A completely earthy bio-plastic flash drive — with 8GB of storage.

You can also find a whole forest of bamboo flash drives online — great as customizable promotional items — by searching for *eco-friendly flash drives*.

Selecting Keyboards and Mice

You won't find a huge range of choices when you go shopping for earth-friendly keyboards and mice, but some companies are doing things right.

If you use a wireless keyboard and/or mouse, use rechargeable batteries to keep your energy use low.

Logitech possibilities

Some of the biggest manufacturers of peripherals take green requirements seriously, as you'd expect them to do. Logitech — a successful maker of mice, keyboards, Webcams, and more — follows the European Union's RoHS directive, which places restrictions on the materials that manufacturers can use in products to be sold in the EU or exported to other countries.

iameco

One intriguing source of natural keyboards and mice (among other computer products) is iameco computers, headquartered in Dublin, Ireland. This company set its sights on developing an ecologically friendly personal computer called the iameco with a wooden case that's biodegradable. That's right — when you finish using it, toss the case out in the compost pile and eventually use it to green your garden.

iameco's designers borrowed ideas from nature's life cycle and worked to minimize the use of natural resources. Also, no scary materials such as lead, mercury, and other hazardous chemicals are used to produce the equipment. To find out more about earth-friendly keyboards and mice (see Figure 7-3) from iameco, visit www.iameco.com.

Figure 7-3:
The iameco
product line
includes
eco-friendly
keyboards
and mice.

Just say no to canned air

Okay, eat a couple of Oreos at your keyboard, and what do you have? Crumby QWERTY keys. You can clean the crumbs (as well as the other grime and gook that accumulates over time), but there's a green way to do it. First, stay away from the canned air. It's packed into the can with stuff you don't want to breathe (including tetrafluoroethane), and it's not good for the environment, either. So clean your keyboard the healthy way by following these steps:

1. **Unplug the keyboard from the system unit or, if you're using a laptop, power down.**

2. **Turn the thing over and shake it (gently).**

3. **Using a dry cotton swab, clean out any other loose debris between the keys.**

4. **To remove sticky spots, use a damp cotton rag with a tiny dot of earth-friendly dish soap.**

There. That wasn't so hard. No forced air required.

Calling Router Rooter

Even though routers aren't actually peripherals, they do exist on your network and you have to consider them as part of your green computing plan. Routers aren't notorious energy hogs, but every little bit of energy savings helps. If you're thinking about consolidating peripherals and sharing what you have, your router is about to become a more important peripheral in your home. First, here are a couple of green computing facts:

- ✔ Your router sips power all the time. It's okay to turn it off if no one is home and your ghosts — er, guests — aren't using it.

- ✔ Consider what your router is made of. Some router manufacturers are looking into earth-friendly materials. (Read on.)

D-Link is d-place to be

A new player in the happy green Wi-Fi world is D-Link, which offers a new series of wireless routers: Xtreme N, which targets big-time online gamers. These routers rely on *Green Ethernet*, a technology that adjusts power consumption based on use.

The routers include a scheduling feature that lets you specify active and sleep times of the day. (Think of the programmable thermostat in your home. The same energy-saving technique can apply to your router.) Also, the company uses only Energy Star power supplies, so the whole ballgame begins with efficiency.

You can find out more about D-Link's green philosophy and the technology behind the products by going to www.dlinkgreen.com.

Netgear Green

Another popular router manufacturer, Netgear (see Figure 7-4), recently turned over a green leaf of its own. The new Netgear Green features of the company's latest routers comply with the 802.11n standard (which is wireless-speak) and are shipped in packaging made of 80 percent recycled materials. In addition to the earth-friendly packaging, Netgear uses Energy Star power supplies and has a simple but elegant feature that many routers don't offer: an On/Off switch so that you can simply turn the thing off when you don't need it. That feature represents simplicity and energy conservation at their finest.

Figure 7-4:
Netgear
went
green with
Wireless-N,
even
including
recycled
materials
in the
packaging.

Making the Purchase — and What to Do Afterward

After you get the peripheral home (or it arrives on your doorstep), and you unbox it and plug it in, here are a few things to keep in mind:

✔ **Enable the power-saving features.** Some manufacturers (including HP) ship their equipment with energy-saving features already turned on; others leave that for you to do. Printers and battery-powered devices generally come with power saving features enabled, other devices probably won't. Take a minute to read the manual or open the information file on the driver disc. Look specifically at the energy-savings section to see whether you need to do anything in particular to take best advantage of energy-efficiency settings.

✔ **Measure the device's energy consumption.** Pay attention to your energy use. If you invested in a power meter like the Kill A Watt, great! Plug in your new peripheral, and see what kind of energy it's really drawing. Peripheral devices, such as printers, have several different power modes. Make sure you measure each mode, such as standby and actively printing, separately. If you don't have a fancy-schmancy device, keep an eye on your electric bill. Is it going down? Do you see any change? Your green education doesn't end with the purchase; the purchase is just part of the path.

Chapter 8

Recycling Your Computer

● ●

● ●

*Y*ou've probably noticed that nothing exists in a vacuum. Each being, each circumstance, each problem, each opportunity is connected to everything else. You see this fact in the food chain and the economy. (Oh, *boy,* do you see it in the economy!) You see it in your home, your work, your health, your pets, and your plans.

This sense of oneness may show up in earth care perhaps more dramatically — and with a potentially longer-term impact — than in any other single area of life. Why? Without too much stretching of the imagination, you can see that we're all in this together. The air in China eventually gets to you, wherever you live in the United States. The water you drink today is part of a shared global water resource (one that scientists are concerned about because it's diminishing, by the way). Without a big effort, you can plainly see that your choices are connected in a very real way to effects in your immediate environment and around the world.

Facing the e-Waste Facts

At first blush, the question of recycling computers may not seem that big a deal to you. If you're just purchasing a new green system, you may have it for . . . what . . . five years or so? Then you'll give it to someone else, take it to a responsible recycler, or maybe just put it out with the trash one day.

Some U.S. states, however, have laws against discarding computers by tossing them out the window with the bathwater. (We hope that you're not tossing your bathwater out the window either, come to think of it.) Illegally discarded computers, known as *e-waste,* represent one of the fastest-growing problems facing the environment today. Recent statistics show that the average home life of a computer is only three years.

Following the *reduce, reuse, recycle* mantra, it's a good green practice to plan to hold on to the computer you've got for as long as you can. Make it work; use it well; and when the time comes to retire it, do so responsibly by using a bona fide recycling program that really does what it says it's going to do. Each choice you make about how you dispose of systems, monitors, and peripherals — not to mention batteries and other power sources — either adds to the problem or helps with the cleanup.

What e-waste are we throwing away?

Anything that you'd call "computer equipment" can be recycled somewhere. In addition, you can recycle MP3 players, cellphones, digital cameras, game systems, and personal digital assistants (PDAs). Right now, however, the majority of electronic equipment goes directly to landfills. It does not pass Go; it does not collect $200.

Here are the statistics, according to the U.S. Environmental Protection Agency (EPA). Be forewarned that they're not pretty.

✔ Americans own nearly 3 million electronic products.

✔ In 1998, an estimated 20 million computers became obsolete.

✔ In 2007, an estimated 37 million computers — almost double the 1998 estimate — became obsolete.

✔ In addition to computers, 304 million electronic devices — monitors, cellphones, and other gadgets — were thrown away in 2005.

✔ Discarded electronics constitute 70 percent of metals and 40 percent of the lead in U.S. landfills.

✔ As of 2007, of the 2.25 million tons of electronic equipment ready to be disposed of, 414,000 tons (or 18 percent) were recycled, and 1.84 million tons (82 percent) were dumped into landfills all across the country.

✔ Only 15 percent of computer equipment was recycled until 2006–2007, when several states started mandatory recycling for electronic equipment.

✔ In the 10 years leading up to 2002, sales of consumer electronics in the United States quadrupled.

✔ Just over half of Americans are aware that recycling electronics is an option.

What's really in computer waste?

If the computer you put out with the trash actually makes it to the landfill, it leaks hazardous chemicals into the ground, and those toxins eventually find their way into the water supply for surrounding areas. Here are some of the problems with the various computer components that are shoved into landfills and covered with dirt (and more trash):

✔ **Lead:** Cathode-ray tube (CRT) monitors contain lead and other hazardous metals. The glass of the screens, when broken, releases a dust that is harmful as well. Lead in the environment can cause respiratory problems and cognitive-development issues.

✔ **Mercury:** Liquid-crystal display (LCD) monitors contain mercury (also used in cellphones, MP3 players, and television sets), which can damage the brain, nervous system, reproductive system, kidneys, and lungs.

✔ **Copper:** Computers contain copper. The process of creating usable copper and etching the wires on the computer boards adds to acid rain and contributes to global warming. High doses of copper can cause headaches, stomachaches, dizziness, vomiting, and diarrhea. It can also cause liver and kidney damage.

✔ **Chemicals:** Each semiconductor used in computer chips includes hundreds (no kidding) of hazardous chemicals, which can contribute to a variety of physical problems in children and adults.

✔ **Plastics:** The treated, flame-retardant plastics used in computers, called polybrominated diphenyl ethers (PBDEs), can contribute to neurodevelopmental problems and some cancers.

Exporting the e-Waste Problem

Around the world, e-waste is a problem of massive proportions. The export business is alive and well, with e-waste being shipped to developing countries such as China, India, and Nigeria, where labor is cheaper and there are fewer restrictions on working conditions than in the United States.

Figure 8-1 shows a diagram produced by the EPA that maps the process that e-waste follows.

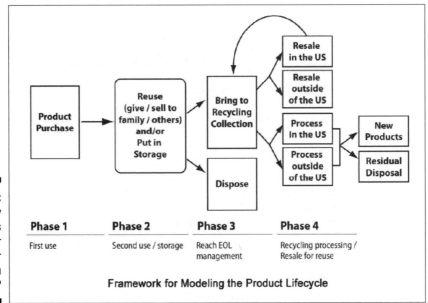

Figure 8-1:
What really happens to your computer after you let it go?

Framework for Modeling the Product Lifecycle

As you can see, the normal life cycle involves purchasing the computer and then giving it to someone else when you don't need it anymore, storing it, taking it to a recycling center, or throwing it out. If you throw the computer away — Dispose, in the diagram — it goes to your local landfill and leaches chemicals into the soil and water supply (refer to "What's really in computer waste?" earlier in this chapter). If you send it to a recycling center, one of four things can happen:

✔ The computer may be resold in the United States.

✔ The computer may be resold outside the United States.

✔ The computer may be *processed* (broken down into its parts) and recycled in the United States in such a way that new products are created and the unusable components are disposed of responsibly.

✔ The computer may be processed outside the United States. In this case, fewer safeguards are in place, and the system may wind up being burned for scrap metal in China, India, or Kenya.

Stories on news programs like "60 Minutes" and video segments on environmental blogs have helped break the story of the villages in China where electronics are broken down to their components and burned for their scrap metal, and the families that do this dangerous work earn the Chinese equivalent of a few dollars a week. Children are exposed to the toxic chemicals, which permeate the air and water in the villages. Don't kid yourself — these toxins travel around the world as well.

Jim Puckett, coordinator of the Basel Action Network (`www.ban.org`), was recently quoted in *ENVIRONMENT: Where That "Recycled" E-Waste Really Goes* by Stephen Leahy (`http://ipsnorthamerica.net/news.php?idnews=1841`). As Puckett says, "I recently watched shipping containers loaded in the U.S. being opened on the docks in Hong Kong. Inside, they were packed with e-waste." Experts estimate that an average 100 containers of e-waste arrive in Hong Kong from the United States every day, and the contents are smuggled illegally into mainland China.

To see a sobering video report on the e-waste problem in China, visit

> `www.engadget.com/2008/11/10/video-chinas-toxic-wastelands-of-consumer-electronics-revealed`

You can read the Basel Action Network's report on its research in Africa, *The Digital Dump: Exporting Re-Use and Abuse to Africa,* at

> `www.ban.org/BANreports/10-24-05/documents/TheDigitalDump.pdf`

Seeing Reasons to Recycle Computers

In the *reduce, reuse, recycle* mantra, *recycle* may sound like the end of the line, where the computer moves beyond your concern and becomes somebody else's problem. In reality, your recycled computer may be somebody else's beginning. A growing market exists (thank goodness) for second-life computers: desktops, laptops, monitors, and peripherals that have been donated, refurbished, and maybe even recertified.

Wonder what the difference is between refurbishing and recertifying? A *refurbished* computer has parts that someone has fixed or updated to make the computer ready to rock again. A *recertified* computer gets similar treatment, except the manufacturer takes a look and gives it the thumbs-up if it meets the manufacturer's standards. So a recertified computer gets a slightly higher-level nod.

When you decide to recycle a computer, you might

✔ Donate the computer to a not-for-profit organization, school, or person who needs it.

✔ Give your computer to a recycler in your local area.

✔ Take or send your computer to a manufacturer's or retailer's recycling program.

The rest of this chapter explores these options in more detail so you can decide what's best to do with the system you've got.

Planning Your Computer's Retirement

We assume that you're all charged up (that's a power phrase, by the way) about reducing your energy use and staying on top of your home computing resources. Perhaps you just purchased a new and greener computer. Good for you! The next step is deciding what you'll do with the old one. Here are some guidelines to help you begin the process of donating or recycling your old system in an earth-friendly way:

✔ **Know what you're giving.** Before you donate a system to someone else, have a technical friend look it over and make sure that someone else can actually use it. Some computers are so old there really isn't anything to do but recycle them. (Kathy had an old Windows ME system a few years ago that was good for little more than propping the window open on a nice day.) If the machine is still usable — in other words, you used it until you got the new one — chances are that it can be a blessing to someone else.

✔ **Know where you'd like to give it.** If you plan to donate your computer to someone in your own circle of friends and relatives, cool. If, however, you want to donate the system to a school, not-for-profit organization, or another charity that you're not personally involved with, it's usually not a good idea to donate the item directly. Consider giving your system to a recycling or refurbishing organization that ensures that the computer works the way it should and has legal copies of software. The recycler can then give your refurbished computer to the school, not-for-profit organization, or charity.

✔ **Know what doesn't work, and find a recycler to take it.** If you have equipment that doesn't work at all — such as a printer with a dead head, a scanner that doesn't scan, or a computer that doesn't power up — find a computer recycler for the item. A computer recycler can salvage the usable parts before recycling what remains. Some manufacturers have recycling programs. (In fact, Energy Star now requires manufacturers qualifying for the Energy Star logo to run their own recycling programs.)

Independent recyclers exist, too, and you may find several in your local area. We tell you more about finding a local computer recycler in "Finding a Reputable Recycler," later in this chapter.

✔ **Include the peripherals.** Donating your computer is helpful, but it's even better for the recipient if you include the keyboard, mouse, printer, and other devices that you use with the computer. Schools and not-for-profit organizations often have very limited tech budgets, and though receiving the computer may be a good thing, if they don't have what they need to go with it, your donation may go unused.

✔ **Include the software.** This point is a confusing one for people who are concerned about honoring the software license on operating systems and packaged software. If you purchased software to run on the computer that you're now donating, it's perfectly fine to send along the software package and CDs. In fact, the recipient will thank you for it — big time. Also, the refurbisher will want to see the documentation and authentic seal on the software package so it knows it's donating legal copies of software.

The same thing applies to the computer's operating system. One big challenge in recycling and refurbishing computers in years past was that "clean" refurbished systems didn't have an operating system installed, and most users weren't interested in systems that were *that* clean.

✔ **Know how to clean off your personal information.** Before you donate your computer anywhere — whether you're taking it to a friend's house, donating it to a school, or delivering it to a recycler or refurbisher — know how to remove all your personal information. You have Web settings, cookies, browsing history, e-mail messages, contacts, documents, files, and much more stored on that system, and even though you may think that you've gotten rid of it by deleting the files, the data isn't actually "all gone." To eliminate it for good, you need to use a disk-cleaning program. (We tell you more in "Wiping Your System Clean.")

✔ **Keep a record of where you took the system.** Yes, this point seems to be pretty basic, but as time goes on, you may wonder where that computer went. Also, if you don't get a receipt or some kind of documentation, you may miss out on a tax break, and every little bit helps. (For more info on donating computers, see "Finding Great New Uses for an Old Computer," later in this chapter.)

Wiping Your System Clean

We begin here by saying that most local recyclers and refurbishers that help you prepare your donated computer for reuse are reputable, but in this age of identity theft, why take a chance? Cleaning off your computer — and getting it *really* clean — is an important step in the recycling process.

Before you give your computer to recyclers or refurbishers, be sure to do the following things:

- Uninstall the software that you intend to use again on another system.
- Move the files and folders that you need to a backup device or new computer.
- Delete files and folders.
- Clear your browser cache (uninstalling software seldom removes all of your data from the machine).
- Remove all user accounts on the computer.
- Use a disk-cleaning program to remove everything else.

We discuss all these steps in the following sections.

Uninstall as needed

Chances are that some programs came bundled with the computer you're about to recycle, and you may want to send them along with the system to its next incarnation. That's fine, but first be sure to remove any personal information (and delete the data files, which we show you how to do in the "Delete the rest" section).

On your Windows machine, the personal information you entered when you registered the software is likely stored in the Windows Registry. Use the following steps to open the Registry Editor, where you can look for personal information:

1. **Choose Start⇨Run.**

   You see the Run dialog box.

2. **Type RegEdit in the Open field and click OK.**

   Windows starts the Registry Editor, where you can look for bits of personal data.

Some programs use initialization files (.ini files) to store the data. You can search for .ini files and open them with a text editor such as Windows Notepad to remove the information.

On a Mac, the information you entered during software installation and registration should be stored in the Preferences folder. The Preferences folder normally contains a list of .plist files that have names in the form of com.[company name].[product name].plist. For example, iTunes has a preferences file named com.apple.iTunes.plist. Simply delete all of these

`.plist` files to remove your personal information. After you get rid of your personal info, uninstall programs as you normally would.

Although it's legal to pass along the purchased copy of software you used on the old system (refer to "Planning Your Computer's Retirement," earlier in this chapter), it isn't okay to give away the CDs and manuals and still continue to use the software on another system. Yeah, we know — lots of people do. But if they jumped off a cliff, you wouldn't. Would you?

Back it up, big fella

Make sure to make backup copies of all the files, folders, and programs you want from the existing computer. You can use Windows Easy Transfer to do this easily on a Windows Vista or Windows 7 computer; alternatively, you can copy those files, folders, and programs to an external hard drive, an online file storage system, a CD, or a flash drive.

If you're using Windows XP, and you've inadvertently (and often) assigned long filenames to files and folders, copying or moving those files may be a pain. You can use Robocopy to do the transfer for you. Originally available as part of the Windows Server 2003 tool kit, Robocopy is available as freeware in several incarnations. The one available at the following link has an easy-to-use interface and does the job:

```
http://web.comporium.net/~gwenanderic/software/EasyRoboCopy101.zip
```

You can discover how to use Robocopy at

```
http://technet.microsoft.com/en-us/library/cc733145.aspx
```

Delete the rest

Do a quick inventory of the places where you expect your files to be. On a Windows machine, your data files — all those files that you created in various applications — are probably somewhere in the Documents folder (maybe in their own subfolders as well). If you're using a Mac, you're likely to find application data files in the Documents folder.

Often, however, people don't stick with the default locations for data files. They wind up scattering files on the desktop, in the application folders, in other folders that they create, and maybe even in the root directory (in the folder for the drive, such as C:) instead of in subfolders.

We won't lecture you. We do it too.

Just take a good, long look around, and make sure that you've deleted everything that looks like you created it. Better safe than sorry.

You can use your operating system's search tool to list all files and then sort them by date, with the newest files at the top of the list. For example, in Windows, you can use Windows Explorer to look through data folders on your machine and sort them by clicking the appropriate column at the top of the right pane. When working on a Macintosh, you search using Finder. This method enables you to scan the dates on the displayed files to make sure that you haven't missed anything important.

Clear your browser files

One nearly-invisible place where your personal information can collect is your Web browser's cache. The *browser cache* keeps track of the sites you've visited; your user preferences for those sites; and information you've entered on those sites, such as passwords, usernames, form data, and addresses.

Most browsers provide a method for clearing the cache. For example, in Firefox you simply click Clear Now in the Private Data section on the Privacy tab of the Options dialog box (display the Options dialog box by choosing Tools➪Options). To clear your browser cache in Internet Explorer, follow these steps:

1. **Choose Tools➪Internet Options.**

   Figure 8-2 shows the Internet Options dialog box for Windows. The Browsing History area stores the files collected online.

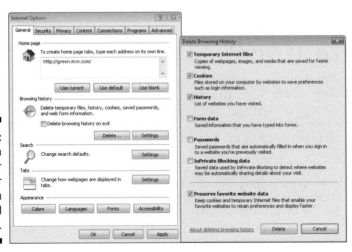

Figure 8-2:
You can delete your browser cache in one fell swoop.

2. **Click Delete.**

   The Delete Browsing History dialog box appears, listing several types of information that may be stored in your browser files (the kind of information that Internet Explorer displays depends on the Web sites you have visited).

3. **Select all check boxes and then click Delete.**

   The files are deleted from the system.

If you plan to continue using this computer, deleting passwords and form data may remove information that you'll wish you had later, but for your purposes here, you want to remove *all* traces of your activity.

Remove all user accounts

If you have multiple user accounts set up on your computer, make sure that you remove all the profiles and passwords that your family members use. You can get to the User Accounts page quickly by typing **user accounts** in the Windows Vista search box and clicking User Accounts when it appears in the All Programs list. Then you can remove an account by following these steps:

1. **In the User Accounts screen, click Manage Another Account.**

   The User Account Control dialog box may pop up; if so, click Continue.

2. **In the Manage Accounts page, click the icon or name of the account you'd like to delete.**

   The Change an Account page appears, displaying several options for working with the user account you selected. (See Figure 8-3.)

Figure 8-3:
Bye, bye account. Here's to greener pastures.

3. Click Delete the Account.

The Delete Account page asks whether you want to keep or delete the files connected to the account you're deleting. (See Figure 8-4.)

Figure 8-4:
You may as well let Windows Vista do the work for you. Click Delete Files.

4. Click Delete Files.

Windows Vista, never the impulsive one, asks you to confirm that yes, you really, really do want to delete the account.

5. Click Delete Account.

That's it! Piece of cake, right?

6. Repeat Steps 2–5 for all other accounts on the computer except the Administrator account.

7. Change the password for the Administrator account to something super-simple, such as 12345.

You change the password so that other people won't start guessing your actual passwords based on the sample you provide. It's important to provide something different from what you normally use. In addition, you want to make the password simple so that the next person to use your computer doesn't have to go through finger gymnastics to access the system the first time.

You'll also want to remove user accounts on your Macintosh. Use the following steps to perform this task.

1. **Choose Apple menu⇨System Preferences.**

   You see a list of system preference options.

2. **Click Accounts.**

   You see the Accounts dialog box.

3. **Open Accounts Preferences.**

   You see a list of account preferences. Some of the settings might appear dimmed. If so, proceed to Step 4; otherwise proceed to Step 5.

4. **(Optional) Click the lock icon. Type an administrator name and password when asked by the system.**

   The account preference settings are no longer dimmed.

5. **Highlight the user account you want to delete. Click Delete.**

   The system asks whether you really want to delete the user account.

6. **Click Delete Immediately to remove the user account and all the user's files.**

   The system deletes the user information.

Be sure to include the account name and password with the computer (perhaps put it on a sticker on the bottom or side of the unit) before you drop it off.

Use a disk-cleaning program to remove everything else

Many users don't realize that when they simply delete a file, it isn't necessarily gone. The index to the file may have been erased, but the file may still be retrievable, even after you reformat your hard drive, as final as that sounds. With the proper software (and dastardly intent), other people can access information on your old computer that you thought was long gone.

Sensitive or personal information means more than love letters you wrote to your special someone. It could also mean your Social Security number, your credit card account numbers, passwords, and preferences. It can include e-mail, your contacts, and any cookies any site ever left on your system.

To make sure that your computer is really, truly clean, you should use a commercial disk-cleaning program such as the following (you should do this in addition to manually cleaning the hard drive because none of these products will catch absolutely every little thing):

- Active@ Kill Disk Hard Drive Eraser (www.killdisk.com/eraser.htm) is freeware that meets U.S. Department of Defense standards for sanitizing disks.

- Blancco PC Edition (www.blancco.com/eng/products/blancco+-+data+cleaner) isn't free ($32), but it offers several features, including a comprehensive erasure report.

- WipeDrive (www.whitecanyon.com/erase-file-index.php) is available for both Windows and Mac machines for $39.95.

- Mac users can also use the built-in Disk Utility program (choose Applications➪Utilities to access Disk Utility). You can read more about Disk Utility at

```
http://www.macworld.com/article/51199/2006/06/julyworkingmac.html
```

Finding Great New Uses for an Old Computer

Many of the computers that wind up in landfills could be happily serving students, librarians, social advocates, and people of faith all over the world right now. This section gives you a range of ideas for possible homes for your old computer, but before you donate, be sure to do your homework and make sure that the refurbisher is a reputable one. We cover both topics in the following sections.

Doing the pre-donation paperwork

Before you donate your computer to some worthy individual or organization, it's important to document it in some way. The person receiving the computer will want to know some information about it. Because we all forget what we're told, it's important to have this information in writing. Use Table 8-1 to help you make the plan for donating the equipment.

Table 8-1		Planning Your Donation	
System: _____			
Model: _____			
Year Purchased: _____			
Where Purchased: _____			
Still Under Warranty? _____			
Extended Warranty Available? _____			
Item	*Working?*	*Original Packaging?*	*Comments*
Computer	Yes	Yes (with manual and CDs)	
Monitor	Yes	Yes (with manual and CDs)	
Operating system	Yes	Yes	

We left a blank row at the bottom. Your plan should include anything you think the recipient might find helpful. For example, does the computer include the manuals? If so, you should document them. When a computer includes additional software, you should include that information too. If you plan to provide other peripherals, document each of them. In short, document every aspect of the computer so the recipient has no questions about it.

Finding a refurbisher

As the green-tech industry matures, some organizations and businesses are getting in on the certification game, which is good because, ultimately, it means that more people care about the standards we expect for quality green products. (This trend also helps educate consumers and safeguard them against greenwashing.)

Microsoft, for example, offers the Microsoft Authorized Refurbisher (MAR) program (`http://oem.microsoft.com/public/seo/mar.htm`) to large-scale refurbishers that take care to wipe computers clean before installing Windows, commit to using only legal software, use adequate security controls, and act in accordance with health and safety regulations for electronics.

Microsoft gives each MAR partner low-cost Windows software to install on each machine before delivering it to the recipient. A version of this program called Secondary PC is available for refurbishers in the Czech Republic, Nigeria, Pakistan, and South Africa.

To find a list of refurbishers in your area, go to

```
www.techsoup.org/resources/index.cfm?action=resource.view_summary&resourcelist_
             id=144&range=10&order=1&start=126
```

Donating to a worthy cause

Many organizations struggle to find good computer equipment at a price they can afford — usually free. The computer you think is outdated and worthless might be solid gold to these organizations. Before you simply toss that old computer away, think about giving it to someone who really wants it. The following sections provide some solid ideas for places to donate your computer.

Not-for-profit organizations

Not-for-profit organizations accept donations of all kinds, including time, treasure, and talent. A computer that you're no longer using would definitely be treasure to someone who needs it, but you can also invest some time and a little of your talent as you think creatively about where to donate and what to give along with it. You may want to check out refurbishers or recyclers in your local area that focus on technology.

Before you run to your nearest not-for-profit, however, do a little calling. First, make sure the organization you have in mind can actually use your old computer. Second, make sure that you ask the organization about other needs it might have. Sometimes you find that an item collecting dust in your closet is precisely what the organization requires.

Here are a few types of not-for-profit organizations that could make good use of your computer donation:

- After-school programs at organizations like the YMCA
- Occupational organizations that train underserved populations in necessary job skills
- Youth development programs, such as Boys and Girls Clubs
- Your local nature organization or parks department (for use in a computer lab or nature center)

If you're shopping for a possible computer recipient at a not-for-profit organization, GreatNonprofits.org (`www.greatnonprofits.org`) helps match needs, talents, people, and purpose, and can help you find out more about the organization you're interested in donating to.

Schools

Everybody knows that students need computers, but not every student has access to one. Consider donating your clean, working computer to a school that may not have the resources of larger suburban districts. Use the Computers for Schools site (`www.pcsforschools.org`) to locate a refurbisher in your area that will help prepare the computer for just the school that needs it. (See Figure 8-5.)

Figure 8-5: Computers for Schools is a refurbisher that helps match your donation with a school that needs your computer.

Here are a few more sites that focus on getting refurbished systems into the hands of kids who'd love to have them: `www.youthfortechnology.org`, `www.giftmypc.org`, and `www.komputers4rkids.org`.

Religious organizations

Increasingly, churches, synagogues, and mosques are teaching their students and followers about computers, and this can mean offering access to Web sites, job training, language classes, healthcare awareness, and even online education. All these missions require computers, at least in the virtual world. You can donate your old computer directly to your favorite religious organization, but be sure to clean the system thoroughly first.

Finding a Reputable Recycler

You may be surprised to discover the number of organizations in your area that offer computer recycling. When you begin to explore this option, keep the following pointers in mind.

Do your research

Your friends may be able to help steer you toward a good recycler. Follow their leads, but also do your own research.

Check large Web sites or those that are affiliated with groups you trust, such as the EPA. Several of the following sites may offer lists of recyclers in your area:

- ✔ E-cycling Central (www.eiae.org; see Figure 8-6.)
- ✔ Earth911.com (www.earth911.org)
- ✔ Find Your Local e-Stewards (www.e-stewards.org/local_estewards.html; see the nearby sidebar)
- ✔ myGreenElectronics (www.mygreenelectronics.org)
- ✔ TechSoup's Donate Hardware (www.techsoup.org/resources/index.cfm?action=resource.view_summary&resourcelist_id=144)

Find your e-stewards

Partnering with electronics recyclers in the United States and Canada, the Basel Action Network (refer to "Legislating e-waste disposal," earlier in this chapter) created the e-Stewards certification program to help consumers find true green recyclers in their states.

To locate e-Stewards in your area or to download a PDF listing all certified recyclers in the United States, go to www.e-stewards.org/local_estewards.html.

Figure 8-6:
E-cycling
Central
offers
electronics
recycling
information
for the entire
United
States.

Ask questions

We don't like to think that recyclers will be dishonest about what they do with the systems they receive, but being part of the e-waste solution means asking questions.

A recycling company that's on the level and not shipping boatloads of toxic e-waste to developing countries will be willing to answer the following questions:

- ✔ **What do you do with the equipment you receive?** The recycling company should be able to offer you a specific recycling plan and the names of places that receive the recycled parts. You can double-check the plan by checking with these companies to make sure the recycler actually does supply them.

- ✔ **Where do you send parts for materials recovery?** Again, look for specific information. Don't be surprised if the recycler ships products overseas. It's better to find a recycler that processes materials locally because overseas processing is usually dirty and environmentally unfriendly.

- ✔ **What do you do with the usable components?** The best answer here is to build up new computers for people to use. After all, the ultimate in recycling is to create something new with the least possible effort.

✔ **Where do the CRTs you receive wind up?** Many CRTs end up overseas. Try to find someone who processes them locally. Make sure that the components are sent to someone for reprocessing into new devices of some sort. Because CRTs are less popular today, don't be surprised to find that the parts end up as something entirely different from computer equipment.

✔ **What do you do if someone's personal data is accidentally left on the system?** It's possible that the recycler exposes the system to a strong magnet — strong enough to destroy any data. If that's the case, then you don't have any worries. The idea is to find someone who assumes the drive has data on it and removes it automatically, even if there really isn't anything on the drive.

✔ **How do you test the equipment before you give it to a recipient?** The words you want to hear, in this case, are "burn-in test." A *burn-in test* is a serious and complete examination of every aspect of the system before it goes to someone else. Using a burn-in test ensures the recipient has the best possible experience with your old computer.

Are you curious about what goes on inside a computer-recycling outfit? You'll find an interesting five-minute video clip called "Recycling Computers," online at

    www.thefutureschannel.com/dockets/hands-on_math/recycling_computers

Know the recycling laws in your area

Not all U.S. states have true recycling laws in effect, but you can be sure that the conversation is on every state lawmaker's agenda. The National Center for Electronics Recycling (www.electronicsrecycling.org) keeps track of legislative changes and posts updates, as well as a diagram of the types of laws at work in different states.

Generally, state recycling laws regulate what citizens can throw away, where it goes, who pays for it, and how it's monitored.

As we're writing this book (in 2009), the following states have enacted recycling laws: Arkansas, California, Connecticut, Hawaii, Illinois, Maine, Maryland, Massachusetts, Michigan, Minnesota, Missouri, New Hampshire, New Jersey, North Carolina, Oklahoma, Oregon, Rhode Island, Texas, Virginia, Washington, and West Virginia. That leaves a lot of room for growth!

Check out the legislative updates and find the info on your own state at

    www.electronicsrecycling.org/public/ContentPage.aspx?pageid=14

Going Back to the Source (Almost)

One of the easiest recycling options — and one that reduces the amount of legwork you have to do — is to use your computer manufacturer's recycling program. Some manufacturers — including Dell, Hewlett-Packard, and Apple — have great recycling programs and a true green commitment. Other manufacturers may be a little late to the party but are no less committed.

In addition to computer manufacturers, some retail outlets (including Staples and Office Depot) provide drop-off recycling programs.

In general, you'll find that computer manufacturers and retailers offer services reflecting one or more of these options:

✔ They provide a take-back, mail-in, or trade-in program.

✔ They partner with local organizations that receive recycled equipment.

✔ They sponsor collection events.

As you might expect, companies set up their programs differently. Dell, for example, doesn't care what kind of computer you're trading in as long as you buy a Dell; other companies want only their brands sent in for recycling.

Most companies seem to know — at least in theory — that maintaining responsibility for their computer equipment through that equipment's entire life cycle is the right thing to do. Some companies, such as Dell and HP, make it very easy for customers to recycle their old systems. You don't hear as much about Toshiba's green efforts, but that manufacturer is making great strides as well. (See Figure 8-7.)

Where are you, Aretha? Rethink!

The Rethink Initiative (http://pages. ebay.com/rethink/index.html) is a program, hosted by eBay, whose members work to encourage best practices in electronics recycling throughout the industry. The initiative hopes to bring business, government, association, and not-for-profit groups together to expand the discussion of the challenges of e-waste and try to come up with feasible solutions.

These partners are currently part of the Rethink Initiative: Apple, Best Buy, Circuit City, CEA (Consumer Electronics Association), Dell, Gateway, Hewlett-Packard, IBM, Ingram Micro, Motorola, Nokia, Toshiba, United States Postal Service, UPS, Verizon, Wireless . . . The New Recyclable (wireless industry association).

Figure 8-7:
Toshiba offers recycling and trade-in programs.

See Table 8-2 for a list of manufacturers offering recycling programs that you may want to investigate.

Table 8-2	Computer Manufacturers' Recycling Programs
Company	*Web Site*
Apple	www.apple.com/environment/recycling
Dell	http://www.dell.com/content/topics/segtopic.aspx/dell_recycling
Epson	www.epson.com/cgi-bin/Store/Recycle/RecycleProgram.jsp
Gateway	www.gateway.com/about/corp_responsibility/env_options.php
HP	www.hp.com/hpinfo/globalcitizenship/environment/recycling/product-recycling.html
IBM	www.ibm.com/ibm/environment
Lexmark	www.lexmark.com/lexmark/content/withoutnav/home/0,7316,204816596_1099884817_0_en,00.html
Panasonic	www.panasonic.com/environmental
Sharp	www.sharpusa.com/about/AboutEnvironment
Sony	www.sony.tradeups.com/Default.aspx
Toshiba	www.explore.toshiba.com/innovation-lab/green

It's great news that more and more manufacturers are getting with the program every day. Bear in mind, however, that this "end game" is only part of the true green life cycle. To make a huge, long-term impact, all computer manufacturers need to work actively to reduce — and eventually eliminate — the hard-core toxic chemicals they use in product manufacturing. Then they can get to work on making their manufacturing process more energy- and resource-efficient, too. Offering a recycling program, however, is a start — a big start — so we're not knocking it.

Recycling Computer Supplies, Too

In Chapter 11, we introduce the possibility of recycling your toner and inkjet-printer cartridges. You can recycle rewritable CDs (by rewriting them, of course). Floppy disks aren't useful any longer and there really isn't a good way to recycle them unless you give them to someone with an older system. Flash drives are more in keeping with the times, but they don't last forever, either.

Finally, don't forget the batteries you use. Rechargeables are givens, but when those have gone to the big power-charger in the sky, you can drop them off at an organization that partners with the Rechargeable Battery Recycling Corporation (RBRC). You can find the RBRC site (shown in Figure 8-8) at

www.rbrc.org/call2recycle/dropoff/index.php

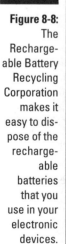

Figure 8-8: The Rechargeable Battery Recycling Corporation makes it easy to dispose of the rechargeable batteries that you use in your electronic devices.

The site tells you more about the various programs; easy partners to spot are Office Depot, RadioShack, and Wal-Mart. According to the RBRC, 6.3 million pounds of batteries were recycled safely in 2007 alone!

Taking Local Action to Clean Up Global Computer Waste

There are all kinds of roads to green advocacy; the journey is limited only by your imagination! How can you help let people know that e-waste is something to care about on a global scale? Here are just a few ideas to get you started:

- ✔ **Spread the word.** The Electronics TakeBack Coalition has a variety of information about global e-waste on its site at `www.electronics takeback.com/problem/export_problem.htm`. You'll find the latest data on tech dumping, as well as a "60 Minutes" video of the deplorable conditions in China (refer to "Polluting poorer countries," earlier in this chapter).

- ✔ **Download the e-waste briefing book.** The Electronics TakeBack Coalition published a briefing book, *e-Waste: The Exploding Global Electronic Waste Crisis*, in February 2009 to help you talk to businesses, government leaders, friends, and family members about the realities of global e-waste. Download the free book at

    `www.electronicstakeback.com/legislation/Ewaste%20Briefing%20Book.pdf`

- ✔ **Find out about the recycling laws that are in effect in your state.** Visit the State by State e-Waste Law Summary at

    `www.electronicstakeback.com/legislation/States%20Summary%202009.pdf`

    to find out what's happening in your area and get involved.

- ✔ **Tell the story your way.** If you're a teacher, design a lesson plan about responsible computer recycling. If you're a painter, create something that inspires people to love the earth and to care about her misuse and underappreciation. If you're a businessperson, make and model green computing choices at work — and when people ask why, share the reasons why.

Even little changes add up to a big difference over time — just like that small inkjet cartridge that you recycled this afternoon and all the hundreds more that you'll recycle over the next ten years. With some good old-fashioned dedication to cleaning up our own messes, building a system that works, and keeping at it 'til we see good things beginning to happen, we can make the world a greener place.

Part III
Greener Under the Hood

"I don't know much about alternative energy sources, but I'll bet there's enough solar power being collected on those beach blankets to run my workshop for a month."

In this part . . .

Starting where you are is a good philosophy for greening your technology. Chances are that you've got more than one or two electronic devices around the house — maybe desktop computers, laptop computers, printers, game systems, cellphones, MP3 players, and digital cameras. Sound familiar? Each item uses some kind of power, either AC, (plugged-in power) or DC (battery life). In addition to the power those devices use, they have already made an impact on the environment simply by the nature of their existence (the manufacturing process uses a lot of resources) and their arrival at your house. (Packing, shipping, and delivery all use materials, electricity, and fuel, which translate to CO_2 emissions.)

In this part of the book, you take a closer look at the computers, devices, and peripherals you already have and explore ways to decrease their power-and-resource impact. Along the way, you'll find out how to dial back your power consumption and manage what you use, reduce the number of trees smashed into pulp for your printouts, and learn how to share resources among the various computers in your house. You might even save a few bucks in the process.

Chapter 9

Optimize Your Computer Power Management

*W*hen you explore the world of conservation, you look at ways you can begin to make an impact on the environment by choosing to green your technology and apply the natural laws of *reduce, reuse, and recycle.* This chapter brings such practices to your fingertips by showing you how to reduce the amount of energy your computer is consuming right now as it whirs quietly in the background. The good news is that you can save half a forest (no kidding — as many as 300 trees per PC) by trading your always-on mindset for a PC power-management plan.

In this chapter, you discover quick ways to reduce the energy your computer swallows needlessly. After those initial energy cutbacks, you shrink your carbon footprint even more by putting a power plan in place — a plan that optimizes your PC's power use but still gives you the performance you need. The process sounds pretty techie, but it's really surprisingly simple, and the Windows power-management plans take you most of the way there.

Taking Your Computer's Temperature

Your computer isn't the only energy-sucking culprit in your house. Anything that's plugged in — whether it's turned on or off — draws at least a little current. To give you a bit of an idea of how much a computer costs when turned off, a typical computer uses 4.8 watts when turned off (see `http://tech reviewer.com/viewpage.cfm/ui/040226130555` for some other statistics — note that these statistics are for an older computer — newer computers use even more power). If you leave it off for 24 hours, that's 115.2 watt/hours or 0.1152 kilowatt/hours. If your electrical utility charges $0.35 per kilowatt/hour, then your computer is costing you around $0.04 per day, even if you leave it turned off. Now, consider that if you just leave your computer turned off, put plugged in, you're spending $14.72 for electrical power every year. That's $14.72 to do absolutely nothing!

In addition to your desktop and laptop computers, you may have a router, printers, a scanner, a digital camera, a camcorder, an MP3 player, and game consoles. What about wireless game controllers? Yep, they use power too. Even though they run on batteries, the receiving unit draws power, and of course, batteries *are* a type of power — a type that needs to be recharged or disposed of properly in a way that doesn't muck up the environment even more.

So even when you think your technology is turned off, it still may be drinking in a steady stream of energy. Take a closer look. If you can read the clock on your DVD player, it's using power. The only way to get the DVD player to stop using power is to unplug it (a great use for the power switch that comes with most power strips is to turn it off — which effectively disconnects everything attached to the power strip when you're not using it).

A plugged-in laptop is a laptop that's using power. Even if you shut your laptop down, if the system is plugged in, it's drawing electricity. To stop the drain-and-replace process, unplug your laptop when it's fully charged.

Energy Appetites 101

Computer manufacturers are the first to tell you that their systems are energy-efficient and green. Well, some are, and some aren't so much. Generally speaking, newer computers *are* more energy-aware than older systems, and operating systems make a difference too. Windows XP with Service Pack 1, for example, was created in an era when we weren't quite so conscious of PC energy drain, whereas Windows 7 — designed in an ecologically awake landscape — provides several easy-to-use tools for power management. Macs in general have a reputation for doing less with more.

In most systems, the amount of power used to start the computer is roughly equivalent to the amount of power that the computer uses in an active state (when you're loading photos, writing a document, or watching a video online, for example). By comparison, Sleep mode uses a small amount of energy!

The message? Power up once during the day, and if you'll be away from your computer for a few hours, let it go to sleep. If you'll be gone three hours or more, shutting the system down can save some watts, but if you'll be back right after lunch, sleep mode is the way to go.

Sleep mode in Windows is a low-impact mode that enables you to take a break from your computer and then go right back where you left off without a lot of drain on power (or the risk of losing data). The "Putting your computer to sleep" section of this chapter tells you how to work with sleep mode.

Energy use in laptops shows up differently from what you see in desktop systems; that's because now you have to consider the effect of using a battery power source. Power consumption doesn't stop when you unplug the system. You may be surprised to see how much power it actually takes to charge the laptop battery.

The University of Pennsylvania keeps a detailed, updated list of power-use comparisons for several top computers (desktops and laptops). You can check out the comparisons by going to

```
www.upenn.edu/computing/provider/docs/hardware/powerusage.html
```

What's going on under the hood?

Things may look pretty quiet as you gaze at the surface of your computer, but a whole "ecosystem" of energy-consuming life is underneath. Each component draws power as electric current runs the length of paths and circuits. Your monitor has the biggest appetite, followed by the chipset on the motherboard, the microprocessor, the graphics card, the hard drive, and the network card. Although you're not likely to cut back on the basic power supply that each of these elements needs to function effectively, you can make a difference in the total amount of electricity that your computer uses by creating a power plan. With just a few clicks, you can control how and when your computer uses the most power, and balance that use with the kind of overall performance you want from your computer.

Table 9-1 compares the amount of electricity your technology uses in various power states, and the following list tells you what those states mean:

- ✔ **Active** means the technology is plugged in, turned on, and in use (as when you're watching an online video).

- ✔ **Active standby** means the technology is turned on but isn't in use (as when the printer is turned on but you're not printing anything at the moment).

✔ **Passive standby** means the equipment is ready for use but isn't active (as when you can turn on your DVD player by pressing a remote-control button).

✔ **Off** means the equipment isn't in standby mode and can't be activated until the power is switched on.

Table 9-1	How Much Energy Your Computer Uses			
Equipment	*Active (Watts)*	*Active Standby (Watts)*	*Passive Standby (Watts)*	*Annual Use (Watts)*
Desktop computer	68	17	4	255
Laptop computer	22	3	1	83
CRT monitor	70	3	2	82
LCD monitor	27	2	1	70
Computer speakers	7	NA	2	20
Modem	6	NA	2	48
Wireless router	6	NA	2	48
USB hub	3	NA	1	18
Printer	9	3	2	15
Multifunction printer/ scanner/copier	15	9	6	55
MP3 player	1	NA	1	6
Digital camera	2	NA	0	3

Chances are that your computer equipment doesn't use an astronomical amount of energy, but when you multiply the number of computers and peripherals you have (don't forget to add your monitors, routers, printers, digital cameras, camcorders, and scanners) by every house on your block, and then by all the blocks in your city and all the cities in your state, you get an idea of how big the savings could really be. In fact, a 2001 study by the U.S. Department of Energy showed that in the United States, technology gobbles up 3 percent of total energy consumption.

On some systems, it may be possible to change the computer's Basic Input/ Output System (BIOS) so that the CPU (central processing unit) functions at a minimal power level. The computer manufacturer determines whether you can control those settings. Messing with the BIOS, however, isn't something you should try unless you're technically inclined or very, very lucky.

Later in this chapter, you find out about Windows Vista, Windows XP, and Mac power management plans (as well as a little about Windows 7), and see how to get your computer on a reasonably healthy diet of balanced energy consumption. The good news is that setting up your power management plan isn't nearly as geeky as it sounds!

Quick Energy Cutbacks for Your PC

You probably want to start with the easy fixes, so this section gives you a look at a few simple ways to begin reducing your computer's power consumption. The first consideration is whether you even need to have the computer *on.* (You're probably reading a book right now — the non-electronic variety — which doesn't require any power usage.) But beyond that basic choice — on or off — you can perform the simple tasks outlined in this section to slow the rate at which you draw watts into your house.

Unplug peripherals

Any device plugged into your computer by universal serial bus (USB) uses your computer's power just by the nature of its connection. If you have a mouse, touchpad, scanner, printer, or flash drive connected to your computer, it's consuming electricity — maybe a tiny amount, but still some.

Before you just yank out all the USB cables connected to your system, however, consider what they connect to — and use the Safely Remove Hardware Wizard in Windows to let them go gracefully. Here's how to do that:

1. **Double-click the Safely Remove Hardware icon in the Windows notification area.**

   The Safely Remove Hardware dialog box appears, listing all peripherals currently connected to your computer.

2. **Select the item you want to remove and then click Stop.**

   The Stop a Hardware Device dialog box appears, as shown in Figure 9-1, so you can confirm that you really do want to disconnect the device. (Yes, Windows wants to be extra careful.)

3. Select the item you want to remove and then click OK.

The Safe to Remove Hardware balloon pops up above the notification area, letting you know that you can disconnect the peripheral safely.

If the Safely Remove Hardware tool doesn't seem to be working right in your version of Windows, check out the fix Microsoft has posted for this tool. Go to http://support.microsoft.com/kb/931619 to find out more.

Dim the lights

Most of us like a nice crisp display, but you may be able to conserve some of the power your monitor uses by lessening the monitor's brightness. You don't have to trade eyestrain for a lower electric bill, though; you can find a happy medium.

The brightness control is actually a hardware feature, which means that you need to look on the monitor itself to change the brightness on your desktop PC. Your monitor may have its own brightness-control buttons, or you may need to use the keyboard to find the brightness controls. Consult your monitor's manual if you aren't sure how to adjust the brightness.

Your laptop may have a function key (labeled Fn) that you press along with another key to adjust the brightness. Typically, the characters on the Fn key are a different color from those on other (non-function) keys so you can locate a chosen key easily. Function-related keys on the keyboard have the same color as the Fn key, indicating that when you press Fn and then press one of these other keys, they perform specific tasks. On my laptop, for example, these steps reduce the brightness:

1. Press and hold Fn.

The name of the Fn key appears in blue letters on screen.

2. **Press F6.**

   The F6 key displays a symbol with a down-pointing triangle and a brightness symbol, which looks like a little sun icon.

3. **Repeat Steps 1 and 2 until you get the brightness effect you want.**

Is the screen too dull now? If so, you can reverse the process by looking for the Fn key combination that enables you to increase the brightness. (On my system, it's Fn+F7.)

When your laptop draws power from the battery, Windows dims the screen by default to conserve power. You can change the display settings as part of your Windows power management plan (see "Set It Up Your Way with Windows Power Management," later in this chapter).

Dump your screen saver

Once upon a time, screen savers really did save your screen from something. They were designed to keep the screen display moving to prevent a static image from being burned into the monitor when the computer was left inactive for long periods. Changes in monitor technology did away with the risk but not with the practice. Screen savers became fun photos of the kids, mazes, puzzles, or nature scenes to cool people down between meetings. Today, however, those cool screen savers are contributing to global warming because they keep your computer running when it could be blanking out and going to sleep.

Here's how to turn off your screen savers in Windows Vista and Windows XP:

1. **Choose Start⇨Control Panel.**

2. **Click Personalize.**

   The Personalize Appearance and Sounds dialog box appears. Here, you can make all sorts of aesthetic changes to your Windows Vista setup, adjusting the color scheme and style of your windows, the mouse pointers, themes, sounds, and more.

3. **Click Screen Saver.**

   The Screen Saver Settings dialog box shows you the screen saver that's currently active on your system. (See Figure 9-2.)

4. **Choose None from the Screen Saver drop-down menu.**

5. **Click OK.**

Figure 9-2:
Blank your
screen
saver in
Windows
Vista.

In Windows 7, you nix the screen saver by following these steps:

1. **Choose Start➪Control Panel.**

2. **Click Appearance and Personalization.**

   The Appearance and Personalization dialog box gives you a range of settings that you can use to customize the look and feel of Windows 7.

3. **In the Personalization area, click Change Screen Saver.**

   The Screen Saver Settings dialog box appears.

4. **Choose None from the Screen Saver drop-down menu.**

5. **Click OK to save your changes.**

Here's one more procedure for good measure. Do away with your screen
saver in Windows XP by following these steps:

1. **Choose Start➪Control Panel.**

   If you're using Windows XP, you see the screen shown in Figure 9-2,
   earlier in this section. If you like the retro look of Classic Windows and
   selected that option in the past, look for the Display applet that appears
   in the Control Panel.

   2. **Click Appearance and Themes.**

   3. **Click Choose a Screen Saver.**

   4. **Choose None from the Screen Saver drop-down menu.**

   5. **Click OK.**

Managing Power in Windows Vista

Even though Windows XP includes a respectable number of power-saving features, Windows Vista is the first Microsoft operating system developed and released in the growing green era. Vista represents a kind of four-way conversation among the software designers, consumers (that's us), the environment, and the machine.

As a result, Windows Vista is in sync with the times, offering you several ways to manage and reduce the energy your system slurps while you work, play, and surf. You get to make the call about how much power you want your system to use to deliver the kind of performance you want. That freedom of choice is important, because optimizing your computer's performance is a subjective thing. You may want to save as much power as possible, and you feel perfectly fine about processing that's a tad slow, but your friend down the hall might blow a gasket if her system doesn't operate at top speed. (You may want to tell her it's time to switch to decaf.) Every computer user needs to be able to make the call for his or her own computing experience.

Using the power-management features in Windows Vista, you can

  ✔ Create a power-management plan that helps you effectively (and easily!) manage the power your computer uses.

  ✔ Change the way your power buttons act.

  ✔ Turn on Sleep mode (and do away with hibernating forever).

  ✔ Reduce the amount of carbon dioxide that you add to the atmosphere.

  ✔ Still get a great look in Aero graphics (the fancy new interface supported by Vista and Windows 7 that includes transparent dialog boxes and the like) without any boost in your power consumption (meaning that you can look great for less).

Putting your computer to sleep

Putting your computer to sleep when you aren't using it is an important part of saving power. A sleeping computer uses less power while keeping your session alive and ready to use. However, Microsoft actually has three terms for sleeping, as explained in the following list.

- ✔ **Standby:** Places your computer in an energy-saving mode. Memory is still active and holds your data. However, hard drives, monitors, and other peripherals are shut down. The processor and many other peripherals are in a low-power state. As a result, your computer uses around 11 watts instead of the usual amount of power.

- ✔ **Hibernate:** Saves all the data for the current session to the hard drive and then shuts the computer down. As a result, hibernate requires about the same amount of time as a normal boot to restore your session. This mode does save more power at around 4 watts.

- ✔ **Sleep:** Initially places your computer in an enhanced standby mode. Sleep uses features found in new computers to reduce power usage more than with the Standby mode found in Windows XP. Instead of 11 watts, the Sleep mode uses around 8 watts. After three hours (the time interval is adjustable using the Power Options dialog box), Sleep places your computer in the equivalent of Hibernate mode (power usage goes down to around 4 watts), so you get the best of both Standby and Hibernate in a single package.

Sleep mode puts your computer into a low-power state that saves quite a bit of energy and still gives you access to your open files and applications — almost instantly — when you're ready to get back to work. (By contrast, Standby mode in Windows XP can take up to five seconds and uses a whole lot more power in its inactive state.) Sleep mode uses only a fraction of the power that an active work session requires to keep your session in memory, and it powers up quickly (in two seconds!) when you press the power button to begin working again.

To put your computer to sleep, click Start; then click the gold Power button on the bottom-right side of the Start menu. (See Figure 9-3.)

To wake up your computer, press your computer's power button, and the Windows Vista opening screen appears so you can choose your user account. Instantly you're returned to the screen as you left it before your system went to sleep.

Figure 9-3:
Goodnight,
sweet
computer.

Click the power button

Checking out Vista power plans

The secret of choosing the right power plan for your computer is knowing what's more important to you: saving a whole lot of energy or getting the best performance possible from your system. Windows Vista gives you a choice of three power plans (for a comparison, see Table 9-2):

- ✔ **Balanced:** Enables you to equalize the energy you use in proportion to performance so that neither one sets any *Guinness Book* records. You can save a healthy amount of energy by giving up just a little high-end performance. The Balanced power plan maximizes power conservation when your system is inactive — and adapts as needed when you need a power boost.

- ✔ **Power Saver:** Puts the premium on energy conservation and worries less about the performance of your computer. You might choose this option when you're using a high-performing system that does well even when it's not running at the top of its functioning, or when the tasks you use the computer to accomplish put only light demands on the system. This power plan helps you get the most out of your battery charge so your laptop is good on the go as long as possible.

✔ **High Performance:** Isn't so worried about energy use and puts all the emphasis on system performance. If you use processing-intensive applications, you may find that your laptop battery drains more quickly. If you're AC-powered, you'll simply draw more current.

You can change your power-management plan at any time. (See the upcoming "Switching your plan" section for instructions.) If you try one and aren't getting the results you want, switch it (or create your own)!

Table 9-2	A Quick Look at Vista Power Plans	
Power Plan	*Plugged In*	*On Battery*
Balanced	Turns off the display after 20 minutes.	Turns off the display after 5 minutes.
	Enters Sleep mode after 60 minutes.	Enters Sleep mode after 15 minutes.
Power Saver	Turns off the display after 20 minutes.	Turns off the display after 3 minutes.
	Enters Sleep mode after 60 minutes.	Enters Sleep mode after 15 minutes.
High Performance	Turns off the display after 20 minutes.	Turns off the display after 20 minutes.
	Never enters Sleep mode.	Enters Sleep mode after 60 minutes.

Choosing a power plan

To put one of the existing power plans into action, follow these simple steps:

1. **Choose Start⇨Control Panel.**

   The Windows Vista Control Panel opens, showing you the variety of categories in which you can fine-tune your system.

2. **Choose Hardware and Sound⇨Power Options.**

   Yes, it seems strange to throw Sound in there. But it's all vibration, right?

3. Select the power plan you want to try.

As you see in Figure 9-4, Balanced is selected by default, so if you opt not to change that setting, you have nothing else to do here. The power and performance indicators on the right side of the window give you an idea of the priorities of each plan.

The plan you select goes into effect immediately; you don't need to reboot (which is a relief and saves power).

The quickest way to choose a power plan — and save a few keystrokes of human energy at the same time — is to click Start and type **power options** in the Search box. You go directly to the power choices in Windows Vista. Nice.

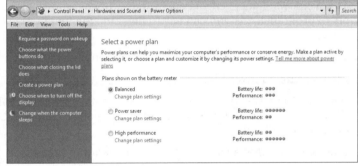

Figure 9-4: Balanced is the default power plan in Windows Vista.

Switching your plan

As you may already know from gym memberships and cellphone contracts, you don't always choose the plan you *really* need the first time out. As you get a little experience with the plan you've selected, you may decide that it's affecting your system's performance too much. Or perhaps you can cut things back a little. Either way, you can remember which plan you selected and make an easy change by following these steps:

1. On your laptop, click the Power Meter icon in the Windows Vista notification area.

The Power Meter icon looks like a little power plug. You can't miss it. A note box pops up, showing you the power plan in effect and giving you a quick update on your system's charge level.

2. To change the power plan, click the one you want.

If you want to read more about the different power plans, click the More Power Options link at the bottom of the note box.

To change the plan on your desktop PC, return to the Power Options Properties dialog box by clicking Start and typing **power options** in the Search box. Select the new power plan you want, and click the Close box.

Creating your own power plan

You can use any of the Windows Vista power plans as they are set by default, or you can customize them to fit the type of power management that best fits the way you use your computer. You can also create your own power plan from the ground up. Here's how:

1. **Choose⇨Control Panel.**

   The Windows Vista Control Panel window opens, showing you the variety of program icons you can use to fine-tune the functioning of your system.

2. **Choose Hardware and Sound⇨Power Options.**

3. **Click Create a Power Plan.**

   Windows Vista shows you the power plan that's currently in place (Balanced is selected by default) and allows you to choose other plans or create a new one.

4. **Choose a plan that's close to the one you want to create.**

5. **In the Plan Name field, type a name for the plan you're creating; then click Next.**

   You can use any combination of uppercase and lowercase letters in your plan name, and spaces are fine. Be sure to name the plan in such a way that you'll easily remember later why you created it and when you should use it.

6. **Specify your settings for display and your sleep settings for battery and AC power use.**

   As shown in Figure 9-5, you click the down arrow for each setting, and choose the setting you want from the list that appears.

7. **Click Create.**

After you create a custom power plan, the plan is available so that you can review and change it easily. If you're using a laptop computer, the new plan appears below the plans shown on the Battery Meter. If you're using a desktop computer, the plan is under Preferred Plans.

Now when you click the Battery Meter icon in the notification area, the new power plan is one of the three displayed there. (See Figure 9-6.)

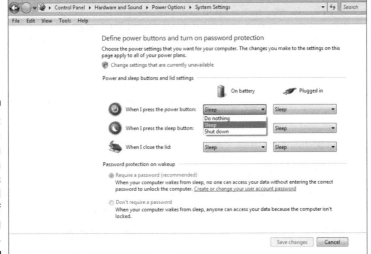

Figure 9-5:
Create a custom power plan in Windows Vista based on one of the existing plans.

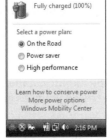

Figure 9-6:
Selecting a power plan to match how you're using the computer.

Energy-Friendly Windows 7

The early power-efficiency reports for Windows 7 are good. Windows 7 extends the power consciousness of Windows Vista and reduces energy consumption even more, in particular when the computer is idle. Windows 7 builds on the idea of smart trade-offs between power and performance by

✔ Adding to the power management plans and settings that you can control

✔ Enabling you to manage your devices' power consumption

✔ Helping you use system resources such as your microprocessor, memory, and hard disk as efficiently as possible

As computers have evolved and improved, so have users. People like instant results. (This is true not only in computing, we might add — hence, the seed of disposability). Few of us are happy to wait for long periods while the computer wakes up; in fact, a slow computer feels like agony. Sleep mode, introduced in Windows Vista, was designed to shortcut that long painful state of awakening by keeping your computer at the ready with minimum power use. Windows 7 continues that objective by improving Sleep mode and giving you additional ways to control the peripherals and internal system resources that go to sleep.

These steps lull Windows 7 to sleep on your computer:

1. **Click the Start button.**

   In the bottom-right corner of the Start menu, you see a right-pointing triangle that appears to the right of the Shut Down button.

2. **Click the right-pointing triangle and choose Sleep.**

   If nothing appears to happen immediately, don't worry. Here's what's actually going on when you put your computer to sleep in Windows 7:

   - Windows 7 copies your programs, open documents, and anything else that's currently saved in your computer's memory to the hard drive.

   - Windows takes a snapshot of the contents of memory, capturing everything so that it can come back quickly.

   - Windows shuts down the hard drive, the monitor, and anything else that drains power, keeping a little trickle going to memory to keep your current work session intact.

One of the perks Windows 7 offers is a more reliable Sleep mode. With Windows Vista, if power is interrupted while the computer is sleeping, everything in memory is wiped out. With Windows 7, if somebody trips over the power cord or your battery goes dead, Windows 7 can grab that snapshot of your data and programs, and take you right back where you left off.

Want to take a peek at Windows 7 power settings? If you've used Windows Vista, Windows 7 won't look too different. Here are the easy steps:

1. **Choose Start➪Control Panel➪Hardware and Sound.**

   You see the Control Panel's Hardware and Sound pane.

2. **Below Power Options, click the link to Change Power-Saving Settings.**

   You see the options shown in Figure 9-7.

Figure 9-7:
Most people
find the
Balanced
settings
to be
adequate,
but if you
really want
to save
energy, you
have to dig
deeper.

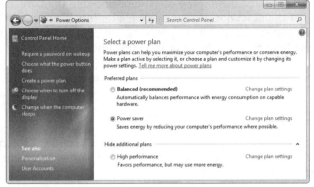

3. **Select the power plan you want to use.**

4. **Click Change Plan Settings if you want to customize the selected plan.**

5. **Choose when you want to turn off the display, and click Save Changes.**

6. **In the Select a Power Plan dialog box, click the Close button.**

   On a desktop computer, the Balanced plan turns the monitor off after
   10 minutes and puts the computer to sleep after 30 minutes. The Power
   Saver plan turns the monitor off after 5 minutes and puts the computer
   to sleep after 15 minutes.

 Microsoft recently published some recommendations that I found fascinating.
If you really want to conserve energy with a desktop computer, be very
aggressive with the monitor idle time — say, two minutes or less — and make
sure that you don't have a screen saver enabled. If you want to conserve
energy with a notebook or netbook, your top priority is reducing screen
brightness.

 Woody introduces you to all things Windows 7 in *Windows 7 All-in-One For
Dummies.* Be sure to check out that book to discover ways to make the newest
Microsoft operating system really sing.

Choosing Power Options in Windows XP

Windows Vista wasn't the first version of the Windows operating system
to care about power consumption; Windows XP includes a fair number of
power management techniques that help you keep an eye on the energy your
system uses and make choices about how you allocate the power (for how

long and to which devices). Granted, Windows XP's initial power management strategy may have been more consumer-oriented than green (as in "We want you to get the most out of your system's battery life so you'll like us" instead of "We care about the planet and are thinking environmentally"), but perhaps both views get you closer to the same end.

Here's how to find and begin working with the power options you'll find in Windows XP:

1. **Choose Start➪Control Panel.**

   The Windows XP Control Panel window opens in either Category view or Windows XP Classic view (depending on which view you used the last time you opened Control Panel).

2. **Choose Performance and Maintenance➪Power Options.**

   The Power Options Properties dialog box opens, as you see in Figure 9-8. This small but mighty dialog box is the hub for the power choices you make in Windows XP. Table 9-3 introduces the tabs and tasks that you find in this dialog box.

Figure 9-8:
Central control for Windows XP power management.

You've probably noticed a little terminology difference here. What Windows Vista and Windows 7 call *power plans,* Windows XP refers to as *power schemes.* The XP phrase seems just a little sneakier, don't you think?

Table 9-3	Power Options in Windows XP
Tab	*Tasks*
Power Schemes	Choose and/or customize the power scheme you want to use.
Alarms	Set alarms that alert you when system power is low.
Power Meter	Check your battery's power level.
Advanced	Choose the actions for power button and whether Windows XP should prompt you for a password when it resumes from standby.
Hibernate	Elect whether to use Hibernate mode to store your work session before shutting down.

Choose a power scheme

Windows XP has a set of power schemes already programmed into the software so that you can choose one that works for you or modify it to better fit the way you like to use your system. Here are the power schemes included with Windows XP by default:

- Home/Office Desk
- Portable/Laptop
- Presentation
- Always On
- Minimal Power Management
- Max Battery

You choose the power scheme you want (or want to begin with) on the Power Schemes tab of the Power Options Properties dialog box. Choose the one you want from the Power Schemes drop-down menu. Notice that the power settings at the bottom of the dialog box change to reflect the power scheme you select.

Each power scheme offers two settings (Plugged In and Running on Batteries) for the following choices:

- When the monitor shuts off
- When the hard disk shuts off

✔ When Standby mode is activated

✔ When Hibernate mode is activated

After you make changes to the plan, you can save the new default settings you've selected or create another plan based on your new settings.

Making your power choices

Here are the steps for tweaking one of the power schemes that come with Windows XP:

1. **In the Power Options Properties dialog box, choose the power scheme you want to use from the Power Schemes drop-down menu.**

   If you don't see *exactly* the one you want, choose the one that's closest to the type of power scheme you think you'll use. Notice that the settings in the bottom half of the dialog box change to reflect your choice.

2. **Click the down arrow next to each setting you want to change to display a list of options.**

   It's a big range of options, isn't it? Find the length of time that works best for you, in minute or hour increments.

3. **Choose new values from the list.**

   You may want to change settings for some items but not for all. You could be more concerned about power consumption when your computer is running on battery, for example. In that case, you would choose shorter time periods for the Running on Batteries settings than you choose for the Plugged In settings.

4. **Click Apply.**

   The power settings are saved as part of the selected power scheme and applied immediately.

You can customize any power plan in Windows XP to suit your preferences, but if you want to keep the original plans intact, click the Save As button below the Power Schemes drop-down menu to save the modified power scheme under a different name.

Saving a customized power scheme

If you want to keep the default power schemes intact, you can save your customized power scheme and apply it to the way that Windows XP manages power for your system. Here are the steps:

1. **Choose the power scheme closest to the one you want to create.**

2. **Modify the power-option settings so that they appear the way you want them (refer to the preceding section).**

3. **Click Save As.**

   The Save Scheme dialog box appears.

4. **Enter a name for the new scheme, and click OK.**

   The new power scheme is applied by default. You can still change settings, apply another scheme, and return to the new scheme at any time by making new changes in the Power Options Properties dialog box.

Alert! Diet infraction!

Power is such a quiet thing — how will you know when your system is running low? One way to check involves using the Power Meter icon in the Windows XP system tray. But what if you're caught up in what you're doing and forget to check? You can avoid those low-power outages that can cost you valuable time and data by using the Alarms tab in the Power Options Properties dialog box.

Windows XP Alarms let you set a low-battery alarm so that when power gets to a certain level (a level that you set), the program notifies you by sounding an alarm or displaying a text message. You can also have the computer go directly to Standby or Hibernate mode, or even shut down completely. (Do not pass Go; do not collect $200.) One further choice that Alarms offers: You can arrange to have Windows XP run a specific program when a power event (such as low battery or going to standby) occurs.

To set alarms for power management in your version of Windows XP, follow these steps:

1. **In the Power Options Properties dialog box, click the Alarms tab.**

   The options shown in Figure 9-9 appear. The defaults set on your system may be different from the ones you see here. Windows XP gives you the option of setting two levels of notification — one as a Low Battery Alarm, when your system power reaches a low level, and the other as a Critical Battery Alarm, when your computer is about to run out of juice.

2. **Select the Activate Low Battery Alarm check box if it's deselected.**

   The slider control and the Alarm Action button become available.

3. **Drag the slider to the percentage of charge you want to set for the low-battery alarm.**

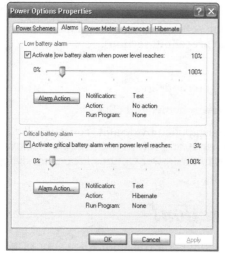

Figure 9-9:
Set alarm
levels and
actions so
you know
when PC
power is
running low.

4. Click the Alarm Action button.

The Low Battery Alarm Action dialog box appears. You're most likely to want to use the Notifications options in the Low Battery Alarm Action dialog box. All settings here are optional.

5. Set the Alarm Actions as follows:

- In the Notifications area, choose whether you want a sound alarm or a text message (or both).

- In the Alarm Action area, choose whether you want the system to stand by, hibernate, or shut down automatically when the low-power setting is reached.

- In the Run a Program field, you can have Windows XP automatically run a program when a power event — such as a low-power setting or a power outage — occurs.

6. Click OK to close the Low Battery Alarm Action dialog box.

7. Repeat Steps 2–6 for the Critical Battery Alarm setting.

Typically, you'll use the Low Battery Alarm simply to call your attention to the fact that your power is draining away, but the Critical Battery Alarm signifies a more dire state. Here you may want to choose an action in the Alarm Action area so your computer hibernates immediately in critical power situations.

8. Click OK to save all power settings on the Alarms tab.

Bring in the batteries

A simple way to keep an eye on your power consumption in Windows involves checking the Power Meter. Click the Power Meter tab on the Power Options Properties dialog box to see information about the battery you're using. This tab shows you your current power source as well as the charge level of your batteries.

Want more info on the battery your system uses? Click the battery icon, and a pop-up window displays your battery's manufacturer's information.

Tell your power buttons what to do

The Advanced tab of the Power Options Property dialog box includes several choices that affect the way your computer behaves when you close the lid (on a laptop) or push the power button. When you close the lid on your laptop, you can have Windows XP do nothing, move into Standby mode, or hibernate.

When you push the power button on your system, you can have Windows XP

- ✔ Do nothing.
- ✔ Ask what you want to do.
- ✔ Stand by.
- ✔ Hibernate.
- ✔ Shut down.

By default, the first check box tells Windows XP to display the Power Meter icon in the system tray. This setting is an easy way to keep an eye on your computer's power level, so leaving that check box selected is a good idea.

Simply make your choices and click OK to save the changes.

Ah, the competition between Windows XP Hibernate and Standby. This sibling conflict has been immortalized in blogs and discussion boards throughout the virtual PC kingdom.

Hibernate and Standby are two options that Windows XP offers when you take steps to shut down your computer. The process goes like this:

1. **Choose Start⊅Shut Down.**

2. **Click the power-down option you want.**

   Figure 9-10 shows the power-down options (Hibernate, Stand By, Turn Off, and Restart) available in Windows XP. Turn Off and Restart are the most commonly used; Turn Off turns off your computer completely, and Restart reboots the system, clearing everything in RAM so that you can start fresh.

Figure 9-10:
Choose
a power-
down
option.

Turn off computer

Hibernate   Stand By   Turn Off   Restart

Cancel

Not all Windows XP computers show the Hibernate option by default. If you don't see Hibernate as one of the power-down options available to you, press and hold the Shift key when the power-down options are displayed. Standby should change to Hibernate, and then you can click that button to select it. If this method doesn't work for you, display the Power Options dialog box, click the Hibernate tab, and make sure that the Enable Hibernation check box is selected.

Hibernate and Standby are two temporary power-down modes. You use them when you're going to be away from your computer for a while, and you want to conserve power and suspend operation.

In Windows XP, the Hibernate option takes a little longer than Standby to resume, but it saves your data and conserves a significant amount of power. Standby mode in Windows XP is okay if you need to suspend operation for a little while (an hour or less), but be sure to save your files first. You won't save much power by using Standby mode.

Another challenge for IT personnel when it comes to using Standby is that there's no way for Standby to be controlled in any kind of group policy. Also, because Windows XP doesn't have a mechanism that enables it to determine automatically when the system is idle, it doesn't kick in automatically (as does Sleep mode in Windows Vista).

Why Standby leaches electricity

Windows XP's Standby mode is designed to let your computer take a little rest from processing without making any drastic moves like saving files to disk. One of the nice things about Standby is that it doesn't require a huge amount of disk storage space for file retrieval. By contrast, Hibernate mode requires a chunk of hard-drive space — roughly equivalent to the amount of RAM in your computer — so it can store the files you're using when you choose Hibernate mode.

By virtue of this very fact — Standby doesn't save items to disk — it must continually draw power to keep RAM awake and functioning. So in Standby,

your computer never shuts down completely — which translates, for purposes of this discussion, to continuous energy consumption.

If your focus is on reducing the amount of power your computer uses and making the most of the battery life you have, and if you're going to be away from your computer longer than an hour or so, use Hibernate instead of Standby. You may wait a few more seconds for the computer to wake up, and you may need to free some hard disk space that you'd rather use for something else. At the end of the day, though, Hibernate is a safer — and greener — choice.

Saving Mac Power

No matter where your sympathies lie in the I'm-a-PC / I'm-a-Mac debate, you have to admit that Macs do a pretty good job with energy conservation. The newer Macs tend to run leaner than many popular PCs do, although all responsible manufacturers are working to shrink their carbon footprints and use safer materials in the systems they offer.

The Mac looks at power a little differently from its PC cousin, in that the Mac includes deep sleep and lighter sleep (Idle mode). When you step away from your Mac, after a brief period of inactivity the system goes into Idle mode. Then, after a further period, the computer goes to sleep.

Hushabye, little Mac

You use the Energy Saver dialog to set your preferences for when the Mac slips off to slumberland. Here are the steps:

1. **In Mac OS X, choose System Preferences.**

   The System Preferences dialog opens. You'll find the Energy Saver icon in the center of the Hardware settings.

2. **Click Energy Saver.**

The Energy Saver dialog opens (see Figure 9-11). In this dialog, you can optimize existing choices or customize power settings. Note that your Energy Saver dialog may look different from the one shown in Figure 9-11.

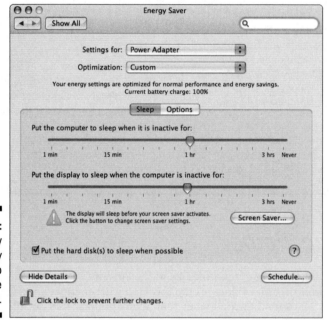

Figure 9-11:
Display Energy Saver to manage Mac power.

3. **From the Settings For pop-up menu, choose Power Adapter or Battery.**

The options displayed vary depending on whether you're making choices for the AC source or your battery. You can set the sleep times you prefer for the different power sources.

4. **Drag the slider to the amount of time you want to set for the Mac's sleep time.**

5. **Drag the slider to reflect when you want the display to go to sleep.**

Do less-energy-conscious people use your computer when you're not looking? You can lock the power-management settings so other users can't modify them: Just click the lock icon in the bottom-left corner of the Energy Saver dialog.

Choosing a Mac power plan

You can customize and then choose power management plans for the Mac by using the Energy Saver dialog box. Similar to Windows Vista (dare we say that out loud?), Mac OS X lets you choose the plan you want based on a balance of performance and power use. You can choose among the following power plans: Normal, Better Energy Savings, Better Performance, or Custom.

Follow the steps in the "Hushabye, little Mac" section earlier in this chapter to display the Energy Saver dialog, and click the arrow on the Optimization pop-up menu to display the list shown in Figure 9-12.

Figure 9-12:
Customize
your Mac
power
settings.

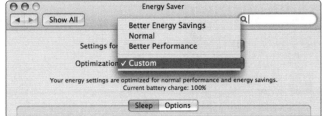

Energy Saver

Show All

Better Energy Savings
Normal
Better Performance

Settings for
Optimization ✓ Custom

Your energy settings are optimized for normal performance and energy savings.
Current battery charge: 100%

Sleep   Options

Click the Options tab to change the way your Mac goes to sleep (you can dim the monitor as Mac dozes off) and also to display the battery status on the menu bar.

Adding Power-Management Software

If you really like managing the way your computer uses power, you don't have to stop with the power-management features your operating system offers you. Power-management software is available from other sources. The software makes it easy for you to keep an eye on the power you're using, whether you're watching your own system resources or coordinating the power for a whole department — or a whole company — of computers.

Power-management software can monitor a computer's activity so that when the system goes into Idle mode, system resources are managed as effectively as possible. In a business, these power-saving strategies can add up and save a lot of money and energy — not to mention the headaches they can save the IT department when they run well!

Monitoring energy for free with Edison

Edison (www.edison.com) is a free, easy-to-use energy monitoring utility that helps you evaluate when you use the most PC power and create a schedule for use. Versions of Edison are available for both Windows Vista and Windows XP.

As Figure 9-13 shows, you can set different power settings depending on the time of day and the types of tasks you'll be using your computer to do. Edison shows you the amount of money, energy, and CO_2 you're saving with the energy choices you make, and it's a great motivator for saving even more!

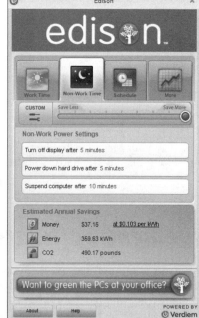

Figure 9-13:
Edison
enables you
to set power
options
according
to your daily
schedule.

Reducing CO_2 with Snap's CO_2 Saver

Snap's CO_2 Saver (http://co2saver.snap.com) is another free personal power management utility that lets you optimize your system's power in its idle state. The tool works with both Windows XP and Windows Vista, displaying a running total of energy savings in a toolbar that includes a search feature you can customize.

As soon as you install CO_2 Saver and set the power options the way you want them, the utility adjusts your Windows power management settings to maximize energy savings for your system. You can choose any of four power-management levels: Mild, Medium, Aggressive, or Custom.

New energy-management gadgets are being developed all the time, so keep your eyes open for new utilities you can add to your Windows Vista Sidebar, download to your cellphone, or use on mobile devices to help you stay tuned in to your power consumption. Awareness is the first step in positive change, so you're already improving your computing karma!

Chapter 10

Greening Mobile Devices

· ·

· ·

*B*efore you do a double-take to check the title on the cover, we can assure you that the book you're holding in your hands is *Green Home Computing For Dummies*? Why then, you may wonder, a chapter on mobile devices, when the focus is on the home?

To many of your gadgets, connecting with your home computer is, to them, the equivalent of resting their heads on the proverbial pillow at the end of the day. That's because many of your gadgets depend on your home computer to do things like keep your contacts and calendar in sync, or transfer music and movies that you can watch on your gadgets on the sofa or the subway, or simply recharge their built-in batteries the greener way, by tapping into your computer's USB port rather than bothering with the wall charger.

In this chapter, we focus mainly on your mobile phone and how you can adjust its power settings to save energy and extend battery life. We also tell you about green options for charging your mobile phone and other handheld gadgets, introduce you to mobile applications for tracking your carbon footprint, and turn you on to converting your mobile phone to an e-book reader or personal GPS navigator. We describe which eco-friendlier factors to look for when buying a new mobile phone, and we tell you how getting rid of your old phone and other gadgets by donating, selling, or properly recycling them when they're no longer of use to you (or anyone else), is the right green gadget thing to do.

Welcome to your green gadgets home.

For the most complete coverage of all things gadget green, pick up a copy of *Green Gadgets For Dummies*, by Joe Hutsko (Wiley Publishing).

Getting a Handle on Energy-Saving Settings

If you turned to this chapter before reading any of the others, we probably know the reason: Blame it on the battery. Are we right?

Let's face it: We've all done it, blaming, or perhaps cursing, our most essential gadget's battery for running out of juice at the worst possible time. It might have happened in the middle of an important phone call or halfway through the motivating song you rely on to help push you to finish your run or workout. In the worst-case scenario, the battery dies, and it isn't until you awaken later than usual and plug in your gadget again that you can call your boss and apologize for being late because your alarm didn't go off.

One way to extend your gadget's battery life between recharges is to adjust or turn off any energy-zapping features you're not using — some of which you may not even know about. By doing so, your battery will last longer between charges.

General battery-draining features

You can less frequently blame your gadget's battery for bringing your productivity or playtime to a standstill if you pay attention to a few elements that most gadgets expend a lot of energy on — often gratuitously — to keep you happy.

Powerfully pleasing — but power-hungry — factors that have the biggest impact on how long batteries last between charges include the ones in this list:

- ✔ **Screen:** The screen, when putting on its brightest face possible, is generally the biggest drain on your gadget's battery life. Adjusting the screen's brightness setting to the lowest comfortable level and setting it to automatically dim or turn off after certain actions or periods of inactivity helps extend your gadget's overall battery life. How you access your screen's brightness setting is unique to your gadget, but Figure 10-1 shows an example.

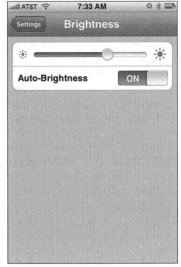

Figure 10-1:
An example
of a screen
brightness
setting.

✔ **Sound:** Lowering your gadget's sound level lengthens battery life. Listening with headphones saves even more power. Shutting off sound completely if you aren't using it offers even longer stretches of time between charges — but keep in mind that turning on your mobile phone's vibrate feature taxes the battery every time it gives you that quiet buzzing feeling.

✔ **Wireless:** Turning off wireless features you're not using extends battery life. The key culprits to look for are Bluetooth, Wi-Fi, GPS, and speedier data service network boosters such as EDGE and 3G. Turn off any of these that you're not using, and then turn them on again only when you need them.

✔ **Heat:** Batteries drain faster when they're hot rather than running warm or at room temperature. Extend your gadget's battery life by keeping it away from too-hot places like car glove boxes or winter-warming radiators.

✔ **Dirt:** Dust, dirt, belly button fuzz, and other debris and impurities that can collect on your gadget's battery contacts can hamper proper contact and charging. Removing the rechargeable battery and gently cleaning exposed contacts with a cotton swab or dust-free cloth dipped in rubbing alcohol can help keep the battery's internal connection strong and unencumbered.

The more specific energy-saving settings described in the following sections can help you eke out the longest battery life possible from your mobile phone.

Saving energy on your mobile phone

This section's heading is sort of a catchall because the reality is that many gadgets nowadays are catchalls themselves. Cellphones are giving way to smartphones, which not only make and receive calls, but also let you stay on top of your schedule and e-mail, browse the Web, listen to music, and watch movies. Of course, using some or all of these extra features means your mobile phone's battery drains faster than just using it to make and receive calls.

If your cellphone's ringtone is the only setting you've ever changed, getting to know its other settings and learning which ones to adjust can reward you longer stretches of time between recharges. Because settings differ from device to device, you may need to poke around to find the individual energy-saving settings on your cellphone or smartphone.

Here are the top mobile phone battery-hogging energy settings you can adjust or turn off if you aren't using them:

- ✔ **On and Off:** Powering off your phone when you know that you won't use it for a while is the basic way to save power.

- ✔ **Brightness:** Turning down the brightness level to its dimmest (but still viewable) level can lengthen your gadget's battery life. Activating your phone's automatic screen dimming and shutoff options to dim or turn off the screen after fifteen seconds or so is another way to extend its battery life.

- ✔ **Auto-Shutoff, Lock, and Sleep:** Similar to the previous setting, setting your phone to automatically lock itself or go to sleep prevents it from waking up in your pocket if you accidentally bump it. You can typically also instantly lock your phone by pressing a button or combination of buttons; check your phone's manual to find out how to instantly lock it on the fly.

- ✔ **Volume:** Turning down or shutting off your phone's ringtone helps save battery life. Adjusting sound effects and alerts for other actions — such as receiving a text or e-mail message or activating your phone's alarm clock — to the lowest level possible can also extend battery life.

- ✔ **Vibrate:** Turning on the vibrate feature can alert you to a call without making a sound, but keep in mind that vibrating uses battery juice if you let it vibrate continuously. Setting your phone to vibrate only once or a few times is an energy-saving option on many phones.

- ✔ **Equalizer:** One often-overlooked, battery-draining option to turn off, if your phone also plays music tracks, is its equalizer, or EQ. When turned on, this option makes your phone work harder to produce the sound-quality effect you want.

✔ **Network:** Sensing your wireless carrier's phone network signal is a task that your phone does continually to keep you connected. Turning off your phone's Network option when you're in rural areas where reception is spotty or unavailable (but you're still using your phone to do other things like listening to music or playing a game) can save power. Note that the Network option isn't the same as the one you can use to connect to a Wi-Fi network and browse the Web on your mobile phone, however. (That option is next on our list, in case your phone has it.)

Leaving the Network option on but turning off data networking enhancements that give you faster Web access or clearer calls (if your phone has those options) can also help extend battery life. An often talked-about wireless carrier enhancement is 3G, which is an abbreviation for third generation.

✔ **Wi-Fi:** Turning off your phone's Wi-Fi connection if you aren't using it to browse Web pages, check e-mail, or download music can help extend battery life. Leaving Wi-Fi on if you regularly use it, but turning off the option to automatically search for and connect to any nearby Wi-Fi networks it discovers, is a good compromise for staying connected, while minimizing power consumption.

✔ **Bluetooth:** Connecting your phone to a Bluetooth handsfree headset saves you from having to hold the phone to your ear, but it also reduces talk time because it uses extra battery juice. Turning off Bluetooth when you're not using it can give your phone markedly longer battery life.

✔ **GPS:** Continually tracking your location by using your phone's global positioning system (GPS) feature is helpful for finding directions or locating a new restaurant in town. This helpful feature also drains your battery, so turn it off after you've reached your destination.

✔ **Infrared:** Although IR (infrared) was more common before Bluetooth arrived on the scene, some new gadgets, such as Palm's Centro smartphone, are still equipped with the infrared option. If you're not using the IR feature to beam your contact card to fellow IR-capable smartphone users, shut it off for battery savings.

Charging Your Gadgets with Green Power

Portable power chargers and extenders can help you keep your gadgets charged and usable when you're away from a power outlet. The ones we describe here are eco-friendly because they rely on the sun (or wind) for a charge, or on good old-fashioned elbow grease to crank a dynamo.

In other words, these gadgets turn natural energy (sometimes your energy when built-in cranks are what charge them) into energy you can use to power your gadgets.

Many chargers can typically charge gadgets that use a USB cable to connect to their own rechargers or your computer. Some come with multiple charging plug tips so you can connect them to a variety of gadgets. Check with the Web sites of these few that we recommend to learn more about specifications and connection options for each:

✔ **Solio Magnesium Edition solar charger:** Unfold the petals of this portable solar charger ($170; available at www.solio.com), shown in Figure 10-2, and you see three solar panels that soak up the sun to give renewed life to your gadget. Use the Solio to recharge MP3 players, cellphones, digital cameras, handheld video-game players, and many other gadgets. Fully charged, the Solio can recharge a typical mobile phone more than twice, or provide more than 20 hours of MP3 music.

Figure 10-2:
The Solio Magnesium Edition solar charger.

✔ **Gaiam SideWinder cellphone charger:** Connect your cellphone to the Gaiam SideWinder ($29) with the included cable and get cranking for up to six minutes of talk time after two minutes of winding. A built-in LED emergency light provides over five minutes of light after 30 seconds of cranking, and included adapter tips work with most models of Nokia, LG, Samsung, Kyocera, Sony/Ericsson and Motorola Razr phones. It's available at www.gaiam.com.

Although the SideWinder isn't meant for full-charge service, its tiny size makes it perfect for camping or other situations when power is out of reach and you need to reach out and call someone.

✔ **Eclipse Solar Gear:** The company offers a wide selection of backpacks, messenger bags, laptop and camera cases, and even a solar fishing-tackle bag (from around $95 to $200). Although you can carry your notebook in one of the Eclipse messenger bags, the company says that the solar panel can't generate enough energy to charge it. It can, however, charge your cellphone, MP3 player, digital camera, or camcorder. Visit `http://eclipsesolargear.com`.

✔ **HYmini wind-powered charger:** Relying on the wind, rather than on you, is how the HYmini wind-powered charger ($50) generates power to juice up your MP3 player, digital camera, mobile phone, and other gadgets.

What, no wind today? No worries. Connect the HYmini (visit `www.hymini.com` for more information) to your bicycle's handlebars or strap it to your upper arm with optional accessories and get pedaling or running to make some wind of your own as you go about your merry, green way. If you buy the optional solar panel, you can also use the sun to charge on windless and bicycle-free days.

✔ **nPower PEG** (`http://greennpower.com`): Pop the nPower PEG into your backpack (or attach it to your hip or leg), plug in your gadget, and presto — instant power, brought to you by *you*! Harvesting kinetic energy (in this case, up-and-down bodily movement) as you move about, nPower claims the PEG charges portable electronic gizmos at the same rate as a wall charger, which means an hour of walking can bring your iPod or other gadget's charge to about 80 percent. As this book went to press, the nPower PEG was available for pre-order for about $150.

Running Mobile Applications to Monitor and Adjust Power

Downloading and running an application to monitor or adjust a gadget's carbon footprint — and your own — can help you do "the greener thing" wherever you are. Check out these popular applications:

✔ **greenMeter:** This application for the iPhone and iPod touch helps lower your vehicle's impact on the environment by weighing parameters such as its tonnage and the price of gasoline against your driving behavior. By tapping into the iPhone's built-in accelerometer to gauge the vehicle's rate of forward acceleration, greenMeter, available at `http://hunter.pairsite.com/greenmeter`, calculates vehicle readings such as fuel efficiency and carbon footprint.

- ✔ **Ecorio:** Running on a Google Android-based mobile phone near you, Ecorio (find more information at `http://ecorio.org`) uses the phone's GPS feature to track your personal carbon footprint. Choosing your mode of travel — car, bus, train, or bike — determines how seriously green you are about getting around.

  Ecorio suggests carpool options by matching drivers and passengers, lets fellow green-gadgeteers keep tabs on one another (in the same town or across the country), and offers an option to buy carbon offsets by way of Carbonfund.org.

- ✔ **Carbon-Meter:** Coming soon to Google Android and Blackberry smartphones, the iPhone version of Carbon-Meter (visit `www.viralmesh.com/carbon-meter`) rewards your green activities and efforts with coupons and specials sponsored by local advertisers, as shown in Figure 10-3. Run, walk, or bike your way to increase your ecosavings — and your savings account.

- ✔ **UbiGreen:** Presently a research project and not yet something you can hold in your hand, UbiGreen (`http://dub.washington.edu/projects/ubigreen`) gauges how you get around to calculate how much CO_2 you generate — and save — during the week. Glancing at the UbiGreen background running on your cellphone can help you put your best foot forward as you take steps to reduce your carbon footprint.

Figure 10-3: Carbon Meter is one of many mobile phone applications for monitoring your carbon footprint.

Turning Your Mobile Phone into a GPS Navigator

A global positioning system (GPS) navigator in your car can help you get where you're going in the most fuel- and time-efficient manner. To find out more about GPS technology and products, check out *GPS For Dummies,* 2nd Edition, by Joel McNamara (Wiley Publishing).

The GPS mapping programs bundled with mobile phones (such as T-Mobile's G1 or Apple's iPhone) don't typically offer spoken turn-by-turn directions or some of the other features found on dedicated navigators like the ones used in cars. They do offer scalable color maps and point-to-point directions.

Of course, you can always add turn-by-turn voice directions to your mobile phone — for a price — by buying or subscribing to, then installing, GPS navigator programs on your mobile phone or PDA.

If your mobile phone doesn't have built-in GPS, you can still run these programs by purchasing an optional (and external) Bluetooth GPS receiver.

Mobile GPS navigator applications that like to be seen *and* heard include:

- **amAze:** This free GPS navigation program has turn-by-turn voice directions, for a variety of GPS-equipped smartphones and PDAs, including Blackberry, LG, Samsung, Sony Ericsson, and Windows Mobile. Visit `http://amazegps.com`.

- **ALK CoPilot Live 7:** Provides natural voice directions in 20 languages on a number of Pocket PC or Windows Mobile smartphones. Check out `http://alk.com`.

- **MapQuest Mobile Navigator:** Voice-guided GPS navigation service is offered by several of the major wireless carriers for about $50 per year. (For more information, go to `http//:wireless.mapquest.com/ mapquest-navigator` or contact your mobile service provider.)

- **TeleNav GPS Navigator:** This one is available from all major mobile carriers for around $10 per month for unlimited service. TeleNav (go to `http://telenav.com`) provides turn-by-turn driving directions, both onscreen and by voice, on a number of popular GPS-equipped mobile phones, including Blackberry, HTC, Motorola, Palm, and other models.

By adding GPS navigation to your phone instead of buying a dedicated device, you can not only save money, but also do more with the device you already have, which is always the green way to go.

Reading E-books on Your Mobile Phone

Reading e-books on Amazon's Kindle 2 dedicated e-book reader is a green gadget alternative to buying traditional books. Choosing more e-books means that less trees are felled to mill paper that would wind up bound in a printed book. E-books also reduce the other drains on the planet's resources associated with printing and distributing books. At the same time, it's worth noting the materials used to manufacture e-book readers, and the servers that you download e-books from, will still have an environmental impact via the resources and energy used to create and use them.

Yet as sleek and eco-friendly as the Kindle 2 is, why introduce yet another gadget into your life when you may not need to? Chances are good that you already own an excellent e-book reader without realizing it: your cellphone, smartphone, or PDA. Browsing, downloading, and reading free and competitively priced e-books on your handheld gadget is merely a matter of installing an e-book reader program.

Here are a few mobile e-book reader programs and electronic bookstores that enable you to browse and download e-books for free or for a price:

- **Mobipocket Reader** (www.mobipocket.com) runs on mobile phones and PDAs that run on the Windows Mobile, Palm OS, Symbian, and Blackberry operating systems. Downloading titles to your computer and then installing them on your mobile device is required for all but the Blackberry version of the program. Downloading books *over the air,* directly to your Blackberry, means you can skip the computer middle-man step.

  The Mobipocket Reader Web site also offers news and other RSS feeds. Tapping into them to create your own, customized electronic newspaper can keep you up-to-date on news and other topics when you're on the go.

- **Feedbooks** (www.feedbooks.com), the universal e-reading platform, is compatible with a wide range of mobile phones and PDAs. Download titles directly to your mobile phone or PDA by opening http://feedbooks.mobi with your gadget's Web browser.

- **Stanza** (www.lexcycle.com) is an iPhone and iPod touch reader, with the ability to connect to numerous online bookstores to download free and for-sale books, including Feedbooks, Fictionwise, Project Gutenberg, SmashWords, and a number of mainstream publishers.

- **eReader** (www.ereader.com) is an e-book reader program that runs on Windows and Mac desktops and notebooks, as well as on many mobile devices running Windows Mobile, Pocket PC, Palm OS, or Symbian operating systems.

The iPhone and iPod touch edition of eReader can download titles directly from your online bookshelf account that you registered with either eReader.com, Fictionwise.com, or both.

eReader on the iPhone is one of the authors' favorite way to read e-books. The text is beautifully crisp, and the display is large and easy enough on his eyes that he prefers reading on the iPhone to reading on a larger, dedicated reader such as the Kindle 2.

Another reason for this preference is the backlit iPhone display, which is pleasant to read in bed with the lights turned off. Like real books, the Kindle 2 and most other dedicated e-book readers are readable only when the lights are turned on, or in daylight.

Dialing In to Green Mobile Phones

You can't turn on the TV, open a magazine, or listen to the radio without hearing about this product's green benefits or that company's efforts in improving the planet by being green. That's because every company under the sun wants to be seen as green. It's the It thing of our era. Sorting through what's real and what's hype isn't so glamorous and can be dizzying.

Choosing the greenest mobile phone starts with you researching the latest models on the Web. Opening your Web browser and going to `www.google.com` to search for *greenest cellphone* or *greenest mobile phone* can turn up a number of results that point to articles or product pages for mobile phones claiming the title.

Knowing whether the claims are still current (or, for that matter, accurate) can be tricky. Was the claim staked last week — or last year?

You can narrow your Google search results to show only recent hits: Go to `www.google.com/advanced_search` and then click the link that says Date, Usage Rights, Numeric Range, and More. Click the Date arrow and select the Past 24 Hours, Past Week, or Past Month option.

Another way to find environmentally friendly mobile devices is to check out the latest Greenpeace Guide to Greener Electronics report (available at `www.greenpeace.org/electronics`).

At the time this book was written, the report gave top honors to the Nokia 6210 Navigator smartphone, followed by the Sony Ericsson G900. Both devices are PVC-free, but the Nokia gadget earned extra credits for its better energy efficiency and lifecycle.

The four mobile phones listed in the text that follows further illustrate what it means to be a significantly green gadget.

Motorola MOTO W233 Renew

Motorola states that the MOTO W233 Renew is the world's first carbon-neutral cellphone, thanks in part to a plastic housing made entirely from recycled water bottles. The phone ships in a small package, and it and all the printed materials inside it are made from 100 percent post-consumer recycled paper.

As the first mobile phone to earn Carbonfund.org's CarbonFree Certification, Motorola's alliance with Carbondfund means that the company offsets the amount of carbon dioxide used to manufacture, distribute, and operate the phone.

Other green perks the MOTO W233 Renew serves up include:

- **Long-lasting charge:** Motorola estimates that you can expect up to nine hours of talk time — which means less tapping in to the recharger and more energy savings for you.

- **Tree planting:** Furthering the phone's eco-friendly theme, mobile carrier T-Mobile will plant a tree in your name if you sign up for the company's paperless billing option. Partnering with the Arbor Day Foundation, T-Mobile reportedly planted more than a half-million trees in 2008.

- **Easy recycling:** To recycle the phone at the end of its life, you can just drop it off at the nearest T-Mobile phone store, or mail it in using a mailing label you create on the T-Mobile or Motorola Web sites.

- **Ongoing sustainability:** Proceeds gained from T-Mobile's handset-recycling efforts contribute to the company's social investments, and to schools participating in Race to Recycle, which is part of T-Mobile's sustainability practice.

Although the MOTO W233 Renew was offered exclusively to T-Mobile customers for six months after it launched in early 2009, your carrier may offer the green mobile phone by the time you read this. To find out, visit your carrier's Web site and browse the selection of mobile phones it supports and sells. For more on the MOTO W233 Renew, go to www.motorola.com.

Samsung solar-rechargeable Blue Earth mobile phone

Designed to look like a flat, well-rounded, shiny pebble, Blue Earth will be the world's first solar-rechargeable touch-screen phone when it reaches production. A solar panel on the back of the phone can generate enough power to make calls and charge the battery.

The gadget is made from recycled plastic extracted from water bottles, and both the phone and its charger — which draws fewer than 0.03 watts after it charges the phone — are free from toxic substances, including brominated flame retardants (BFRs), beryllium, and phthalates.

The Eco mode option adjusts the brightness, backlight duration, and Bluetooth energy efficiency settings with a single touch. The Eco Walk function counts your steps with a built-in pedometer and calculates how much CO_2 emissions you reduce by hoofing it rather than driving. Go to www. samsung.com.

Nokia 3110 Evolve and N79 eco

Featuring biocovers made from more than 50 percent renewable materials and a charger that draws 94 percent less power than Energy Star requires, the Nokia 3110 Evolve is a good example of a green mobile phone — in part because the 3110 Evolve charger notches down power consumption to next-to-nil after the phone is all charged up.

Charging the Nokia N79 eco when you take it out of its minimal, eco-friendly box isn't an option — unless you plug in a charger you already own. Nokia, figuring that it's greener to reuse an existing charger, doesn't include one with the N79 eco.

Neither phone was available in the U.S. at the time this book was written, but buyers in the United Kingdom can feel good knowing that Nokia donates 4 pounds sterling to the World Wildlife Fund for each N79 eco it sells. Visit www.nokia.com.

Disposing of Gadgets the Green Way

When it's time to get rid of a gadget such as a smartphone that's broken beyond repair (or too expensive to fix) — or that you're replacing because you just have to have the newest model that came out, for reasons all your own — it's time to consider the three Rs: Reduce, reuse, recycle. Just because you want to get rid of something doesn't automatically translate to invoking the third R — *recycle*. Not in the classical sense of, say, hauling piles of old newspapers out to the curb on pick-up day. That's because when we talk about *recycling* a gadget, we don't necessarily mean it will be broken down into parts and ground up, melted, or otherwise destroyed.

When it comes to gadgets, the terms *recycle* and *reuse* are sometimes interchangeable. For example, if you have someone repair or update a working gadget or computer that you don't want or need and then put it back into someone else's hands, that process qualifies as both recycling and reusing.

Why do we talk more about trying to reuse or repurpose gadgets instead of sending them off to a recycler? Well, we think there's a bonus fourth R — *rethink*ing. Think about recycled paper. It comes from existing paper that is collected, processed, and then repurposed as new paper. By selling a gadget or giving it away, you're repurposing it, but you're also essentially recycling it. What's cool here is that you're skipping the processing part of breaking down a gadget the way a recycler would when the gadget has truly reached its end. What's more, reusing or repurposing a gadget means not having to purchase a new product to replace it, which in turn means you're *reducing* the resources and energy required to manufacture, package, ship, and use a new gadget.

Looking to just unload your mobile phone or gadget's dead recyclable battery and not the device itself? Point your Web browser to www.rbrc.org to search the Rechargeable Battery Recycling Corporation's Call2Recycle database for a drop-off center near you.

Erasing your personal information

Before we list your options for getting rid of gadgets the green way, something you don't want recycled is any personal information you might have stored on a gadget you're saying goodbye to. Most repurposing programs promise to securely erase your personal information from your gadgets before they send them to their eventual recipients.

Zapping your personal information from your mobile phone

If the gadget you're giving away is a mobile phone, smartphone, or MP3 player that has no built-in hard drive, erasing your past is a cinch.

Restoring most mobile phones to factory freshness generally requires keying in a series of symbols and numbers and then pressing the Call button to carry out the wipeout.

On the other hand, you zap a Palm smartphone and PDA by holding down a button while powering on the device. On some devices, choosing an option from the device's Settings menu erases and restores the gadget to factory freshness.

Check the manual's index for the word *resetting* or *restoring* or *erasing,* or search the Web for your particular device and the phrase *factory restore* or *factory reset.*

On some cell phones or PDAs, erasing personal data and settings is often accomplished by tapping a few keys or holding down a button or three while powering on the gadget. Voilà! The gadget then has straight-from-the-factory freshness and is ready to start a new personally rewarding relationship with a fresh face (and fingertips) — just like it was when you turned on the gadget for the first time.

If you're unsure how to completely erase your personal information from your mobile phone, let your fingers do the walking to the nearby sidebar, "Zapping your personal information from your mobile phone."

Getting rid of mobile phones and gadgets

Here are the most common options for getting rid of your broken or unwanted, but still useable, mobile phones and gadgets:

- ✔ **Wireless provider's retail store:** Drop off your working but unwanted mobile phone so that it can be repurposed or properly recycled. (Don't forget the charger and any accessories you no longer want.)

- ✔ **Gadget manufacturer's Web site:** Check to find out more about the manufacturer's take-back, trade-in, and recycling programs.

- ✔ **Donations:** Several organizations gladly accept unwanted cellphones so that victims of domestic abuse, the elderly, or other persons in need can call 911 at no charge. Cellphones can also be reset to provide free or limited service for those in need, or sold to raise funds for not-for-profit groups, charities, or causes. Four cellphone donation organizations are

- *Call to Protect:* This national philanthropic program is aimed at combating domestic violence. All donated phones are sent to the group's partner, ReCellular, where they're refurbished and sold or recycled, and one hundred percent of the net proceeds are used for grants to national organizations working to end family violence. All phones donated that are obsolete or damaged are recycled according to strict environmental standards. Visit `www.wireless` `foundation.org/calltoprotect`.

- *Cell Phone Trade-Ins:* This site lets you dispose of your cellphone and help those in need, or just pad your wallet a little bit with cash. The service also welcomes iPod trade-ins. Either way, check the site to see whether your phone or iPod model is one they want. If so, you can print a prepaid label to mail your unwanted gadget to Cell Phone Trade-Ins, and soon thereafter, you'll get a check in the mail if you opted for payment. Go to `http://cellphonetradeins.com`.

- *CollectiveGood:* This mobile device recycling service makes a donation on your behalf in exchange for your unwanted cellphone, pager, or PDA. Charity choices include The United Way, The Red Cross, Friends of the Congo, and several others. Go to `www.` `collectivegood.com`.

- *Wirefly.org:* Wirefly.com's sister site claims that it sells more cellphones every day than any other online authorized dealer. So it's only fitting that its dot-org site offers a trio of options for getting rid of your unwanted cellphone: recycling for charity, donating (via Cell Phone Trade-Ins), and paying you cash. Charities include the ASPCA (American Society for the Prevention of Cruelty to Animals), Livestrong, Sierra Club, and several others. Visit `www.` `wirefly.org`.

✔ **Electronics trade-in Web sites:** Visit `www.eztradein.com` to see whether your still-working but unwanted gadgets can earn you cash or credit toward a new purchase. Three more trade-in sites are

- *BuyMyTronics:* Trade in your iPod, cellphone, PDA, video game machine, laptop, digital camera, or camcorder and get a check in the mail a few days after BuyMyTronics (`http://buymytronics.` `com`) verifies that what you sent is as you described. Opting for electronic funds transfer by way of PayPal instead of getting a check in the mail makes your exchange of unwanted gadgets for e-cash all the more green.

- *Consumer Electronics Recycling:* Accepts trade-ins of working or broken cellphones, smartphones, PDAs, iPods, and Zune media players, and assuming that your gadget is in the condition you say it is, the company sends your check within as little as one or two business days. That's fast money! Visit `www.cerecycle.com`.

- *Flipswap:* Trade in your iPod or cellphone for in-store credit or a check sent to you, or a charity of your choosing, if you prefer. Or type your zip code to locate a nearby Flipswap partner retail store to walk in with your trade and walk out with a little more green in your wallet. Visit `www.flipswap.com`.

✔ **Your local newspaper's classified ads or an Internet auction:** Sell your unwanted gadgets, computers, and other working but unwanted electronic products in your local newspaper's ads or on the community classified Web site Craigslist, or you can sell or auction them on eBay or another auction Web site, such as the following:

- *Bonanzle:* Bonanzle (`www.bonanzle.com`) refers to itself as an online marketplace for buying and selling items faster while having more fun, stating that its specialty is "helping you buy and sell items that aren't shiny, new, and mass-produced." Posting items is free, and Bonanzle charges low final offer value fees that range from fifty cents for items under $10, and $1, $3, and $5 for items under $50, $100, and $1000, respectively. Anything more than that costs sellers only $10.

- *eBid:* Charging no listing fee and a final value fee of only three percent to basic free members, the growing eBid member base (`http://ebid.net`) makes it worth taking a look at. eBid eliminates the final value fee for members who pay for Seller+ privileges for as little as $1.99 per week to $59.99 per year. At the time of this writing, eBid.net has a lifetime Seller+ membership offer for $49.99.

- *PlunderHere:* This company (`www.plunderhere.com`) says that its goal is to become the go-to marketplace for buyers and sellers. With no fee for listing items and a small final value fee from .01 to 2.5 percent, it may well be where you go to sell your gadgets. PlunderHere also charges small fees for listing options, such as adding video, or for spotlighting your item on the site.

✔ **A nearby or nationwide reputable recycler of e-waste** *(e-cycler):* Properly disposing of broken or otherwise hopelessly useless electronics rather than throwing them in the trash reduces potential hazards to the environment, and it may also reduce waste if parts and materials can be extracted and reused or manufactured into new products. Visit Earth911.com — which calls itself "your one-stop shop for all you need to know about reducing your impact, reusing what you've got, and recycling your trash" — to find an e-cycler near you. Other ways to find an e-cycler include

- *Your state or city Web site:* Most states follow the `.gov` Web site address format. For instance, typing `www.nj.gov` will take you to one of the authors' home state's Web site, where a search on *recycle* turns up links to a directory of statewide recyclers.

Visiting www.usa.gov/Agencies/State_and_Territories.
shtml provides links to every U.S. state's Web site. And you
can find a complete set of links to Web sites for American cities,
counties, and towns at www.usa.gov/Agencies/Local_
Government/Cities.shtml.

- *The Environmental Protection Agency (EPA):* Checking your state's
  environmental agency Web site for electronics recyclers is another
  option. Go to www.epa.gov/epahome/state.htm to access the
  Environmental Protection Agency's directory of state agencies.

Many state and city Web sites also link to national recycling organizations
and programs. For instance, type what you're getting rid of and your zip code
on Montana's Where to Recycle Web page (www.deq.mt.gov/Recycle/
Where-to-Recycle_New.asp), and a list of nearby e-cycling organizations
and facilities opens, compliments of Earth911.com.

Chapter 11

Print Less, Breathe More

● ●

In This Chapter

▶ The hungry printer

▶ How duplexing saves the planet

▶ 20 green printing tips

▶ DIY: Filling printer cartridges

● ●

*W*e can all agree that technology is fundamentally a good thing. It saves lives. It makes you more productive. And it can help you reduce the size of your carbon footprint significantly — and that makes the planet smile.

As with anything else in life, getting the real green benefit from technology involves keeping things in balance. Not overdoing it with the power supplies. Not indulging in the latest-and-greatest machinery just because it's the new thing. Weighing out wants and needs and coming up with some sort of reasoned, rational decision about your green efforts.

We know that doesn't sound particularly exciting.

Anyone who has been on this planet awake for any amount of time knows that life isn't all logic — perhaps not even mostly logic. There are reasonable, fact-based reasons to weigh our actions in terms of how they impact the global climate, just as we consider our behaviors and words before we inadvertently do something we'll regret. But there are also heart reasons (*"the heart has reasons that reason does not know"* — Voltaire) that have to do more with being part of this blossoming life and less about how to manage it.

This chapter takes a rather ho-hum idea (reduce your number of print jobs and make the planet a greener place) and looks closer, exploring all the different ways you can use technology to streamline what you do and reduce the impact you're making on the environment. And the big payoff is not a number but a feeling — that sense that through simple, thoughtful, caring actions, you are part of the greening of your planet. And that makes us all breathe a little easier.

Rate How Much Your Printer Eats

The thing you have going for you as a home computer user is that it's likely you don't depend too awfully much on your printer as it is. You may print the following things:

✔ Letters and reports

✔ Schoolwork for the kids

✔ Copies of Web pages you want to keep

✔ Spreadsheets and bookkeeping items

If you run a small business from your home, your printer tasks may increase exponentially. You will likely have

✔ Business planning documents

✔ Reports for professional service providers (such as your accountant, your attorney, a business consultant, and so on)

✔ Spreadsheets for financial reporting

✔ Payroll and tax reports

✔ Letters to clients, vendors, and contacts

✔ Marketing materials for your business

What you might not know is that the average office worker in the United States uses 10,000 sheets of paper per year. And, ramping it up, the U.S. — which has roughly 5 percent of the world's population — uses 30 percent of the world's paper.

To capture a picture of your current printing habits, make a list of all the things you print. If you can't think of everything, just go about your day, week, or month and make notes as you go. When you're ready, use the following questions to get a sense of how you use your printer. You can then make a plan to weed out any unnecessary printing you're inadvertently doing:

✔ Which items must you print?

✔ What printouts are really optional?

✔ Have you made any printouts that you're not sure how to classify as necessary or optional?

Understanding the Impact of Paper

It's super-easy to grab a stack of paper, put it in the printer, and print chapters, reports, presentations, spreadsheets, Web pages, and more. Need directions to the dollar store? Use MapQuest and print the directions. Simple enough.

The trouble is that paper comes from trees, and manufacturing that paper uses up a lot of valuable resources. In fact, consider these manufacturing factoids:

- It takes one and a half cups of water (imagine a can of soda) to make every single sheet of paper you use.
- Roughly 40 percent of all wood pulp created goes to the production of paper.
- Paper makes up 25 percent of the garbage tossed into landfills — even with current recycling efforts.

Here's a staggering statistic: According to the Environmental Defense Fund, creating one ton of virgin, uncoated paper uses *three* tons of wood, over 19,000 gallons of water, and produces almost 2,300 pounds of solid waste.

Choosing Good Print Alternatives

Not long ago, people printed everything. Did you purchase something online? You probably printed the receipt. Did you create a spreadsheet to set up a household budget? You probably printed it out and filed it away.

We filed everything: printed letters, e-mails from friends, recipes, reports.

Lots of paper. Lots of accordion folders. Where are they now? In a landfill somewhere? Or up in the attic, collecting dust?

Many people — especially Baby Boomers — like the feeling of having something tangible in their hands. That means paper, books, and CD cases. While that's understandable, it may also be a luxury we really don't need, if the tradeoff is mowing down forests full of trees to provide backup printed copies for things we don't really need anyway.

What we need for good print alternatives

People who argue for keeping backup printed copies of everything often have a good reason for their argument — they don't want to lose valuable stuff. When it comes to legal documents, important household papers, and ideas and documents you just don't want to trust to electronic media, fine — print it out.

But as a matter of course, there are other ways you can safeguard your important files without pulverizing trees to preserve them. Here's what we need to know about the files we save if we store them only in electronic format:

- ✔ The files are stored on media that won't be obsolete in a few years.
- ✔ The files we write today we'll be able to read tomorrow.
- ✔ The files will be easy to access and safe no matter how technology may change.

The PDFs Have It

In recent years (especially since the introduction of Microsoft Office 2007), saving, sending, receiving, and opening PDF files has become easier. PDF stands for Portable Document Format, and that's just what it is — a format that enables people to view your document with the correct format (just as you saved it), no matter what type of computer they may be using to view it. You can install free software — such as the Microsoft Office 2007 PDF add-in or CutePDF — and print your document to a PDF file instead of printing to your printer.

Depending on the software you have installed, some PDFs can also be editable. You can even embed links in the document so people who receive your document can click links and go to your Web site, find another document, launch a presentation, or do whatever else you want to rig in there.

The point is that you can do a lot today with PDFs and they provide a portable, easy, and low-footprint way to share professional-looking documents with others. People who receive your PDFs can print them if they choose (we hope they don't, though, right?) and you'll never miss the fact that you didn't print the document for them.

Collaborating with online documents

Another development in the last couple of years involves working collaboratively with shared workspaces online. This type of online collaboration enables multiple users to view, edit, comment on, and revise a single electronic document. This saves probably not just one printout but many — think how many individuals might print, mark up, and revise a document while working as a team.

One example of this kind of document collaboration is offered by Office Live Workspaces, a free tool that enables multiple users to upload, modify, share, and assign document- or project-related tasks. (See Figure 11-1.) For more about online collaboration tools, see Chapters 15 and 16.

Figure 11-1: Online document sharing can save printing.

Why Duplexing Is Good for the Planet

Duplex printing is big — in fact, it's so big that it is now part of the Energy Star standards for new printers. In order to be considered *Energy Star-compliant* (which means the manufacturer can put an Energy Star logo on the printer packaging), the company needs to demonstrate that the printer is capable of duplex printing.

So is a *duplex* like a double-sided condo? Well, you got the "double-sided" right. When a printer is capable of duplex printing, it can print on both sides of the page. This may seem like an impossible task for your low-end HP all-in-one printer, but you may be surprised just how easy this is to do.

Setting up duplex printing

To set your printer up for duplex printing when using Windows, follow these steps:

1. **In your favorite word processing program (we're using Word 2007 here), choose File⇨Print.**

   The Print dialog box appears, offering you all kinds of choices about how much, where, and what to print.

2. **In the Printer Name: box, make sure your printer is displayed.**

   If your printer name doesn't appear in the box, click the down-arrow and choose your printer from the list.

3. **Click the Properties button.**

   The Properties dialog box appears, displaying the Printing Shortcuts tab. Click the down-arrow labeled *What do you want to do?* to display the range of options for your printer. (See Figure 11-2.) Note that the items you see in that list will depend on the capabilities of your installed printer.

4. **Click Two-sided (Duplex) Printing.**

   The options in the dialog box change slightly to reflect your choice.

5. **Click the Print On Both Side down-arrow and choose Left Edge Booklet.**

6. **Click OK.**

   The changes are saved with your printer preferences, and the Print dialog box appears once again. If you're ready to print something as a test and you have a test document open on the screen, you can click OK and print it. Otherwise click Close.

Figure 11-2:
Choose
duplex
printing in
the Printing
Shortcuts
tab.

Doing a Double-Take: Duplex Printing

So it sounds fancy, like something only people who speak copy-machine lingo can adequately describe, but it's really pretty simple. Duplex printing is just printing on both sides of the page.

Some printers are equipped to do this easily — the technology supports the process so the page is fed back through the printer (with the help of software) and the next page prints like a dream on the other side of the paper. Office-quality printers are sure to be able to handle duplex printing, but you may be surprised to know that many ordinary home printers — in particular, laser printers and all-in-one printers — are able to do this as well.

Of course, you don't have to have a duplex printer to print documents and use both sides of the page. You can print the odd-numbered pages first, turn the printed pages over, and then print the even-numbered pages. This is known as *simplex* printing, and even though it takes a little patience, it's a good way to save a few extra pages. You'll get the hang of it.

Calculating duplex savings

You can check out how much money you'll save — and how many trees will thank you — by calculating your duplex-printing savings at `www.brother.co.uk/g3.cfm/s_page/106450`. Just plug in the amount of pages you currently print per week (this will be a higher number if you run a small business from your home, but don't worry). Figure 11-3 shows you the impact of duplexing one good book manuscript — and how much it can save.

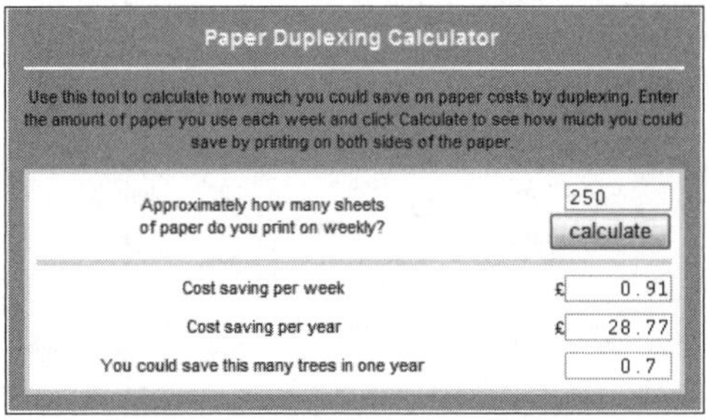

Figure 11-3:
Calculate the dollars and trees you can save by duplexing.

Paper Duplexing Calculator

Use this tool to calculate how much you could save on paper costs by duplexing. Enter the amount of paper you use each week and click Calculate to see how much you could save by printing on both sides of the paper.

Approximately how many sheets of paper do you print on weekly?	250
	calculate
Cost saving per week	£ 0.91
Cost saving per year	£ 28.77
You could save this many trees in one year	0.7

You can find out about the whole range of duplex printers on the Energy Star site (`www.energystar.gov`), but these printers are popular because they are duplexers *and* they're fast (which means they print more pages in less time — and that means energy savings):

- ✔ Canon PIXMA MP530
- ✔ HP Color LaserJet CM1017
- ✔ Lexmark E350d
- ✔ Xerox CopyCentre C118

Print . . . If You Must

So are there creative ways you can reduce your printing pattern and still make sure your electronic documents are just as good? With a few common-sense adjustments and some easy print techniques, you can reduce your paper consumption by up to 50 percent (more if you run a small home business). Here are a few ways you can reduce the resources you're using when — and if — you print:

✔ Choose a shade of gray for printing to lessen the amount of black toner you use in that inkjet cartridge (it's not as noticeable as you may think).

✔ Reduce the print size (if your eyes can take it) to fit more on a page.

✔ Go even smaller and use booklet-style printing (reduced-size and double-sided, mind you) to reduce paper consumption even further (you may need to buy a magnifying glass or get longer arms, though).

To print more than one page on a single page of paper, follow these steps:

1. **Prepare your document as usual and choose File⇨Print.**

   The Print dialog box appears.

2. **Click the Pages Per Sheet down-arrow and choose the number of pages you want to print on one page.** (See Figure 11-4.)

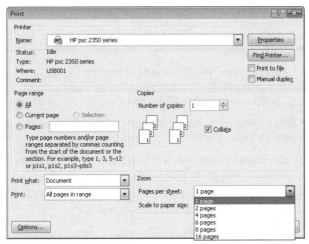

Figure 11-4:
You can print multiple pages on one page if your eyes can stand it.

Unless you have a superhero's vision powers, you probably won't want to choose more than 2 pages per page if you plan to read the document fairly comfortably. If you simply want thumbnails that display the general format of each page, choose as many as you want.

3. **Click OK.**

   The document prints as usual — except you have more than one page (as it would be in traditional-size duplex printing) printed on your paper. This means you get double the printing for half the page use. Nice.

Tree-Saving Printing Tips

Sure, there are going to be things you still need to print. Here's a set of tips to help you make the most of what you *do* print when you feel the need:

✔ **Set your print expectations.** Only you know how many pages are too many — but think through what you want to print before you print it — and then do your best to stick to that.

✔ **Have a standard for what's okay to print and what isn't.** If you're not sure where to start, begin with the basics. Agree with the family not to print Web pages, e-mail messages, or silly photos of animals with large eyes.

✔ **Keep the printer unplugged until you need it.** This may seem like a pain but it will make you think twice about whether you *really* need to print . . . and it will conserve energy that your printer may be sipping while not in use.

✔ **Use recycled paper and recycled (or soy-based) ink cartridges.** See the related sections in this chapter.

✔ **Proofread and preview your document before you print it.** (It's an extra painful waste of paper when you have to throw out a document because of spelling or formatting errors.)

✔ **Do a test print.** When you have to print multiple copies of something, print one first to make sure it looks right before printing the whole job.

✔ **Print only the pages you need.** If you need only the table on page 2 in a 20-page document, just print that page.

✔ **Earn cartridge karma.** Return your empty inkjet cartridges for recycling. We cover green cartridge practices later in this chapter.

✔ **Give up hard-copy edits.** Edit documents, reports, and presentations on-screen instead of printing them and marking them up on the page.

✔ **Go electronic.** Send documents by e-mail, in PDF format, whenever possible. Don't print e-mail messages you receive. Save them electronically and include them in your regular backups. Fight the temptation to print Web pages; instead, save them to your Favorites folder.

✔ **Make the page bigger.** The margins of your document are probably set by default to 1.25 inches, all around the page. You can reduce the size of the margins to 1 inch and fit more words on the page.

✔ **Change your type, change your life.** Change the font and reduce the size to create a more compact document that is still readable.

✔ **Turn any paper forms you use into electronic forms.** You can easily do this in Word 2007 and there are a number of free online Web-form tools you can use as well.

✔ **Duplex printing is double the fun.** See the earlier section in this chapter.

✔ **Use it again.** Recycle your used paper (the backs of early drafts and saved documents) whenever possible.

✔ **Get a whiteboard.** Want to share notes, calendars, or messages with others in the family? Instead of printing items — or even writing them by hand on scrap paper — get a whiteboard and some colorful whiteboard pens. We all need a little more doodling in our lives anyway.

The Ins and Outs of Recycled Paper

Although we hear about recycled paper more often these days, in reality more than 90 percent of the printer and copier paper used today in businesses and homes is not recycled paper.

Myths abound — but they are, in fact, myths — about recycled papers jamming your printer, leaving a dusty residue, or smearing or smudging characters. In the early 1980s, when recycled papers were first becoming available, there was a slight drop in quality compared to non-recycled papers. But today that challenge is long gone — in fact, recycled papers are high-quality, available in a variety of forms (including letterhead, special sizes, and envelopes), and often are acid-free, which means a longer life and better appearance.

Also, printing with recycled paper can have a positive impact on the environment. When you use recycled paper, you

✔ Save trees, energy, water, and landfill space.

✔ Protect entire forests, wetlands, and natural systems.

✔ Reduce the amount of CO_2 pumped into the atmosphere.

✔ Continue to offer energy and resource savings because the paper can be recycled over and over again.

✔ Reduce the use of toxic chemicals by choosing chlorine-free paper.

Go to any office-supply store and you'll find a whole collection of recycled papers there, ready for your purchase. How can you tell one from another — and how do you know what you really need? Is this more greenwashing at work? A few details on the label can tell you what you need to know:

✔ **Postconsumer Waste (PCW):** You'll see some papers with *20 percent PCW* somewhere on the page. PCW stands for "postconsumer waste" — and that means the waste that your neighbors put out at the curb (or take to the recycling center). So that paper you're holding is made from cereal boxes, coffee filters, junk mail, and other products that went out with the trash a few weeks or months ago.

Look for papers that are at least 30 percent PCW for a good green impact (with good-quality print). Look for the postconsumer waste symbol.

✔ **Processed Chlorine Free (PCF):** If paper were left to its own devices, it wouldn't be white. To get the nice white page that stares back at you so invitingly, traditional paper manufacturers throw chlorine into the mix. When you see PCF on the wrapper of the paper you're buying, it's a good thing. It means no chlorine or chlorine-related chemicals were used in the making of that paper — this time around, anyway. And that means less bad stuff in the environment.

Greening Your Printer Supplies

Greening your printing practices at home involves more than simply unplugging your printer until you need it and buying recycled paper (oh, yeah, and printing on both sides). In addition to your paper supply, you may also print family photos, invitations, postcards, birthday cards, brochures, mailing labels, and CD labels and covers.

Chances are that you'll be able to find a recycled version of these various items — but if not, you can be inventive and recycle some of them from other things. (Well, okay, you may be out of luck on the photo paper.) Especially for artistic items like invitations, cards, and CD covers, you can piece together interesting images or create your own. And the recipients will love you all the more for it. (Really, we will.)

Recycling your print cartridges

A number of print vendors and office supply companies offer free cartridge recycling programs that enable you to put your used cartridge in a postage-paid envelope and return it to the vendor for recycling and refilling. Staples offers Inkdrop, a free recycling program that makes it easy for you to send in your empty cartridges and receive a refilled one for free. The only thing you ever purchase is the cartridge that you refill. To find out more about the Staples Inkdrop program, go to `http://tinyurl.com/dk62os`. Other office-supply companies have similar programs, so ask at the counter or visit your favorite store's Web site for details on what it's doing.

Why not make some green while you're going green? Castle Ink (www.castle ink.com) offers a recycling program for ink cartridges, offering up to $4 per cartridge for virgin cartridges.

What's up with soy-based ink?

Yes, we know — soy is showing up in everything, but there's a reason for that. Soy is a readily available, low-cost, and environmentally friendly option, an alternative to the toxic chemicals used in the petroleum-based inks used in standard print cartridges.

Regular inks contain VOCs (Volatile Organic Chemicals) that have been linked to health hazards, and pose a threat when they find their way into landfills on newsprint and other papers that are thrown away. Soy-based inks are made from soybeans — safe, biodegradable, and — well, edible. Other vegetable-based inks are also being used today, but both eco-friendly inksets are still used only by the commercial printing crowd. So when you need to have a yard sign printed or you have the neighborhood newsletter done at your local printer, ask whether they have soy-based inks available instead of the hard stuff.

Makes you wonder what an earth-friendly, sustainable ink might look like for our home printers, doesn't it? An earth-friendly ink that is truly sustainable

✔ Uses renewable resources.

✔ Creates less waste.

✔ Reduces VOC emissions.

✔ Is biodegradable.

✔ Doesn't include additives.

This type of dream ink may not be available in your favorite inkjet cartridges yet, but keep your eyes open! It won't be long.

Chapter 12

Seamless Sharing across Systems

● ●

In This Chapter

▶ Reaping the benefits of a home network

▶ Choosing and setting up a network

▶ Sharing your devices and files

▶ Loving the earth with Windows Home Server

▶ Keeping your home computing footprint small

● ●

*C*onserve, conserve, conserve. Reduce, reduce, reduce. Think about what you're buying before you buy it, and when you do prepare to whip out that debit card or write that check, ask yourself whether you're buying the greenest, most earth-friendly item you can.

Yes, you have a lot to weigh for what could be a simple, gotta-have-it purchase. But you can see where our gotta-have-it lifestyle has brought us: to a world with brimming landfills, an atmospheric sauna, and a rapidly depleting supply of natural resources.

Gosh, that's a depressing way to open a chapter.

The good news is that with some thoughtful planning, you can put together a home network that makes the best use of the resources you've got, cuts down on the resources you use, and makes safeguarding your data easier.

This chapter is just the tip of the melting iceberg when it comes to home networking capabilities, so be sure to get your hands on some references if you want to take things a step farther. For the latest info on home networks, check Web sites such as `http://computer.howstuffworks.com/home-network.htm` and `http://compnetworking.about.com/cs/homenetworking/a/homenetguide.htm`. In fact, the Internet is overloaded with useful information for anyone who wants to set up a home network.

Sharing at Home: The Networked Way

We start this section with a little quiz. Which of the following is a home network?

- A: A bunch of computers connected by telephone cords to wall outlets
- B: A set of systems, printers, monitors, and technological miscellanea all trading ones and zeros via wireless routers
- C: A group of computers and game systems connected by cable to all sorts of boxes and gizmos and switches

The answer is, none of the above! A bunch of systems connected to a router (see the sidebar "Network lingo," later in this chapter) to get access to the Internet doesn't necessarily make for a very sharing network. Oh, it's considered a network, all right, but if you are not currently sharing resources on the network you have, you're missing the big, green boat.

This section gives you the big picture on home networking, providing resources, a smattering of procedures, and some great references to use when you do the deep dive.

Benefits of networking

If you have more than one computer in the house, a network will help you reduce the resources you're using by reducing each computer's power use. Other benefits include

- **Peripheral sharing:** When your systems are networked, you can easily share the printer; scanner; and even DVD, CD, or hard drive on any system in the house. (See Chapter 7 for the lowdown on peripherals.)

- **Media sharing:** Here's a neat idea. You've got a great collection of MP3 files on your main system, and your teenage daughter is having a slee-pover in the family room tonight. Instead of burning all the Jonas Brothers tunes to CD and taking the disc downstairs for the kids to play on the family-room computer, you can simply turn on the network and let the girls access the media files on the hard drive of the main system upstairs. They'll have a great slumber party, complete with tunes. No hassle. Nice.

- **Backups:** You can store all your valuable files in a single location on the network and copy them to an external hard drive or another backup storage device. The difference between a network backup and a single computer backup is that you back up all of the computers to one central location. Using this approach means that you can share a back-up process between all computers, saving both time and money.

The big green bottom line is that you can reduce the number of devices you use by storing files in one central location and using the other systems and peripherals only when you need them. You'll see a dip in your power consumption, extend the life of the computers and peripherals, and store your important files in one easy-to-find spot. Simplicity is good — and green.

Types of networks

Networking sounds a lot harder than it really is. When you use your cellphone, you're accessing a network. (You've seen the commercials.) When you turn on your lights, you're using power that flows through what could be said to be a utility network. Things are connected to other things, so resources flow from one thing to another (and vice versa). That's a network.

When you set up a home network so that your computers can talk to one another and share resources, you have three basic types of networks to choose among. The type you choose depends largely on the type of technology you have (or want).

Here are the basic three:

- ✓ **Ethernet:** An *Ethernet network* is a setup in which the various computers are connected by cables. Yes, that's right — geeky gray or black (occasionally white, blue, or yellow) cords stretching under rugs, over door frames, and around corners. Ethernet is fast, however, so it was the networking standard until wireless muscled its way into the picture.

- ✓ **Wireless:** A *wireless network* is the kind you can access at places like Panera Bread and Starbucks. You take your laptop in with you and open the lid. Instantly, the system searches for a wireless connection; when it finds one, it asks whether you want to connect. A home wireless network works the same way. It's simple, invisible, and flexible, with no cables to trip over or to keep the cat from chewing through. Wireless networks are very popular (and won't be losing that popularity any time soon) because of the sheer freedom they offer.

- ✓ **HomePNA:** A *HomePNA (HPNA)* network is a network that's created throughout your house, using the phone lines that are already in your walls. This technology works fine and is likely offered by your telephone service provider (such as AT&T). Kathy had an HPNA system for a while, and although it could be a bit clunky, it got the job done.

What you need to get started

Each type of network requires different stuff. The goal is always the same — get the computers talking to one another and sharing resources — but the hardware and the technology differ from type to type.

For the play-by-play and the ins and outs on getting the components you need and assembling your home network, see Woody's books (depending on which operating system you're using) *Windows 7 All-in-One For Dummies (or the Windows Vista or Windows XP version).* To find out everything you need to know (and then some) about wireless networks, take a look at *Wireless Home Networking For Dummies,* 3rd Edition, by Danny Briere, Pat Hurley, and Edward Ferris.

Ethernet ingredients

For an Ethernet network, you need the following items:

- ✔ One Ethernet network adapter for each computer you want to add to the network

- ✔ An Ethernet router, if you want to share an Internet connection (you only need one of these for the entire network)

- ✔ An Ethernet hub or switch with enough ports to connect all the computers you're adding (again, only one for the entire network)

- ✔ Ethernet cables (one for each computer, plus one for each external connection)

In the market for network adapters? Pick up the USB versions. They're fast, easy to use, and keep on cranking.

I want my wireless

For a wireless network, you need a wireless router (one per network) and wireless adapters (one for each computer) for the computers you're going to connect to the network. The end.

No, HPNA isn't your medical record

To set up an HPNA network, you need one telephone cable and one HPNA device for every computer you want to connect to the network.

Okay, we'll stop being obtuse: *HPNA* stands for *Home Phoneline Network Adapter.* Yes, we know that this translation is unimpressive. The secret's out.

Network lingo

Are you running into some terms you haven't seen before? Here's the short scoop:

✔ **Adapter:** You plug a network adapter into the computer you want to add to the network. This device enables the network to "see" the system.

✔ **Cables:** Well, cables are cables — you know, cords. An Ethernet cable is bigger than a regular phone cable and resembles a snake if you're not expecting to encounter one on the floor in the dark late at night. (Don't ask.) For an Ethernet network, you need lots of Ethernet cables, because that's how the information gets from one place to

another. For a wireless network, you don't need 'em.

✔ **Hub or switch:** A *hub* has several ports and enables you to connect several devices on the Ethernet network. A hub can send and receive information but does only one task at a time. A *switch* functions like a hub but is a little higher end; it can recognize the different systems on the network and can send and receive info at the same time.

✔ **Router:** An Ethernet or wireless router enables your systems to access the Web through a single Internet connection. Simple is good.

How to pick a network type

You may wonder why, if Ethernet has a laundry list of required items, and wireless and HPNA networks need only a few items apiece, anyone would ever go to the trouble of setting up an Ethernet network. The answers, my dear Watson, are speed and reliability. Use Ethernet when you need a solid connection for gaming or other high-performance applications.

Each technology has its benefits, however. We personally dig the freedom of being able to work anywhere in the house — a wireless perk — but Ethernet is fast and consistent, and it makes lots of home networkers happy. Wireless continues to improve but can still be affected by varying signal strength, competing flotsam in the airwaves (microwave some popcorn, and you may lose your Web access), and routers that occasionally cash in the chips. Use wireless when you want maximum flexibility for casual computing and speed isn't quite as big an issue.

HPNA offers a few benefits of both Ethernet and wireless. You can plug into HPNA anywhere you have an outlet, so it offers most of the flexibility of wireless. However, because you're using a wired connection, you also get Ethernet reliability. Okay, the whole story isn't rosy: HPNA can suffer from noise problems, and you don't get Ethernet speed from it. Use HPNA when you really do need to have a connection in every room and require Ethernet reliability for applications such as home control or letting the kids use a single printer.

Setting Up a Home Network

When you've settled on the type of network you want and have all the components you need to create your home network, you're ready to make the magic happen. Many people are terrified about setting up their new network because they see all of the hardware for it and think it's simply impossible. Think again! Setting up a home network is doable — and perhaps even a little fun — using the information found in the following sections.

Getting your computers talking

To set up a home network of PCs using Windows, follow these steps:

1. **Turn on the computers you want to network, along with any routers, switches, and hubs you want to use.**

2. **Make sure that your Internet connection is working properly.**

   If you're using a router (both Ethernet and wireless networks use routers), connect the router to the computer and to the wall outlet and make sure the router is turned on.

3. **Connect the remaining computers to the router.**

   The process varies, depending on which type of network you use. Choose your favorite flavor:

   - *Ethernet:* Connect your Ethernet router (or hub or switch) to the computers by cable.

   - *Wireless:* Run the Set Up a Wireless Router or Access Point Wizard, which leads you through the process of adding other computers and devices to your home network.

   - *HPNA:* As soon as you connect the computers to the phone jacks, your system should be ready to rock.

4. **Test the network on each computer by choosing Start⇨Network.**

   The window that appears should show you the computer you're using, as well as all the other computers connected to your home network. (See Figure 12-1.)

Figure 12-1:
See?
Computers
together
in one big
happy
family.

Networking for Windows XP and the Mac

Not everyone has a Windows Vista or a Windows 7 machine. Many people have a Windows XP or Mac setup instead. This chapter doesn't cover either operating system in any depth. The general information in this chapter applies to all operating systems, but for specific procedures you'll need to go elsewhere.

Windows XP doesn't support some advanced Windows Vista and Windows 7 features, such as network mapping and network discovery. If you want to set up a Windows XP network, check out the setup procedures at www. microsoft.com/windowsxp/using/ networking/setup/default.mspx and www.microsoft.com/windowsxp/ using/networking/default.mspx. When you want to share your printer over

the network, check out the article at www. microsoft.com/windowsxp/using/ networking/expert/honeycutt_ july2.mspx.

On the other hand, if you want to set up a Macintosh network, check out the setup procedures at www.google.com/search? as_q=Macintosh%20Network%20 Setup, http://pangea.stanford. edu/computerinfo/macintosh/ network/, and www.stolaf.edu/ services/iit/resnet/mac/setup. html. The Web site at www.apple.com/ support/leopard/printing/ discusses network printing issues you need to know about.

Mapping your new network

When all your computers are connected and talking to one another, you can ask Windows Vista or Windows 7 to map the network to show you how everything works together. This helpful tool lets you see all the systems that are awake in your house and drawing power.

To display the network map, follow these steps:

1. **Choose Start⇨Control Panel⇨Network and Internet.**

   A whole collection of networking options greets you.

2. **Select Network and Sharing Center.**

   This option is the first one smack-dab at the top. (What, exactly, *is* a smack-dab?)

3. **Click View Full Map.**

   This option is on the far-right side of the page, just above the Internet icon.

   The computers and devices that are part of your network (and turned on) appear in the network map. (See Figure 12-2.)

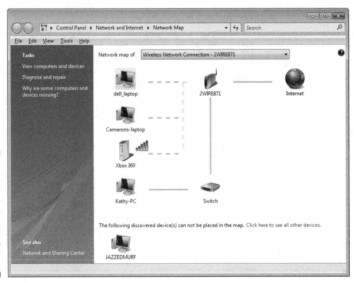

Figure 12-2:
It's alive! All systems — well, almost all systems — are go.

If not all the computers and devices in your network appear on the network map — or if some are left alone at the bottom of the page, like the one shown in Figure 12-3 — make sure that Network Discovery is turned on (see the next section for details). Alternatively, if one of your network computers is running Windows XP, your firewall settings may be getting in the way or you might not have all of the required software installed. The troubleshooting procedure found at `http://winhlp.com/node/179` provides detailed instructions for fixing Windows XP interactions with Vista.

Discovering the joy of Network Discovery

The preceding two sections help you get all your computers happily connected and then view them in the network map. If any computer didn't get mapped properly, you need to check its Network Discovery setting to make sure that the computer is open to finding out that it's part of the bigger plan. Here's how:

1. **On the computer that didn't show up in the network map, click the Start button; type** Network and Sharing Center **in the search box; and press Enter.**

   The Network and Sharing Center page appears.

2. **Click the Network Discovery button.**

   When you turn on Network Discovery, Windows changes your network configuration and adds some new network discovery features to it. The Network Discovery setting makes it possible for the current computer to recognize other devices on the same network, and vice versa.

3. **Select Turn on Network Discovery.**

4. **Click the Apply button.**

   Windows makes the changes you made permanent. This step actually makes the Network Discovery setting active.

5. **Select View Full Map in the top-right corner of the Network and Sharing Center page.**

   Windows Vista or Windows 7 should show you the full network, with this newly discovered computer in its proper place.

Securing the wireless airwaves

If you have a wireless network, it may seem counterintuitive that you can secure a system that sends information through the air, but you'll just have to trust us on this one. In fact, securing wireless networks isn't something that you kinda-sorta should do, but something you *have* to do, because wireless is notoriously unsecure unless you do something about it.

Now that wireless is getting to be more commonplace, users are getting savvy about the tricks and traps of wireless transmission. In the early days (and no doubt it is still happening more often than we'd like to think), people used to drive from one point to another to find somebody's open wireless network — a process called *wardriving.* Then the wardriver piggybacked on the signal — or, worse, gained access to both the unsecure network and lots of private information that the network owner didn't mean to share.

You can secure your wireless network by using a series of simple techniques:

✔ Change your router's password.

✔ Change the default system ID.

✔ Use a WEP (Wired Equivalent Privacy) key so that the data will be encrypted and off-limits to people who are trying to tap into your wireless network. You can discover more about WEP at `www.networkworld.com/details/715.html`. Use the vendor instructions that come with your device to perform the WEP configuration.

✔ Use WPA (Wi-Fi Protected Access) if your setup supports it. WPA overcomes some problems with WEP where outsiders can gain access to your system by hacking it (essentially, picking the lock as a thief would do to access your home). Discover more about WPA at `www.networkworld.com/details/4802.html`.

Sharing the Easy Stuff

In Chapter 11, we suggest that you downsize to one printer (and an all-in-one printer, at that) instead of using a variety of printers plugged into different computers in your house. Making that kind of change means that you need to do a bit more coordinating if you're a family of people who print a lot, but you can make the whole process relatively pain free by setting up printer sharing. After you get that process squared away, you can set up file sharing too. We discuss both procedures in the following sections.

Sharing printers

Picture a printer on a psychologist's couch, talking about its difficult childhood. Oh, wait — wrong kind of sharing. *Printer sharing* is simply the process of making one printer available to the other computers on your home network.

To share a printer on a network using Windows Vista or Windows 7, follow these steps:

1. **Turn on the printer and make sure it's ready to use.**

2. **Click the Start button on the computer that has the printer attached; type** Network and Sharing Center **in the search box; and press Enter.**

   The Network and Sharing Center page appears.

3. **Click the Printer Sharing button.**

   The printer-sharing options appear.

4. **Select the Turn on Printer Sharing radio button. (See Figure 12-3.)**

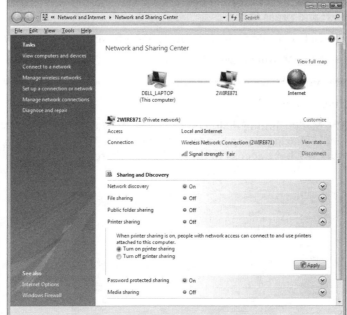

Figure 12-3:
Turn on printer sharing to allow other computers on your network to share the printer.

5. **Click Apply in the Network and Sharing Center page.**

   Windows applies the changes you have made and permits printer sharing.

6. **Set the Password Protected Sharing option on or off.**

   When this option is turned on, anyone who wants to use the printer connected to your computer must have a user account and password on your system. To let other people access your network printer without a password and user account, turn this option off.

7. **Click the Apply button.**

Now when you view your network by choosing Start➪Network, you'll notice a small symbol on the printer's icon, indicating that printer sharing is turned on.

Sharing media files

Remember the Jonas Brothers example we used earlier in the "Benefits of networking" section? This section is where you make such happy file sharing a reality. The steps for configuring Windows Vista or Windows 7 are super-simple:

1. **Click the Start button; type** Network and Sharing Center **in the search box; and press Enter.**

   The Network and Sharing Center page appears.

2. **Click the Media Sharing button.**

   The Media Sharing options appear.

3. **Click Change.**

   The Media Sharing dialog box appears, as shown in Figure 12-4. The Media Sharing dialog box lets you know that the computers on your network will have access to the media you share.

Figure 12-4:
Enable other computers in your network to access the media on your system.

4. **Select the Share My Media check box, and click OK.**

   Windows makes the changes required to share your media. You see the Network and Sharing Center page.

5. Click Settings in the Media Sharing options.

You see the Media Sharing – Default Settings dialog box, which enables you to customize the settings for the media files you share. (See Figure 12-5.) You can choose whether you want to share music, pictures, or video (the default is all three); and you can determine which types of items are available for sharing.

Figure 12-5:
Enter the settings you want to put in place for media sharing.

6. Click OK.

Now when you view your computers in the Network window (the window that shows network resources, rather than the Network and Sharing Center page), a media icon appears on the system icon, letting you know that media sharing is good to go. (You access the Network window by clicking Network on the Desktop.)

Streamlining Your Whole Setup with Windows Home Server

Imagine this scenario: Your family members are media enthusiasts. They like homemade video and movies on demand. They have a million MP3s (all legal, of course), not to mention so many photos that it would take the entire Butler Bulldogs marching band a full summer to put them into photo albums. They have several computers (all of them usually on), plus several printers, a couple of scanners, and an Xbox 360. Have we forgotten anything?

Windows Home Server was introduced in 2008 for families just like yours. The idea behind it was that something smart and safe needed to be done to safeguard the wealth of digital media that people are collecting and to make it easy (think low footprint) to enjoy, share, organize, and back up all that great stuff.

Of course, the question is why you even need a server. By centralizing data storage, you make it easier for everyone to find the files they need, which means that you only need a few computers running, rather than every computer in the house. Reducing the number of computers also reduces your carbon footprint, which makes using a server the ecologically friendly solution for centralized data storage and management. What a server really does is let everyone share a little of a central computer while using their own computers for local tasks. I explain more about the green aspects of Windows Home Server in the "Getting green with Windows Home Server" section.

Figuring out what it is: hardware, software, or both?

Is Windows Home Server hardware or software? Well, actually, it's both — sort of. It was designed as software that makes your regular computer act like a server, collecting your digital files in one central location, making backup and restoration easy, and giving you access from anywhere. Most people, however, buy this software preinstalled on . . . well, a Windows Home Server.

Confusing? Yep, but as the Dalai Lama says, without inconsistencies, life wouldn't be interesting. The brain melt happens when you try to connect a real metal-and-capacitor server to Windows Home Server, which is software that can run on your regular computer . . . *or* on a Windows Home Server like the Hewlett-Packard MediaSmart. (See Figure 12-6.)

The plan behind Windows Home Server was for PC manufacturers to bundle the software with their own hardware and then sell complete home servers — hardware, software, and all — which HP has done, apparently with great success. You can check out some fun demos and even download a trial of the software (that is, Windows Home Server) by going to www.microsoft.com/windows/products/winfamily/windowshomeserver.

Windows Home Server won't help you set up a network, which means that you need to have one working before you install the software.

Figure 12-6:
The HP
MediaSmart
server
features
Windows
Home
Server
software
and makes
digital life
sexier.

Getting green with Windows Home Server

You may think we'd have to pick through compost to find some good, solid green things to say about the perks and benefits of investing in Windows Home Server, but this technology does have some good green ideas behind it:

- ✔ Centralized storage of all your digital files means that you don't have to have all your computers on all the time.

- ✔ Your data and files are backed up regularly, with no intervention from you.

- ✔ Backups and restorations are streamlined and easy, taking less time and using fewer watts.

- ✔ You can access your files from anywhere, which means that you can reuse what you already have. When you have a group of single machines, you usually download files multiple times and then need multiple CDs to store it all — all this duplication is no longer necessary with Windows Home Server. Reuse reduces processing (and, in some cases, manufacturing cost and waste), and that's green.

- ✔ The personal Web site you get free with Windows Home Server makes it easy for you to share your favorite digital media files with whomever you choose, which saves the printing, ink, and/or mailing resources you would otherwise use to produce the files and send them to friends and relatives.

Windows Home Server Power Pack 2 is now available, offering improved features for accessing your files remotely, collaborative features for systems running Windows Media Center, and support for Media Center Extenders. Read about this download at www.neowin.net/news/main/09/03/24/windows-home-server-power-pack-2-now-available-for-download and http://blogs.technet.com/homeserver/archive/2009/03/23/windows-home-server-announcing-power-pack-2.aspx. The update is available through Windows Update.

Backing up and restoring

Windows Home Server isn't kidding around when it comes to backups. You can restore an entire hard drive with almost no headache at all. It's a thing of beauty, really.

You can also add more hard drives to your system. Thus equipped, Windows Home Server will mirror your backup data, putting separate copies of the backup on multiple drives. Nice.

What's more, the backups aren't saved in some arcane format that nobody ever heard of, but in good old-fashioned .zip files, so you can get into them with any old decompression utility if you need to.

Sharing data

Working with shared folders is easier with Windows Home Server than it is with either Windows XP or Windows Vista. (You don't have to go too far to be folder-friendlier than Windows XP, of course.) Windows Home Server creates a few shared folders for you, but you can add to them easily, and other users on your network can access them as well.

Managing disks the easy way

Go get a cup of organically grown coffee, and let Windows Home Server do the rest. That about sums up disk management. Windows Home Server does the work; you just enjoy your digital files. You don't have to worry about drive volumes and folders; Windows Home Server manages the details. All things in life should be so easy.

Taking your media on the road

One big feature of Windows Home Server that Microsoft touts is its capability to let you access your favorite digital files almost anywhere, whether you're in the house or out on the road. Whether you're using a mobile device or a laptop, or remoting in from the office, you can log into your home computer and listen to the new release you purchased last night.

Windows Home Server's Remote Access feature takes a bit of effort to get going, but when you've got it, you've got it. You can log on to your server and move files around, upload and download them, listen to files — do whatever from wherever. Very cool.

Keeping your system healthy

Here's an idea that smacks of greenness, so we like it: Windows Home Server continually monitors all the computers on your network and provides a health report that clues you in about needed updates and software patches. It also tells you if a computer is running out of space, which is a green issue because a clogged computer works more slowly — and uses more processing power.

Keeping Your Footprint Low at Home

Some basics apply to all computer users, whether you're trying to be green or not. You should always do the following things:

- ✔ Back up your data.
- ✔ Remember to clean up your mess.
- ✔ Pay attention to how much you use.

Each of these items helps you be more effective, more productive, and maybe even faster in what you do, which can translate (we hope) into less time at the computer and more time outside growing organic pumpkins.

Working with backups

Show us a person who has lost a hard drive without having a backup, and we'll show you someone who'll never forget to do a backup again.

If you do a quick poll of computer users, you might be surprised to see a blank look come across their faces when you ask them when was the last time they backed up their files. Most likely, you'll hear something like "Oh, yeah — I've got to do that" or "I did it in 2008. How often are you supposed to do it?"

If you work for a company, it's doing regular backups of everything (if its IT department is worth its salt). But what about you? How will you back up your green computers and your home network?

In Chapter 15, we discuss the availability of cloud computing to do many things, from word processing to data backup. If you have a fast Internet connection, and you don't mind storing your data on a gigantic company's computer, you may want to consider backing up your files to the cloud. Several companies, including Google and Microsoft, are offering online storage options that seem to be well received.

Windows Vista makes backups easy by providing the Backup Status and Configuration tool in System Tools. You can choose among three options:

✔ Back up Files

✔ Restore Files

✔ Complete PC Backup

To set up automatic backups and complete your first one in Windows Vista, follow these steps:

1. **Choose Start⇨All Programs⇨Accessories⇨System Tools⇨ Backup Status and Configuration.**

   If you haven't set up your system for automatic file backups, Windows Vista prompts you to do that.

2. **Click Set up Automatic File Backup.**

   The Back Up Files window appears, asking you to choose where you'd like to store the backup. You can choose a hard disk or DVD/CD, or a location on your network.

3. **Click the Browse button to see your backup options on your new network.**

   The Browse for Folder dialog box shows you the various locations you can designate for the backup files. (See Figure 12-7.)

Figure 12-7: You can back up to a system on your new home network.

4. **Select your backup location, and click OK.**

   Backup Status and Configuration saves the backup location information and displays a window where you choose the files you want to back up.

5. **Choose the type of files you want to back up, and click Next.**

   Note that all file types are selected by default.

6. **Specify the schedule for your backups (what day, what time, and how frequently you want to back up your files).**

7. **Click Save Settings and Start Backup.**

   Windows Vista makes a backup copy of all the file types you selected and stores the backup files where you specified. Incremental backups will be repeated according to the schedule you set up during the process.

Cleaning things up

Cleaning the bits, pieces, and file fragments off your hard drive is a very green thing to do, because it helps your computer process information faster and more smoothly, thereby requiring less processing power and using less energy.

In Windows XP and Windows Vista, you have access to two cleanup tools named Disk Cleanup and Disk Defragmenter. To find them, choose Start➪All Programs➪Accessories➪System Tools. Start either application by selecting its entry in the System Tools folder.

Disk Cleanup scans the files on your hard drive to see how much space you can save by cleaning up unnecessary files.

Disk Defragmenter puts back together all the files that were scattered hither and yon on your computer's hard disk. You have the option of setting up a schedule for regular defragging of your hard disk, which generally is a good idea. (Just schedule defragmentation for a time when you're not using the computer, because the process takes a lot of processing power and can really slow your system down.) You can force a defrag at any time, schedule or not, by displaying the Disk Defragmenter dialog box and clicking the Defragment Now button. (See Figure 12-8.)

Get your backup with Windows 7

Windows 7 offers four types of backups (which is actually more intuitive than it sounds):

✔ **Shadow copies:** Windows 7 automatically keeps *shadow copies* (previous versions or backup copies) of your data files.

✔ **Data backups:** *Data backups* are partial backups that you create by using the File and Folder Backup Wizard.

✔ **System Restore:** You use System Restore points to back up most of your computer's internal settings, drivers, and certain key system files. Windows 7 creates a new restore point every day.

✔ **Image backups:** Image backups are snapshots of your drive(s) contents.

Figure 12-8:
Disk Defrag-
menter puts
scattered
files back
together
and gives
you a nice
clean block
of storage
for new
files.

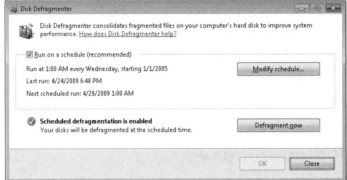

Monitoring your resources

Windows 7 has a great feature called Resource Monitor that lets you see —
in full graphic color — how your system is using the resources that it consumes. If your system suddenly slows down and you think that something
might be hijacking it, or if you want to see how much memory is being used
and when, Resource Monitor is the place to start.

To peruse the internal behavior of your system, follow these steps:

1. **Click the Start button, type** resmon **in the search field, and press
   Enter.**

   The Overview page appears, giving you the big picture.

2. **Click the Average CPU column heading.**

   This step reorganizes the processes and puts the biggest culprits right
   at the top of the list.

   If one of your programs has frozen, you can right-click it in this list and
   choose Analyze Process from the contextual menu to get a little insight
   that just might get you unstuck.

3. **Click the Memory tab.**

   The Memory Tracker shows you how the memory is being used in your
   system.

4. **When you're done, close Resource Monitor — but remember to return
   to it if anything looks fishy later.**

Part IV
Telecommuting, Teleconferencing, and Teleporting

The 5th Wave   By Rich Tennant

ADVANCED COMMUNICATIONS IN THE LUPINE COMMUNITY

My Den

"Woo!"

In this part . . .

Some of us are looking for a good reason — *any* good reason — to telecommute. Think of it: the wind in your hair, meetings at outdoor cafes, the free life. Others almost run in horror from the idea of being on their own, without a structure or schedule, out of sight (and maybe out of mind) of those in charge of hiring and firing. Okay, so telecommuting isn't without its challenges; but it is a great opportunity for reducing the amount of energy you use, the volume of CO_2 your car is pumping into the environment, and the amount of gas you pay for. We'll let you weigh out the pros and cons, but this part is all about the possibilities of telecommuting, for fun, profit, *and* saving the planet.

Chapter 13

Making the Case for Telecommuting

*H*ow does this sound? You get up in the morning as the sunlight is just beginning to stream in the windows. You shuffle to the kitchen, in your favorite pajamas and slippers, and get a cup of coffee. Sipping on the coffee, you walk over to the laptop and check your e-mail. One, two, three messages from coworkers. You dash off a quick response, send the report one colleague was asking for, and after a moment, head upstairs to take a shower.

Yup, no commute. No business casual. Just comfort, sunlight, coffee, and quiet.

Welcome to working at home.

Working at home, or working remotely, for a company — also called *telecommuting* — has been around for a long time, growing slowly in mainstream business. Growth has been slow for a number of bottom-line reasons, and the perception of less employee control is a big one. (How can you make sure your employees are working if you can't see them?) But today the justification for telecommuting is better than ever — as we explain in this chapter. The savings in gas, CO_2 emissions, time, and energy is a big deal. Here you get some of the facts and figures, find out how to approach your boss with the possibility, weigh it all out, and put a plan in place.

Telecommuting: Its Time Has Come

For most people in midsized companies a little more than a decade ago, working at home was a bit of a challenge. Sure, computers and the baby Internet made it possible to connect, trade files, and work on things here or there. But unless you were a one-person team or an entrepreneur, collaboration was clunky and managing all the files you needed, hither and yon, was a pain. Plus working at home back then was isolating (even for us introverts); it was hard to keep up with the group, offer the kind of meet-me-at-the-water-cooler easy access, and stay in sync with your colleagues.

Today everything's different. With the advent of blossoming and always-on Web technologies that make teleconferencing, instant communication, and data warehousing easy and intuitive, you never have to feel out of touch with anyone. Whether you're working in the office or out, tools are available to keep you in continual contact, provide you with the data and processing power you need, and enable you to complete the tasks you're charged with completing, whether you work in an office down the hall or in a house across town.

The green aspect of telecommuting makes it an even more viable option for employees: It's a greener way to work. Here are just a few of the big-ticket savings that telecommuting offers individuals and businesses:

- ✔ **Saves time:** Americans in cities of all sizes across the country lost more than 4.2 *billion* hours waiting in traffic in a single year!

- ✔ **Saves energy:** Whether we're talking about personal, get-yourself-ready-and-the-kids-in-the-car-on-time energy or the amount of energy you use getting to the office, powering up your system, flipping on all the lights, and warming (or cooling) yourself with the climate control system, staying in one place is less of a drain on energy resources.

- ✔ **Saves gas:** Ah, gas. With the $4-per-gallon price tag etched firmly in our recent memory data banks, we all realize reducing the amount of gas we use is a good thing. And longer term, it has ramifications for import and export issues and greenhouse gas emissions, too.

- ✔ **Reduces CO_2 emissions:** Cars on the road are a huge contributor to the gasses that are causing the greenhouse effect around the planet. The logic is simple — reduce the number of cars on the road, reduce the CO_2 emissions. You do the math.

- ✔ **Reduces in-the-office resources:** You may not think you take up a lot of space or use a lot of electricity (or oil, or coal, or water) in the office, but if you're there, you're leaving a footprint. If, on the other hand, you've invested in energy-efficient equipment and done the work around your house to lower your footprint size, the amount of energy you use in a home office may be significantly lower than a similar use at the workplace (especially if your office hasn't taken any steps toward green yet).

Working at home has a number of benefits, but none may have a larger impact on the immediate environment than the CO_2 you save by not driving to work every day. The 2007 Mobility Report published by the Texas Transportation Institute revealed some staggering information:

- ✔ Traffic congestion costs the U.S. $78 billion annually.
- ✔ Traffic jams result in 4.2 billion hours of wasted time and 2.9 billion gallons of wasted fuel.

The report went on to say that when you're doing the drive-and-stop in rush hour traffic, you are spending an extra 38 hours per year — and 26 extra gallons of gas — just because you're stuck in traffic with everybody else. That translates to an average of $710 extra per driver per year, and that doesn't even take into account all the waits you have because of wrecks, work zones, and other events.

To get the full scoop and the not-so-pretty picture that appears in the results from the 2007 Mobility Report from the Texas Transportation Institute, go online to `http://mobility.tamu.edu/ums/media_information/press_release.stm`.

We're not saying you have to stop driving altogether, of course, or even that working at home should be a full-time option. But if you consider — and perhaps make the case for — working at home one day a week (or maybe even *two* days a week), you might find yourself a little more relaxed and feel a little greener in the work department, too.

Telecommute or virtual office?

For many practical reasons — green in both environmental and financial ways — startups today are often considering alternatives to the traditional build-the-office-and-they-will-come approach to day-to-day operations.

Instead of leasing a large office space, complete with its heating and cooling systems, lighting fixtures, water supply, and interior decor (not to mention security systems, technology, and more), some startups are opting for the virtual office — a nonphysical location where employees can "meet" online to share files, have meetings, chat, meet at the water cooler, host presentations, and strategize.

Using readily available teleconferencing, cloud, and shared workspace technologies, the team can collaborate easily while living and working in remote locations all around the globe. The business can be doing business literally 24 hours a day and offer always-on customer service. The business has no leased overhead (which helps keep costs down), and the footprint is little more than the individual personal footprint each person accrues.

In this chapter, we focus on telecommuting, which is working for someone else while you use telecommunications tools to work remotely. But the virtual office is a good idea and is demonstrating its worth. The approach is working for a lot of companies now (and the number is sure to grow in the future).

Rating Yourself: Could You Work at Home?

Not everybody *can* work at home. A nurse in a large hospital, for example, has to be where the patients are. But the bookkeeper in a doctor's office could do some tasks remotely (and probably does). A painter needs to drive to the site of the home she's painting to do her job, but the person who schedules the jobs and orders the paint could probably work at home.

You get the idea. If you work more with information than you do people, chances are that you can do at least part of your job at home. Table 13-1 gives you a look at some of the different kinds of tasks you might be able to do at home and provides a sampling of the technologies that can make it all possible.

Table 13-1	Work-at-Home Possibilities	
Category	*Possible Work-At-Home Tasks*	*Technology/Software Needed*
Accounting	Bookkeeping Scheduling Billing Insurance	Spreadsheet, contact manager, custom database, Web technologies, form generation, reporting
Administrative	Reports Scheduling Operations Communications	Spreadsheet, word processing, scheduling, contact management, billing and payables, e-mail and Web technologies, backup and security software, general application software
Banking and financing	Financial analysis Reporting Charting Customer service Research Statistics	Spreadsheet, custom software, database management, Web technologies, reporting software, form generation
Creative	Graphic design Web design Writing and publishing Editorial services Music production Video production	Graphics editing software, Web design software, word processing, blogging, layout, audio editing, video editing

Category	Possible Work-At-Home Tasks	Technology/Software Needed
Customer service	Customer service calls Tech support Order entry Follow-up calls Appointment setting Customer interviews Scheduling	VoIP (Voice over Internet Protocol), Web technologies, database management, call center software, scheduling software, word processing, spreadsheets
Engineering	Design specs Schematics Prototyping Reporting	CAD software, spreadsheets, reporting software, product lifecycle management, custom software
Health care	Scheduling Reporting Performance reviews Communications Customer service Exit interviews	Contact management, customized software, reporting, performance review software, e-mail and Web technologies, VoIP, form generation, word processing, spreadsheets
Human resources	Reporting Research Developing training materials Web support Research for new hires	Database management, performance review software, presentation software, Web technologies, spreadsheet, word processing
Information Technology	System design and specs Support material preparation Creating training presentations	Graphic design/workflow software, presentation software, training development, word processing, spreadsheet, Web technologies and programming, security administration tools
Nonprofits	Volunteer research and management Scheduling Training (Web-based) Grant research and proposal writing Communications Material design and production Event planning	Contact management, database management, scheduling software, presentation/training software, word processing, spreadsheet, e-mail and Web technologies, graphic design and layout software

(continued)

Table 13-1 *(continued)*

Category	Possible Work-At-Home Tasks	Technology/Software Needed
Sales and marketing	Customer contact Order entry Presentations (Web-based) Design and produce marketing materials Communications Scheduling Follow-up	Contact management, form generator, database management with e-commerce or secure order entry, presentation software, design and layout software, e-mail and Web technologies, scheduling software
Web design and promotion	Design Web specs Web prototyping Presentation (Web-based) Content creation Customer review Hosting and promoting	Web design software, hosting service, Web analytics, security administration

Note the emphasis on technology in Table 13-1? Technology is what makes telecommuting possible. Here are just a few ways in which technology connects the world and makes it easier than ever to be productive, efficient, and a model employee, all without changing out of your Bart Simpson jammies:

- ✔ You can be on time for any meeting anywhere in the world through teleconferencing.

- ✔ You can offer instant customer service response via e-mail, instant messaging, or VoIP.

- ✔ You can develop and share strategies, business plans, presentations, and more in real time, collaboratively, using Web conferencing software.

- ✔ You can schedule projects, assign tasks, report on progress, and evaluate results in real-time using Web-based group management software.

- ✔ You can find, review, modify, and share documents seamlessly and securely using cloud computing technologies.

Exploring the Upside(s) of Working at Home

There are a lot of great things about working at home, and you won't have to look far to find them. The green quotient — the fact that you've already power-optimized your home, created a green home office (oh wait, we show you how to do that in Chapter 14), and discovered how to reduce the power you use and maximize the power you've got — already goes a long way toward energy savings.

 If you have kids at home, you know that the benefit of being there in the morning when they leave and in the afternoon when they come home is a huge perk. Plus, you know if they're raiding the fridge. Telecommuting enables you to work *and* be there — instead of working *or* being there, which is a big stress-inducer for many parents. Relax and enjoy and play a little Mario Kart with the kids when you've got time for a coffee break.

In addition to the obvious energy-and-lifestyle benefits, you may see an upswing in your own work productivity, more creative and flexible energy, and a chance to test those fashion risks you never got up the nerve to wear to the office.

Heightened productivity

If you're like us, you may have noticed something curious in your workplace. Whenever there's a huge deadline and people really need to get things done, they work at home. Why is that? Simple.

When you need to really focus, you need to be able to control your environment and limit the input your surroundings are blasting at you. If you have pre-meeting meetings, meetings, and post-meeting meetings, chances are that you don't get a lot of focus time in your office. And if your workplace is a social one, take another slice away from the Me Time side of your balance sheet.

Working at home — unless you have more than a few kids under four — provides a more or less quiet, controllable space where you can say what gets your attention and what doesn't. Yes, you still need to respond to e-mail, but you can choose the *when*.

Economy of effort: laundry and lattes

With the "Reduce, reuse, recycle" refrain playing in the background, you can think through all the different ways you save energy, time, gasoline, and effort when you telecommute a day or more a week. Soon you get into a routine and know how to keep things moving seamlessly, from laundry to lunch to lead generation software.

Adjusting to working at home does take a little time and effort, but you learn to balance what

you *need* to do with what you *want* to do over time. You discover ways to prioritize and economize so that the day flows smoothly, errands are completed, and kids get picked up in a way that works together pretty well. (It really does happen once in a while!) And underneath it all, you're doing something good for the planet in a tangible way. Sounds like win-win-win all around, doesn't it?

For many telecommuters, this ability to focus translates to a heightened sense of productivity, reduced feelings of "scatteredness," and a noticeable increase in that peaceful, easy feeling. You can set your tasks in your Outlook calendar to reflect the priorities *you* need to work on today. (See Figure 13-1.) Now that's freedom.

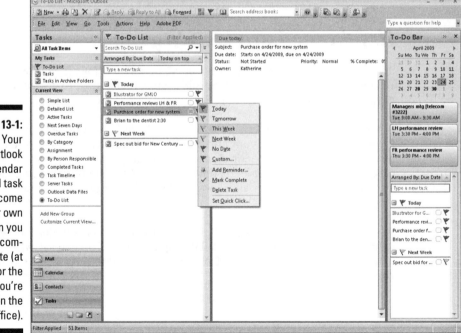

Figure 13-1: Your Outlook calendar and task list become your own when you telecommute (at least for the days you're not in the office).

Flexibility and creativity

Having the freedom to focus on your priorities has the curious effect of free-ing up some portion of your brain for more creative efforts. You will probably notice on your work-at-home days (after you get used to the change) that your thoughts are clearer, plans seem more obvious, and problems are less daunting when you've tuned out the static and can hear yourself think.

Focusing on the things that are most important to you creates a kind of shift that enables other solutions, ideas, and possibilities to bubble to the surface. The temptation may be to follow every good idea down a winding road and get distracted (and then you're back to your in-the-office scatteredness!), but here's a nice trick for managing those creative vibes: Use Microsoft OneNote (see Figure 13-2) so that whenever an idea bubbles up that you want to follow, you can capture it and give it your attention after the end of the business day. If it's a good idea, the energy is still there when you're ready to work on it. If it's not such a good idea, it dissipates and you'll be glad you didn't chase it all afternoon while you should have been doing your *real* work.

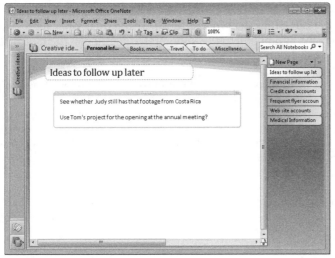

Figure 13-2: Microsoft OneNote is a simple way to capture ideas — as text, audio, or even doo-dles — and save them for con-sideration later.

Closer to family

Even though we've made some strides in this country in terms of family friendliness, the basic us-or-them attitude (in terms of family-versus-work) is still prevalent in many workplaces. The Family Leave Act mandates a certain value set in which employers must (by law) allow their employees to be human, to have human family needs, and to allow time off for life events that need their attention.

But the tension between work and family — how do you care for your family to the best of your ability and still be a "team player" at work? — still exists, and probably always will. Telecommuting can help reduce some of that tension by enabling you to be present at home, with the family, even if you are busy working on a report or building a CAD model.

One of the tricks to telecommuting successfully with the family around is to talk about expectations right off the bat. What does it mean for you to work at home? How accessible will you be — for baseball carpooling, babysitting, fixing dinner? Think it through early before you get too far down the road or you'll have a lot of renegotiating to do.

Bunny slippers-to-work day

Some telecommuters get up at the same time every day, take a shower, put on business casual work clothes, and sit down at the computer promptly at 8 a.m., the same time everyone else is starting their work days. Others are more flexible, stumbling to the computer sometime in the morning, bleary-eyed, in their bunny slippers.

Chances are you may be somewhere in the middle. In general, timing is an important factor — you want to be visible, accessible, and "in there" with the rest of the team, even if you're remoting in. The bunny slippers, they may not care so much about. And even if you're using Windows Live Messenger (see Figure 13-3) to stay in touch with colleagues, they aren't likely to see your slippers unless you point your Webcam in that direction. (We cover Windows Live Messenger in more detail in Chapter 16.)

Some telecommuters feel the way you dress has a direct impact on the way you work. Kathy was wearing a "Rocky Mountain Bulldogs" T-shirt while she was working on this chapter.

Figure 13-3:
Windows
Live
Messenger
is an instant
messaging
program
that enables
you to
send quick
text, video,
and voice
messages,
share files,
and more.

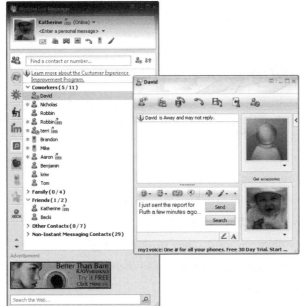

Managing the Challenges of Telecommuting

It would be easy to write this chapter from the *try-it-you'll-love-it* perspective because, well, we've both worked from home for many years and it has turned out well for us. But not everybody is comfortable living and working in the same place, looking at the same surroundings, seeing the same person in the mirror every day, day in, day out. (Feeling claustrophobic yet?)

Some of the big challenges you're likely to encounter as you begin to tele-commute for the first time include these:

- ✔ Setting up expectations
- ✔ Managing your time effectively
- ✔ Setting up boundaries while everyone gets used to the new routine
- ✔ Staying in the loop
- ✔ Demonstrating your value
- ✔ Being on the radar for promotions

This section tackles each of these challenges and offers tech-related solutions to help you clear the hurdles easily.

Establishing expectations

Knowing what your employer expects of you — and what you expect of yourself — is a good thing to start with as you negotiate the possibility of telecommuting. Here are a few questions to ask as you're doing a little fact-finding:

- Are any employees in your company telecommuting now?
- Is anyone in your department telecommuting?
- If yes, how is workflow handled?
- How many days a week do they work at home?
- Do employees have remote access to their computers in the office?
- What challenges have cropped up?
- How have those challenges been resolved?
- What kinds of lessons have already been learned from telecommuting experiences in your workplace?

It's a good idea to think through your own expectations about telecommuting, including all the pros and cons. For example, your list might go something like what is shown in Table 13-2.

Table 13-2	Pros and Cons of Working at Home
Pros	*Cons*
Won't need to drive to the office Mondays and Fridays	Will miss special lunches with staff every other Friday
Can use my green laptop to access my work files remotely	Will need to schedule database work for Tuesday–Thursday, when I'm in the office
Better use of time for creative projects	Will be able to meet with vendors only on Tuesday–Thursday
Easily accessible via remote access, IM, and cellphone	Won't be there for quick meetings on work-at-home days

When you talk to your supervisor about the possibility of working at home, demonstrate that you've done your homework by talking to peers, finding out what worked well and what was a challenge, and share your pros and cons. Helping the person charged with making the call see that you're looking at it from all sides will, we hope, help "reduce and recycle" any resistance that might be lifting its ugly head.

Managing time effectively

One of the challenges in adjusting to telecommuting involves learning to manage the freedom that comes with it. When you are controlled by schedules and deadlines, it's easy to think, "If only I didn't have all these restrictions, life would be so much better!" But then when some of those situations relax, you are still faced with the question of how best to use your time.

A smart way to begin adjusting to a telecommuting schedule involves sticking pretty close to the in-the-office routing. Because you need to demonstrate that you really are there and really are working, you need to be accessible via e-mail, instant messaging, and more. You may participate in phone conferencing or Web seminars, but in general, you need to stay in sync with life at the office. Here are a few ideas to help you do just that:

✔ If you are able to remote in to your office system, keep your daily calendar up to date and share it with others on your team. This helps them see what you have planned for your time at home. You can also use a simple Web-based calendar in a tool like Microsoft Office Live and enable others on your team to have shared access to it.

✔ Send an e-mail message to your team leader or supervisor in the morning to give a quick update on your projects and let him or her know what you're focusing on that day at home.

✔ Let team members who are waiting on items from you know instantly when you send something in. You can send an e-mail message or ping someone with an instant messaging program such as Windows Live Messenger or AIM. (More on those programs in Chapter 16.)

✔ Participate in conference calls, interviews, and any other group or leadership event remotely (or make arrangements to go in for a portion of the day). Being available and flexible is an important part of reassuring your employer that you want to make telecommuting work for everyone.

✔ Keep track of the fuel and CO_2 you're saving as you work at home. This encourages you and reinforces the decision — plus it's something to toss around at parties to inspire other folks.

Distractions and boundaries

As soon as your neighbors learn that you're working at home a couple of days a week, you may begin getting strange requests. Sylvia calls and asks you to let her dog out. Randy is worried he'll miss the cable guy and wants you to let him in if he arrives early. Brian's mom hopes you'll bring him home from soccer. Don't all these people know you work for a living?

In the house, you'll have other challenges. Home means *home*, right? The kids want you to take a turn on Super Mario Bros. Your spouse didn't have time to pick up the laundry from the cleaners. Could you please start dinner a little early so you can all be done before *American Idol* comes on?

As you begin to learn how to set and keep the schedule for your work-at-home day, you also need to think through how you will communicate and reinforce your working boundaries so those you love at home (and those you *like* in the neighborhood) will know what to expect.

What works:

✔ Setting formal "Don't-disturb-me-unless-your-hair's-on-fire" work hours

✔ Creating a work-at-home calendar to post on the fridge

✔ Communicating to your family why you want to work at home, what you need to accomplish during the day, and how they can help

✔ Communicating your expectations clearly to your colleagues at the office — when it's okay to call, when it isn't, when you can be available for online meetings, and when you can't

What doesn't work:

✔ Shouting, "Will you guys just *leave me alone*?!"

✔ Locking everyone out of your office

✔ Trying to take it all in stride and letting yourself get interrupted 10 times an hour (sooner or later that's going to show up in your stress level, your health, or your general outlook toward life in general)

✔ Giving up and going back to the office full-time

The eyes have had it

One problem you may not anticipate from working at home is also one of the benefits — lack of interruptions. If you sit for long hours in front of your monitor, staring at the screen, you may discover that your eyes get more tired than they did in the office. Without distractions, you can stare intently at that gleaming screen for hours at a time, and during that time you tend to blink less frequently. Lack of refocusing and blinking can cause vision problems — and at the very least, exhaust your eyes and lead to blurry vision.

To help keep your eyes energized, some experts recommend the 20-20-20 rule. Every 20 minutes, look at something at least 20 feet away for 20 seconds. The refocusing enables your eyes to switch gears for a few seconds, blink, and be refreshed, ready to start again.

Slipping through the cracks

One challenge you are likely to face sooner or later is the feeling that you're missing something by being out of the office. And you are! But what you're saving — energy, fuel, and greenhouse gas emissions — is definitely worth the effort.

Although many people see the benefit of telecommuting, some still have a hard time seeing working at home as "real work" and don't think it has the same value or structure as work done in the office. Although it's not your responsibility to change the misconceptions of every person in your workplace, you do need to demonstrate your effectiveness as a telecommuter and make the effort to keep yourself in the loop in things like decision-making, team planning, and departmental reviews. Your visibility — and the effort you make to be involved — goes a long way toward keeping you on the radar screen as a full-time, valuable employee.

Another challenge that goes along with working at home can be a sense of social isolation. While you used to joke, lunch, and meet with others on your team face-to-face, now your communication may be more limited to electronic communication (depending on how many days a week you work at home). If you start to feel like you're being left out in the cold, schedule some time in the office and go out to lunch with the gang. You'll feel more in sync and ready to tackle your next telecommuting day feeling reconnected.

Out of sight, out of mind?

The office furniture manufacturer Steelcase recently completed a Workplace Index Survey. It found that 64 percent of remote workers felt that the fact that they didn't have daily contact with their employers reduced their chances for a promotion when the time for raises rolled around.

Whether this is a perception or a reality, it's worth remembering that if no one sees the work you are doing at home, they may not realize how much you're doing for the company or for your department. If it's your job to handle customer service queries and you handle them all so nicely and neatly that no one else has to deal with them, you should still send a report to *someone:* "I responded to 15 customer queries today; 10 were resolved satisfactorily; 3 I'm still researching; and 2 are returning their products." That way, someone can measure your work and know that you're providing a valuable service — whether or not you are visible.

You're Set to Telecommute: Now What?

So hopefully all goes well and your employer is open to you telecommuting for a day or two a week. What should you do next? The most important step involves spelling out how the arrangement works and making sure you and your employer are on the same page. Questions you might want to consider up front include these:

- How many days a week will you work at home?
- Which days?
- How will you report on your progress (and to whom?)
- Will you be able to access your computer remotely? If not, how will you handle the licenses of any software you may need at home?
- How will you stay in touch with the office? E-mail, phone calls, face-to-face meetings?

Arrange for data exchange

One of the big considerations right off the bat involves how you will arrange to receive, work with, and transmit files. If your work involves reports, documents, images, and spreadsheets that you create, modify, and share using common applications like Word, Excel, and PowerPoint, you can likely move files back and forth from your work computer to your home computer by e-mailing them or transporting them on a flash drive.

For earth-friendly flash drives, check out Woody Bamboo, the EcoFlash Drive, at www.memotrek.com/blog/usb-flash-drives/bamboo-usb-eco-friendly-usb-flash-drive.html.

If you are working with sensitive information in a secure system, or you need to access customized database software on the corporate servers, you need to use remote connectivity to access your work system. In Chapter 16, we show you how to use Microsoft's Remote Desktop Connection to access your office computer and work like you're sitting right there at your office desk.

Sorting out software licenses

Another consideration worth thinking through involves the use of extra software that requires specific license seats. For example, you might be able to use Adobe Dreamweaver CS4 at the office, but will you need it on your home computer? If so, how will that be handled? Talk with your system administrator to get any questions you have answered before your telecommuting begins.

Meetings here, there, and everywhere

Telecommuting successfully means being as present as possible with as low a footprint as possible. On days when you're out of the office, you can still attend important meetings by participating by phone or on the Web. In Chapter 16, you learn about various remote technologies — including Skype and WebEx — that help you be present even though you're physically in another location. Weird.

Resolving difficulties

In an ideal world, everyone would communicate perfectly, we'd all get our work done, and there'd be no such thing as global warming.

And then we'd wake up.

As you begin working through the details and start telecommuting, problems will pop up. Chances are that whatever issues arise, they have something to do with one (or more) of the three Ps:

- People
- Projects
- Process

Disaster preparedness

One of the perks of working in the office is that chances are, someone else — like your system administrator or IT person — takes care of regular backups, security, and more. When you work at home, it's up to you to safeguard the data and equipment you use and make sure you keep regular backups.

Talk with your system administrator about backup utilities and procedures that are compatible with those used in the office. Ask also about whether you should deliver backups of files you've created and worked on at home to be archived with the company system.

Each of these three areas presents you with a different set of hurdles to overcome, but we've got another set of three consonants — the three Cs — that can help keep things as smooth as possible. Whether you are facing people challenges, project snafus, or process pitfalls, you can take the sting out of the issue right away and drop the tension level instantly by using *clear, compassionate communication.*

Clear communication starts with a simple statement of what the problem seems to be. "It sounds like I threw a wrench in things when I ordered the new supplies from home. Did that cause a problem?"

Compassionate communication means you try to understand why it's hitting the person the way it is (or how this could have possibly happened to mess up your project or process). "Oh, I understand — that would frustrate me too. Sorry about that; I'll remote in and use your form next time."

And communication, of course, just means you're willing to talk about it openly instead of sticking your head in the sand (which may be tempting when you're out of the office and no one can see you anyway).

If you're the first person in your department or company to telecommute, consider keeping a journal or composing a Word doc of your adventures as a telecommuter. You could include startup struggles, schedules, software challenges, and more. That way, when someone follows in your footsteps (and someone surely will), he or she will benefit from having a guidebook to the trail you've already cleared for them.

Tracking Your Green Savings

After you get the process down, the convenience and flexibility of telecommuting is considerable, but the best news of all is reduction of the impact you're making on the environment. Your example is sure to inspire others to do the same thing.

Sun Microsystems is a computer and software manufacturer that encourages telecommuting — 19,000 of the company's employees currently working around the world have access to "flexible offices." Sun recently did a study to determine whether telecommuting actually saved energy and impacted the planet or simply shifted energy costs to employees who worked at home. Here are some of the significant results of their research:

✔ Their employees saved $1,700 per year in gas and vehicle maintenance by working at home 2.5 days a week.

✔ They consumed less energy because equipment in the office drew two times the amount of energy (130 watts per hour compared to an average of 60 watts per hour).

✔ The savings in the footprint size for the employee was enormous, reducing 98 percent of the employee's carbon footprint for work.

✔ Each employee reduced energy normally used at work by 5,400 kWh (kilowatt-hours) each year.

✔ Working from home saved employees 2.5 weeks of commute time in a single year.

Very encouraging, isn't it?

To get the full benefit of your telecommuting (and be able to tell your story to others), do your own data gathering. You can use the following list for your data collecting:

✔ **Track your drive to work:** Include the number of miles, how many times a week, approximate drive time, number of minutes per week, gallons of gas used, price of gas, gas consumed per week, CO_2 emission (from your carbon footprint).

✔ **Track your time at the office:** Include kWh at the office, systems used, utility cost per employee for working hours (if available).

✔ **Track your work at home:** Track values for kWh at home, systems used, utility costs for working hours.

Create an Excel spreadsheet to track the various data elements over time; this enables you to calculate your green savings and create charts based on your findings.

Chapter 14

Telecomm Central:
The Green Home Office

• •

• •

Depending on your personality and natural abilities, you may either love the idea of designing and setting up a home office — or hate it. Some people approach the creation of the home office the same way they think about where to put the dirty laundry — anywhere's fine. Others put a lot of thought and energy into creating the space that will support the focus, efficiency, and ultimate productivity of their days. Can you tell which group we belong to?

It's worth the effort — for you, your family, and the planet — to spend a little time and effort creating a green home office that enables you to get the most out of your technology (without sapping all your energy — internal and external), that creates a small CO_2 footprint, and that uses earth-friendly materials. That's what this chapter is all about: good ideas and some great resources for designing, setting up, equipping, and beautifying your home workspace.

Peering Through a Green Lens at Your Home Office

So you've probably already heard — *ad nauseum*, we bet — that the basic principles of greening involve reducing your consumption, reusing what you can, and recycling the rest. This approach works not just for technology but also for the furniture and surrounding environment that supports it — and you.

Use the following lists of questions to help you look at your needs for office space through a green lens:

Reduce

✔ Can you reduce the amount of tech equipment (laptops, printers, scanners, and more) you use on a daily basis, sticking perhaps with one laptop and turning on the printer only when you need it?

✔ Can you consolidate the area you use to create a compact but comfortable workspace?

✔ How can you use natural lighting to reduce the amount of electricity pumping into the area?

✔ Can you use blinds and floor coverings to help manage room temperature so you can turn the thermostat up (or down)?

✔ Do you have a reduction plan that helps you minimize the use of paper and plastics in your work area?

✔ How can you go electronic whenever possible? One possible option includes making backups on reusable media or online.

Reuse

✔ What do you already have around the house that you can use for a desk, a chair, storage, and bookshelves?

✔ What in your home or current workspace can be reused to support your work effort?

✔ How can you share resources in a way that benefits the rest of the house?

✔ What items in the attic could be given a second life in a home workspace?

Recycle

✔ Do you have older equipment in your workspace that you want to replace with newer, greener equipment? Recycle the existing equipment using a service offered by the manufacturer, using a retail outlet like Best Buy, or by looking up a local reputable recycler on Earth911 (www.earth911.com).

✔ Are you planning to recycle all office supplies you can — toner or inkjet cartridges, paper, books, and more?

✔ How often do you take a look at what you're recycling to see whether you can ramp it up a bit?

TIP

Your workspace doesn't have to be all function and no fun. Use fabrics and textures to put some life on the walls and add visual interest. The colors and patterns keep your brain awake and help give you a productivity and energy boost.

When to reuse, when to buy

It may be a natural human tendency — or worse, genetically encoded into our DNA — that when we start something new, we want to buy new stuff to go along with it. Green efforts would suggest that this consumerist lifestyle is more fabricated than inborn. We don't *really* need a brand-new desk, a $700 ergonomically designed earth-friendly office chair, and a completely new super-green laptop to telecommute successfully.

Your office can be green without a $2,000 investment. In fact, some would say that the more you spend, the less green it may ultimately be. So knowing when to reuse what you have and when to buy something new is part of the equation you need to weigh as you set up your home office. Simple is good, but efficient is just as good if not better. Here are some points to consider as you think through the whole reuse-versus-buy thing:

- Is the computer (or monitor, printer, desk, chair, lamp) working now?

- Does it do what I need it to do?

- How much power does it use?

- Is it missing any features I really need to have to work successfully?

- What materials were used to make it?

- Does it emit any toxic chemicals into my environment?

- Does it have a greener counterpart?

- How much energy does the possible replacement use?

- What is the replacement made of?

- What is the cost (in dollars and CO_2) of using this computer (or monitor, printer, desk, chair, or lamp) over time?

- What is the cost (in dollars and CO_2) of using the replacement instead?

Chances are that as you work through this list, some items jump out at you as deal breakers, either for or against buying the new system. Think through the costs — in terms of your own financial considerations and the longer-term planetary impact — before you decide either way.

One other idea to think about: If you or your employer is at all tentative about the work-at-home thing, hold off making an investment in a new greener computer system or renovating a green workspace until you know the idea is going to stick (unless you plan to continue doing some work at home, regardless).

Figuring Out What You Need to Work Efficiently

In keeping with the low-footprint model, think through what you really need in your home workspace to be most effective telecommuting. What types of tasks does your job involve? Perhaps you'd choose a few from this list:

- E-mail and Web research
- Writing and editing documents
- Talking with customers and vendors on the phone
- Graphic design and layout
- Designing and offering Webinars for clients and colleagues
- Proofreading legal documents
- Designing new product prototypes
- Managing accounts
- Doing bookkeeping tasks
- Creating media — audio and video — productions

Although different types of tasks bring up different kinds of needs, in general, if you're going to work at home, you need a space that offers room for three primary elements of the work-at-home space:

- Room for computer system(s) and peripherals
- Room for research
- Room for conversation (virtual or face-to-face)

Envisioning the Layout

You might want to sketch a few possible configurations for the space you've got, showing traffic flow, wall outlets, and where you can get natural lighting during the day. (This impacts where you put the monitor so you don't pick up glare on the screen.)

Instead of running to the store and buying a pack of grid paper you'll never use again, use Microsoft PowerPoint to sketch the layout of your room. Here's how to do that:

1. **Choose Start➪Microsoft Office➪Microsoft Office PowerPoint 2007.**

   The program launches and displays a blank opening slide.

2. **On the Home tab, click Layout in the Slides group.**

   A drop-down list of slide layouts appears. (See Figure 14-1.)

3. **Click Blank.**

4. **Click the View tab and click Gridlines.**

   A grid of dotted squares appears on the slide. By default, the gridlines are set at 1-inch intervals, which equate nicely to square footage for your office space.

5. **Use the grid and the Shapes tools on the Insert tab to draw the elements for your office.**

   Remember to start with a rectangle or square for the size of the room, and indicate the wall outlets, the door, and windows before you add furniture. Your layout might look something like Figure 14-1. See, no grid paper needed!

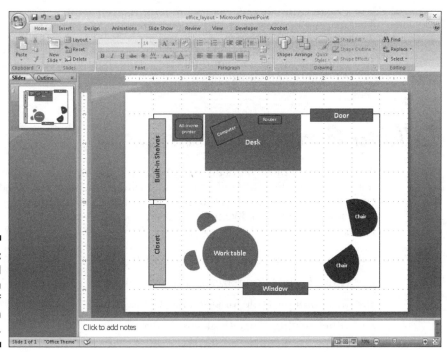

Figure 14-1:
Use the grid
to design
the layout of
your green
office.

Choosing Your Office Location

You don't need a huge space for a green home office — in fact, efficiency is really the name of the game. If you can create a space that meets your needs for technology and focus in a corner of your dining room, more power to you! With a little thought about the way you put it all together, you can create an earth-friendly spot where your work-at-home efforts can flourish.

In general, as you choose the spot for your workspace, keep these ideas in mind:

✔ Your computer and peripherals need access to power, a router (Wi-Fi or wired), and each other.

✔ Your work area should be off the main traffic flow of the house so that contracts don't get mixed in with coloring pages.

✔ If your workspace is part of another room, consider using a credenza or creating shelves with cabinet doors so you can put away your work when you're not working.

✔ Create your workspace in an area that is well-ventilated and gets fresh air whenever possible (your technology will thank you).

✔ If you have an extra room or want to create a space for your home office, plan to go as green as possible with paint, lighting, floor and window coverings, and furnishings.

Talking Green Furnishings

After you know the general layout of the room and have checked out where the outlets are, how the traffic flows, and where your sources of natural light come from, you can start to think about what kinds of furnishings you need. Depending on how you like to work, you're probably looking at the following pieces:

✔ A desk, a chair, and maybe a bookshelf (or two)

✔ A small printer/router/miscellaneous table

✔ An additional table for spreading things out

✔ Other seating, if you think you'll have visitors

✔ Lighting

✔ Window treatments

✔ Stuff for the walls

After you've thought through all the items you hope to collect for your office, you can put together a shopping list and start the scavenger hunt — er, resale shopping. The following sections help you get started with a few green ideas.

Start with the desk

The options for your desk are limitless — you can use anything from an old door on two boxes (done that) to plastic milk crates (which you can consider green if you're reusing them) to a $1,200 (or more) designer desk. In general, to stay as green as possible and find something that is comfortable and healthy for you to use, use the following ideas as a guide:

- See whether you can make use of something you already have — a desk, dresser, credenza, table — before you go out and buy something new.

- If you do buy new, stay away from cheap pressboard computer workstations. They are often treated with varnish that includes formaldehyde, which flies around in the air for you to inhale.

- Consider shopping second-hand. Why not make use of a desk someone else doesn't need anymore? When you get it home, clean it with eco-friendly cleaners and arrange it in the room. You just might find a great deal (which is half the fun) and put something to good use that was just taking up space in a resale shop.

- Find a desk to suit your work style. Some people like gargantuan workspaces; others prefer the smallest tabletop possible. Still others prefer laps for laptops. (If you do that, though, get a lap desk to help mitigate the heat and buffer any unwanted vibes.)

- Make sure the desk is the right height for you. An adjustable chair helps with this, of course, but if you've purchased a bar table for your office and you get sick of raising the chair and having your feet dangling whenever you work, you're not going to be too productive.

- Find a desk big enough to give you room to work comfortably even if you have other components — the laptop, your router, other peripherals — taking up space.

- Are you really, really, *really* tight on space? Think about getting a transformer desk, which can be transformed and used for other things when you're finished using it as a desk. (No kidding.) For a fun article on transformer furniture, see the WebUrbanist page at `http://weburbanist.com/2008/02/24/10-more-pieces-of-clever-transforming-furniture-from-tetris-tables-to-rooms-in-a-box/`.

If you decide you want to buy a new green desk for your computer equipment, here's what to look for. A green desk is

- Built to last a long, long time
- Designed with the environment in mind
- Made of earth-friendly materials
- Made without any kind of hazardous finish (like the cheap glue and polish on pressboard pieces)
- Easy to set up and repair, if necessary

Find the chair

People who love a good chair will tell you — until you are inclined to agree — that spending $500 on a place to put your backside for hours at a time is a great investment. Your family doctor might agree as well. The chair you sit in — and the length of time you sit in it — has a lot to do with your posture, your comfort, and the way you feel (sleepy or awake? scattered or focused?) as you work.

But for every person who swears by a fine ergonomic chair, someone else is sitting on an exercise ball. And another person kicks back in a recliner with a laptop on her knees. So don't take any chair recommendations as gospel — go try a few, and take your laptop if you can.

Chances are that you can pick up a good deal on cheap executive seating. Start by looking online at places like FreeCycle.com (www.freecycle.com), craigslist (www.craigslist.com), or eBay (www.ebay.com). (Remember, however, that if you don't buy locally, you'll pay shipping charges and add CO_2 emissions as well.)

Although the general characteristics of a green chair are similar to that of a green desk (built to last, uses earth-friendly materials, and no toxic chemicals), chair-dom has another consideration: the Cradle-to-Cradle certification. When you're looking for a green chair, you have the added benefit of looking for manufacturers who are making the effort to

- Use materials that are safe and healthy for the environment
- Employ materials that can be reused, recycled, or composted
- Use renewable energy in the manufacturing of the chair
- Maximize energy efficiency in manufacturing

Yes, there really are manufacturers already doing this. You can find out more about Cradle-to-Cradle certification at `www.c2ccertified.com`. Similar to the EPEAT certification for green technology, Cradle-to-Cradle (C2C) certification offers gold, silver, and bronze standards. For example, the Steelcase Think Chair and Stool (`www.steelcase.com`) received a gold rating from Cradle-to-Cradle certification. The designers are quoted as saying that they considered where the chair comes from, how it is made, and "what it will be when it is no longer a chair." The chair is 99 percent recyclable, easy to disassemble, made of 44 percent recycled material, and certified for indoor air quality. Pretty impressive array of greenness, all in a single chair. You may work better just by *looking* at it.

Bookcases and more

Sure, wood is beautiful and warm, and it adds that feeling of home to the room. But if you had the option of looking at a beautiful tree growing outside your window or seeing that same tree across the room holding your books, which would you prefer?

Although we can't do much about the trees we're already using to store books, albums, CDs, and our various technological components, reusing what we already have — and not consuming any more trees — is a good, green practice. You can make your own bookshelves, of course (like you did in college) with bits and pieces of flotsam and jetsam you find around the house.

Or you can try cardboard. Earlier in this chapter, we mentioned a design company called Nothing that created their office space from cardboard. The fun thing about this is that of all the disposable-sounding materials we have to work with, cardboard sounds the most wasteful of them all. Who can make anything durable out of cardboard? It gets soggy and limp; it's not sturdy; it's temporary.

Today's green furniture designers disagree. Case in point is cardboard-design's SHELVES55 cardboard bookshelf. The cardboarddesign company uses a honeycomb cell shape to create furniture that is very sturdy and lightweight as well. All pieces — which include everything from tables to bookshelves to vases and more — are made of recycled cardboard (which reduces the waste going into landfills) and use natural adhesives to hold everything together. In the end, the entire piece can be recycled and turned into another table or bookshelf, if you like.

Similar to bamboo in its ubiquity, as well as in the way it can be used to replace many traditional materials, cardboard makes up a huge percentage of recycled material and doesn't use any toxic chemicals — or trees.

To find out more about cardboarddesign and see the other kinds of furniture they have available, visit www.cardboarddesign.com.

Adding Green Touches

So are things beginning to come together? Moving from the big picture — designing the layout and adding the furniture — we're narrowing in on some of the more specific green items now. In this section, you get to think about the way you set up your lighting, temperature controls, and air quality to support green work-at-home conditions.

Lighting

The lighting in your workspace may have a lot to do with when you work and the brightness level of your laptop monitor. (Here's a hint: Sitting in a totally dark room staring into a laptop screen at full brightness is not good for your eyes. Remember how your mom wouldn't let you sit closer than three feet to the television screen? The same rule applies.)

The greenest lighting you can find is, of course, natural light. Depending on where your office is in the house, you need something to help you manage and reflect that light, however. For example:

- Using natural blinds both helps reduce glare and reflect light into the room.
- Painting the walls a natural, light color helps brighten the room and makes better use of natural light.
- Positioning your desk so that it receives reflected — not direct — sunlight reduces monitor glare and makes reading easier.

Still having a problem with monitor glare? Here are three things to try: Angle or turn your monitor screen slightly so the angle of the reflection changes; adjust the blinds upward to catch and reflect the light instead of allowing it into the room; and use a lamp instead of natural light to stop the glare on the monitor.

If you don't have natural lighting — or you need to work after natural light has long since gone to bed for the night — your next greenest option is using CFL (compact fluorescent light) bulbs. Get rid of those incandescent bulbs once and for all. CFLs are just a little more expensive upfront and last more than 10 times longer.

Here are a few other lighting tips to help you stay as green as possible and maximize your use of electricity for lighting:

✔ Only turn on the light you need for the task at hand.

✔ Consider solar-powered lighting where possible.

✔ Remove and safely dispose of any halogen lights you may have (they're energy guzzlers).

✔ When you *can* use reflected sunlight, turn off the other lamps in the room. You can create ambience another way.

Circulation and temperature controls

So what's the temperature in your house? Depending on the location of your home office, what kind of air flow it gets, and how your home is heated, you may be boiling like a sausage or freezing like an icicle in your work-at-home space.

Like everything else in green-dom, the least amount of intervention, the better, so if you can work with the natural elements — by opening windows, using a ceiling fan, or working in your office during optimum temperature times — so much the better. If you need to do something to manage the temperature of your work environment, use these tips to make low-footprint changes:

✔ Start with what you're wearing. Add a sweater or take one off.

✔ Block out the heat by closing blinds or curtains.

✔ Increase the temperature of a room by opening curtains wide on a sunny day.

✔ Make sure windows are well caulked so that drafts aren't getting in — or out.

✔ Open windows whenever possible — in the cool of the day, for example — to get fresh air flowing into the space and even out the temperature.

✔ Use air flow from the rest of the house to keep the temperature more constant. You can do this by thinking of the air circulation patterns in your home now and making sure vents and doors help bring the air to where you're working.

✔ Use an air filter to keep the air fresh, clean, and moving.

Know your energy use

In Chapter 2, we discuss how to figure out how much CO_2 you are responsible for adding to the planet. In Chapter 3 and Chapter 9, we show you how to keep an eye on your power consumption and begin to manage it more effectively.

In your home office, you have a unique opportunity to find out just how much power it takes to do what you do for a living — and then find out how to correct that by reducing what you can and offsetting the rest.

Invest in a Kill-A-Watt power meter so you can keep an eye on the number of watts you're using in your office, and use a smart power strip to automatically turn off any peripherals that are leaching power. Be sure to use the power management settings in your computer (set this up on your Energy Star monitor and printer, as well) and get a good read on the energy you're using. You may be pleasantly surprised! (Or, you may find room for growth.) Either way, it's a good story to tell at the staff meeting in the office next week — and it helps reinforce the good vibe for telecommuting for those who follow in your path.

Don't forget the plants

Decades ago, research showed that plants have feelings and respond to other life forms in their environment. You can add to the living green essence of your workspace by inviting some green growing friends to cohabitate with you.

Certain kinds of plants are known for their ability to clean the air and improve the quality of the breaths we take. Here are a few of the most popular plants, along with a description of what they do for our environment:

 ✔ The Areca palm is a slender and graceful plant that removes chemicals from the air and releases significant moisture into the air.

 ✔ The Peace lily is a beautiful plant that removes air toxins and "breathes out" moisture into the air. The range of chemicals it cleans is amazing: alcohols, acetone, trichloroethylene, benzene, and formaldehyde.

 ✔ The Boston fern is best at removing chemicals from the air but it can be a little fussy — it likes to be misted regularly or the leaves go brown along the edges.

 ✔ The lady palm has a fan-like leaf that can get very large (up to 12 inches). It is resistant to insects and cleans the air very effectively.

 ✔ The bamboo palm cleans the air of toxins such as formaldehyde and humidifies the air.

> ✔ The rubber plant is easy to grow and requires little light, so it's a good candidate for a home office with few windows. Like the other plants listed here, it is a good air cleaner, removing chemicals and other toxins from the air.

Sustaining Green Practices

Part of keeping your green workspace green involves making sure your daily work practices stay green as well. In the office, the procedures you follow for things like printing, recycling, changing the thermostat, and purchasing probably have some kind of protocol that everyone follows. What will you do at home?

As you begin to work in your home office, think about the green aspect of common work practices to help give yourself a green guide to energy and resource-friendly approaches. Here are a few ideas to get you started:

✔ **A print plan:** Only print items that you must review on the page — and only use paper with a high percentage of post-consumer recycled material. When you do print, print double-sided, use all the scrap pieces you can, and go electronic wherever possible.

✔ **An energy use plan:** Know which items you want turned on as a matter of course in your office and which should remain unplugged until you need them. Set your computer and all peripherals to shut off instead of hibernating or sleeping if you plan to be gone for more than two hours.

✔ **An energy acquisition plan:** Buy renewable energy if you can — your local utility company may have an option that enables you to purchase a certain amount of your electricity from renewable resources. The costs are just a little higher than normal utility rates and, well, it's *green*.

✔ **A resource use plan:** Bottled water. Need we say more? We all knew the massive proliferation of plastic bottles was going to catch up with us someday. Use an earth-friendly refillable bottle — or here's an idea, use a glass! — for the water you drink during the day. Another resource savings — use rechargeable batteries whenever possible for devices, mice, keyboards, and more.

Buying Green Office Supplies

Now that you've got this great green space to work in, you need a way to keep it fresh and clean. Instead of using traditional cleaning supplies that include bleach and chlorine, with just a little effort you can find earth-friendly products that help keep the dust bunnies at bay.

The Green Office Web site (`www.thegreenoffice.com`) evaluates products based on their green claims and lets you know — through the use of the rating system shown in Table 14-1 — in what ways the supplies really are eco-friendly. You can search for all kinds of supplies, add your own comments on things you've tried, and find out more about what it means to go green. (See Figure 14-2.)

Figure 14-2:
The Green Office helps you find green office supplies and uses a rating scale to show you what you're getting.

Table 14-1	Know Your Green Office Rating Symbols
If You See This	*It Means*
	The product contains recycled content.
	The product is biodegradable or compostable.
	The product includes reduced toxic chemical content.
	The product is third-party certified.

Chapter 15

Collaborating and Cloud Computing

*G*ood communication is the heart of collaboration. No matter how many people may be working on your team, what continent they live on, or what kind of technology they use, if you have the means to connect, communicate, and work to understand each other, your relationships will grow, and you will get stuff done.

This chapter continues to build your green telecommuter toolkit by offering a number of ways you can ramp up your communication so that you're truly in sync with your colleagues, across town or around the world. The fact that you can share these tools from anywhere — as with Web-based and cloud computing technologies — makes them green, flexible, and easy to scale up for a friendlier and greener planet.

Communicating with the Office

When you first talked to your employer about the possibility of telecommuting, you probably agreed to stay in seamless touch — or as close to seamless as you can get — by being accessible to your colleagues via e-mail, cellphone, and more.

Depending on the nature of your job and your position in the company, you may need to handle a variety of communication types, styles, and media. The nature of the team you're collaborating with also makes a difference. One type of communication might be best for quick one-to-one questions; another might be more suitable if you're working as part of a global, largely remote team.

Real-time communication includes face-to-face conversation, online chat, instant messaging, phone calls, and more. Take a look at Table 15-1 for a quick comparison of different types of communication you may use to stay in touch with colleagues at the office or around the world.

Table 15-1	How Do You Communicate
Type	*Description*
Asynchronous communication	Communication that can occur anytime — not necessarily in real time
E-mail	Electronic messaging sent instantly that may be read and responded to at the receiver's convenience
Electronic mailing list	A discussion board that enables multiple people to post entries in response to a question or reply
Internet forum	Another form of discussion board that uses posted messages participants can view and respond to on their own time
Blogs and wikis	A type of public communication that posts information on a Web page. Wikis tend to be more organic and collaborative than blogs, but you can create shared blogs for multiple participants.
Synchronous communication	Communication that needs to occur in real time with another person
Instant messaging	Instant short messages that pop up in the recipient's workspace
Web chat	A real-time chat that enables users to converse in real time using a pop-up chat window
Web conferencing	A meeting or an event hosted online that offers chat, application, and phone-in components
Video conferencing	A meeting or an event hosted online that includes a video component in real time

Meeting the Remote — and Globally Green — Team

Just a few years ago, working collaboratively around the globe was something unusual, something only huge mega-conglomerates with dozens of worldwide offices had to worry about. Today, not only do companies collaborate often and easily across continents, but individuals working on smaller projects — whether for fun or profit or both — are collaborating easily, in real time, unrestricted by geographical distance.

Telecommuting enables you to work virtually anywhere, reducing travel times and CO_2 emissions, helping you save time, money, and resources (which gives your happiness vibe a boost). Simply being able to do whatever you do from wherever you are is already a green effort! Nice.

Whether you have a team that works together continually for a single business or you have a more fluid team that organizes and then disbands following the lifecycle of a project, you can keep green computing at the heart of what you do. A green team, for example, should

- Have a plan about when to meet and how often
- Establish standards for the use of resources (what to print, what to share electronically)
- Make energy efficiency and reusability important priorities
- Look for ways to streamline processes
- Incorporate green ideas in their work and computer practice

Finding Out What Makes Your Effective Team Tick

Whether your team is a collection of in-the-office and at-home members, or a more flexible grouping of people logging in from remote places all over the world — some by smartphone, some on laptops, others through Web-based interfaces on office computers — connection is the name of the game.

E-mail cc etiquette

To cc all or not? Few of us like to read through a dozen different e-mail messages that really don't pertain to us. Perhaps two team members are talking about which shade of orange should be used on the new logo. Do you really want to weigh in? And yet in terms of team formation, having access to the entire conversation — whether you participate or not — is an important part of feeling a part of the group. So press Delete if you want, but be glad you're in the loop.

No matter how you all connect, the point at which you come together is where productivity happens. Whether your group is a new collection of coworkers or a team that's been together for years, you can ramp up your productivity and get things done faster (which is green because it uses fewer resources in terms of both energy and time) by keeping a few team basics in mind:

- **Know your common goal.** It's that focus on the thing that's bigger than we are that helps pull a team together and get them moving in the same direction. That goal might be the next big conference you're working to pull together; or it might be a new initiative your company is launching in the fall. Whatever your goal, make sure all members of the team understand it clearly and are working toward that end. In your team communications, regularly include progress reminders and updates. How close are you to reaching the goal? How far do you have to go?

- **Coordinate your process.** Each member of your group is an individual, but when it comes to team building, having similar processes — for checking in, reporting on progress, updating the group, and so on — helps create the shared experience that reinforces the group. Establish some norms right off the bat that everyone can use to complete basic group tasks and watch how the team begins to gel.

- **Keep communication clear.** Good communication is at the heart of every healthy relationship, and building connections with and among team members is no exception. Communicate regularly, consistently, and often — through e-mail, by phone, in Web conferences, on your SharePoint site — by whatever means your team prefers. Regular communication builds trust and helps everyone feel that the team is making progress and that they are an important part of the team. With those pieces in place, your group is well on the way to meeting its goal.

Exploring Communication Options

Depending on the expectations of your workplace and those on your team, you may use a variety of ways to stay in touch with the office. Each of these technologies offers a green alternative to driving there and participating face-to-face. That's the good news.

Adding your work e-mail address to a Web-based account

Sending e-mail messages is the most common way to stay in touch with members of your team, whether you are working on a shared project, updating a manager about a recent change, checking on the status of an order, or something else. You can use e-mail to carry on the normal work of the office and stay up-to-date on last-minute changes.

You may want to use Web-based e-mail to send and receive messages from work. Some Web-based message clients, like Windows Live Hotmail, enable you to include your work e-mail address as a proxy address so that clients, vendors, and colleagues who may not recognize your Web-based e-mail recognize your work address. Use the following steps to include your work e-mail address on the messages you send from Windows Live Hotmail:

1. **Open your Web browser and navigate to your e-mail account.**

   This might be Windows Live Hotmail, as shown in Figure 15-1, or another Web-based e-mail tool.

2. **Click New to begin a new message.**

3. **Click the arrow to the right of the From line.**

   A drop-down list shows you the current e-mail address and the option Add an E-Mail Address.

4. **Click Add an E-Mail Address.**

5. **Click Add Another Account to Send Mail From.**

   A page appears so that you can enter your work e-mail address in the Add an E-Mail Address line. Windows Live Hotmail sends a message to your account so that you can verify adding the account.

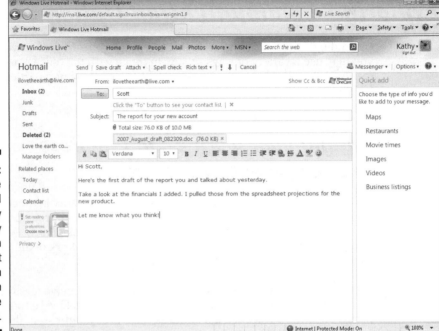

Figure 15-1:
Free
Web-based
e-mail may
be the way
to go when
you want
to stay in
touch with
the office
easily.

6. Click Send Verification E-mail.

In just a few seconds, an e-mail message arrives in your work e-mail Inbox. If you can remote in to your system to click the link and verify the e-mail account, do so now. If you're not able to remote in, simply click the link the next time you're in the office and the e-mail account will be available in Windows Live Hotmail.

Now you'll be able to choose the work e-mail account to add to the From line when you send an e-mail message.

Some free e-mail tools insert a line of advertising at the bottom of the sent e-mail messages. If that bugs you, check out the e-mail settings for your service.

Just-in-time messaging

Another way to be immediately accessible to the office involves using the right-now approach of instant messaging. A number of instant messaging clients are available — all free and all able to give you quick access in popup boxes on the user's desktop. If your message recipient is looking at the screen, she will see your message pop up. And hopefully — if she's not in the middle of something — she'll answer it.

Popular instant messaging programs include these:

- ✔ Windows Live Messenger
- ✔ AOL Instant Messaging
- ✔ Yahoo! Messenger
- ✔ Skype

The idea behind instant messaging is very simple. You build a list of contacts you connect with regularly; the instant messaging program shows you which of your contacts is currently online. You can then double-click the name of one of your online friends to open an Instant Message window, type a message to the person, and click Send. (See Figure 15-2.)

Figure 15-2:
Instant messaging enables you to ask teammates quick questions in real time.

Dos and don'ts for office IM

Some people love the convenience and easy access of instant messaging, and some people really don't. Some IT professionals don't like the security issues that this type of access can bring with it as well. Just to make sure you're on the right side of chat etiquette, follow these simple IM rules:

✓ Keep it short and sweet. A quick question, a quick answer, and you're done. Nice.

✓ Use it only when nothing else will do. If you can wait an hour or a day for a response, send e-mail rather than interrupting your colleague with an instant message.

✓ A little smiley goes a long way. One or two emoticons, okay. (See first bullet.)

Only put in an instant message something you'd be glad for the whole team to see. I know of one incident where a colleague vented some frustrations about a project in an instant message, not knowing that the person she was writing to was demoing new software for the entire workgroup. Her IM popped up in a message window in front of 20 people.

Instant messaging may be here-today-and-gone-in-a-second, but you can keep a log of messages that functions as a transcript of your chat sessions. To check the settings in your instant messaging program, look for a Message History option in the program's settings or preferences.

Keeping your colleagues clued in

One of the clear benefits of being in the office is proximity. Nan gets the design samples for the new magazine cover: Can you come to a quick review meeting in the conference room to share your thoughts on the design? Uri asks when you'll be in next so the two of you can plan a strategy for the next e-mail marketing campaign. If your colleagues had easy access to your calendar, they would be able to check your availability and know when to plan so you can attend important meetings.

Sharing is the next best thing to being there

You have several options for setting up and working with your calendar:

✓ If you are able to access your office computer from home, you can use your office software (perhaps Microsoft Office Outlook) to maintain your calendar; others at work can then tell which times are available for you.

✓ Without remote access, you can use a private, Web-based group site built perhaps on Microsoft SharePoint technology to work collaboratively, share calendars, and more. We cover SharePoint later in the section, "Boring Name, Big Benefit: Windows SharePoint Services 3.0."

✔ You can also use a free, Web-based service (part of the *cloud computing* universe, which we explore more fully later in this chapter in the section, "Sticking Your Heading in the Clouds: A Smart Way to Work") like the one shown in Figure 15-3 to give colleagues easy access to your always-up-to-date calendar. (Now you just need to keep it always up to date.)

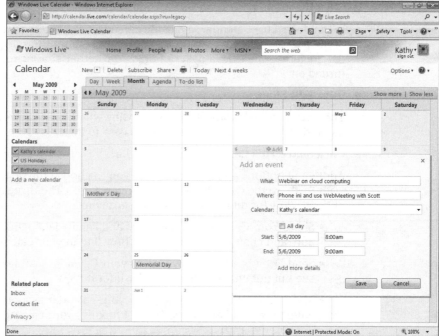

Figure 15-3:
Web-based calendars also enable you to share your schedule with others.

Some calendars let you sign up to receive a daily e-mail schedule of all the events you have planned for the day. It's a nice perk — especially if you have such a full day you don't want to take the time to check your calendar. You can have the message sent to your phone, too, if you're going to be out and about.

Setting up calendar sharing

Before your coworkers are able to view the calendar you set up online, you need to turn on the sharing feature. In Windows Live Calendar (available through Windows Live Hotmail or Microsoft's various other cloud offerings such as Microsoft Office Live or Office Live Workspaces), this is a simple task. Here are the steps:

1. **Point your browser to your calendar site.**

   For this example, we're using Windows Live Calendar, available at `http://calendar.live.com`.

2. **Sign in if you are prompted to do that.**

   Some sites keep you signed in automatically so they recognize you when you return. (You set this up in your site preferences.)

3. **Click the name of the calendar you want to share.**

   In Windows Live Calendar, available calendars are listed on the left side of the page. A page displays more information about the selected calendar, including the title, a description, and whether sharing features are turned on.

4. **Click Edit Sharing.**

   The next page walks you through choosing whether to share your calendar and, if so, who you want to have access to it.

5. **Click Share This Calendar.**

   Additional options appear that enable you to choose the people you want to share the calendar with. (See Figure 15-4.) The three different options allow for different levels of permissions:

   - Share Your Calendar with Friends and Family lets people view, add, and change the information they find in your calendar.

   - Send Friends a View-Only Link to your Calendar enables people to see but not change your calendar information.

   - Make Your Calendar Public posts your calendar as a public link so anyone can find and view (but not modify) your calendar.

6. **Click Send Friends a View-Only Link to Your Calendar.**

   Now your colleagues can view your calendar without logging in or signing up for a Windows Live ID.

7. **Click Get Your Calendar Links.**

   Windows Live Calendar reminds you that this publishes your calendar to a private space.

8. **Click OK to continue.**

   The final page provides you with links you can use to preview the calendar in a browser window, import the calendar into another calendar application, or view the calendar as an RSS feed.

9. **Click Save.**

   That's it — you're done. Now you're ready to share the URLs with colleagues so they can find your available working-at-home times easily.

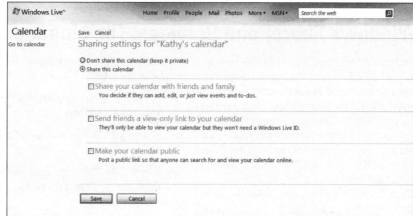

Figure 15-4:
You can
share your
calendar
with
selected
members of
your team to
keep every-
one in
the loop.

Boring Name, Big Benefit: Windows SharePoint Services 3.0

Windows SharePoint Services 3.0 is a Microsoft solution for collaborative teams that are working in any location — locally or remote. It's a bit left-brained and orderly, not a wild free-for-all on a Web page, but given that you're trying to get things done in a somewhat efficient and orderly manner (aren't you?), it's a good, scalable tool.

Here are just a few of the tasks your team can tackle using Windows SharePoint Services:

✔ Share documents, images, and data files online.

✔ Build lists of tasks, events, announcements, and more.

✔ Create and post to blogs.

✔ Create a team wiki.

✔ Set up alerts so you know whenever new contents are added to the site.

✔ Set up tasks for team members so you can keep each other up-to-date on the progress of your project.

✔ See when other members are online so you can contact them directly.

✔ Add a variety of Web parts.

✔ Customize the interface to fit your team or company.

✔ Export data lists and documents easily for use in other business applications.

Windows SharePoint Services: The bigger picture

Windows SharePoint Services 3.0 is a big topic — so big, in fact, that many books have been written about it. In this chapter, we wanted to give you a quick look at some of its capabilities, but there is a lot more to explore. To find out about the different services available with Windows SharePoint Services, see the Office Online article, "Which SharePoint technology is right for you?" at http://office.microsoft.com/en-us/sharepoint technology/FX101758691033.aspx.

You can also check out these *For Dummies* books on the topic:

✔ *Microsoft SharePoint 2007 For Dummies*, by Vanessa L. Williams

✔ *SharePoint 2007 Collaboration For Dummies*, by Greg Harvey

✔ *Office 2007 All-in-One Desk Reference For Dummies*, by Peter Weverka

Windows SharePoint Services 3.0 offers a number of different levels of service so that companies and organizations with different needs can choose the level that best fits what they need. In addition to the basic features in SharePoint 3.0, you can add social networking features and enterprise solutions.

Designed to help teams collaborate as easily and as effectively as possible, Windows SharePoint Services gives you a variety of ways to work with team members, files, and group information. You can set up specific permissions for team members, fine-tuning the privileges needed for viewing, adding to, or modifying site information. Figure 15-5 shows the variety of items you can create and change using Windows SharePoint.

The task and scheduling feature in Windows SharePoint Services offers one way of keeping everyone on the same page as far as project progress goes. When each team member tracks their progress, the entire group can see easily what's been accomplished and what still needs to be done. The steps for setting up a new task are simple:

1. **Log in to your Windows SharePoint Services site.**

2. **In the left navigation bar, click Tasks.**

   The Tasks list for your team appears in the workspace. The Assigned To column shows the person responsible for each individual task, and the Status, Priority, Due Date, and % Complete columns help you see the progress on each assignment.

3. **Click New.**

   The Tasks: New Item window appears, as shown in Figure 15-6. Here you will add the details of the task, assign it to someone, and add a description so that others can understand what it's about.

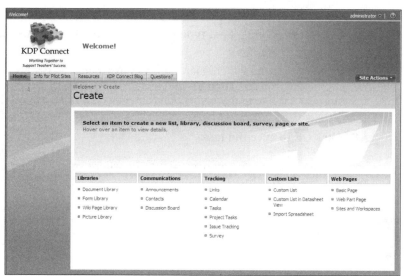

Figure 15-5:
Windows
SharePoint
Services
enables you
to build and
share with
your team
a full Web
site with
document
libraries,
task lists,
wikis, blogs,
and more.

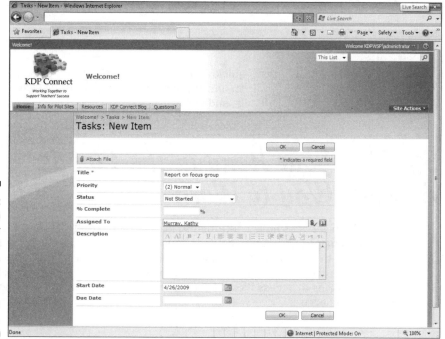

Figure 15-6:
Set up
tasks for
individual
team mem-
bers and
track prog-
ress as a
group.

4. **Fill in the task details as completely as you can.**

5. **In the Assigned To box, type the name of the person you want to assign the task to.**

   If you aren't sure which user names to use, click the Browse button to the right of the Assigned To line to see a list of team members on the site. Click the teammate you want and click OK to add her name in the Assigned To box.

6. **Click OK to save the task.**

The task list appears on any page in the site where you have added the Tasks module. (See Figure 15-7.)

Figure 15-7:
Updated tasks appear after you add the Tasks list to the page.

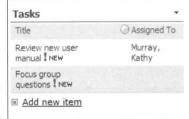

You also can add tasks quickly without going to the Tasks page by simply clicking the Add New Item link at the bottom of any Tasks list. Just click the link, fill in the task details, and click OK.

Sticking Your Head in the Clouds: A Smart Way to Work

As Web services have continued to propagate fruitfully and our mobile life-styles have continued to get more and more. . . well, mobile. . . it's not sur-prising that the way in which we define both *how* and *where* we work would change. The easy access and always-awake nature of the Web makes it pos-sible for us to access files, events, and each other from wherever we have Internet access.

Cloud computing is the ability to get the services and software you need without being tied to a specific place or hard drive. Cloud computing services provide you with a collection of software services — for example, the Calendar and Web-based e-mail tools we described earlier — when you need them, from wherever you happen to be. (See Figure 15-8.) And there are multiple ways to access the services, too. You can check e-mail on your phone; post a blog item via e-mail; or look up your favorite Shostakovich song and download it so you can add it to your Window Media playlist, even though you're accessing your account through your sister-in-law's iPhone.

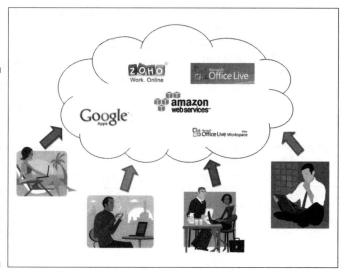

Figure 15-8:
Cloud computing enables individuals and teams to work with Web service applications from any point of access.

Discovering how cloud computing is green

Cloud computing is a just-in-time, scalable alternative to having millions of computers on desktops that individual people use to do what they need to do. Sure, we'll still need computers, but who's to say what they will look like? Mobile phones, PDAs, perhaps smart interfaces in your electric car — what would the limits be if you could work anywhere, using powerful Web-based applications that enabled you to access your own files easily, from any point on the globe?

Paperless office? Er, um . . .

So do you think it's possible that one day your offices — your home office and your work office — will go paperless? Cloud computing may bring this closer than ever, and faster than you think.

✔ If you're used to functioning in a cloud, where will you put the pages you print?

✔ If you can access a document 24/7 with a click of the button online, do you really need to download it and print it on that noisy, resource-hogging, paper-spewing gray device? (What's that thing called, again?)

✔ And if you can simply point others to the link where the document is stored (giving them the right permission to be able to view it, of course), do you really need to print it, put it in an envelope, pay the ever-increasing U.S. postal rate, and mail it to them? (Especially considering they'll have to wait three to five days to receive it, when the link gives them access instantly?)

Paperless isn't just a wave in some far-off distant future — it's becoming a reality fast enough to save a few trees today.

By reducing real-world hardware requirements, cloud computing — in theory, anyway — could potentially help to slow the rate at which our landfills and small villages are filling up with illegally dumped computers. Because cloud computing enables sharing reusable resources globally and is a scalable technology, the lion's share of the power consumption happens in the data centers supporting the cloud.

Google Apps

One of the earliest offerings in the cloud computing skies — long before people were using the term, too — was Google Docs, a free online word processor that Google enthusiasts could use to create, edit, print, and share simple documents. At first blush it was unsupported, which meant users had to tough through it on their own, but it was free and it worked. Not bad.

Today, Google Apps (www.google.com/apps) offers a number of free online applications that help individuals and groups accomplish all sorts of computing tasks. Whether you want to send e-mail, schedule appointments, share documents, or talk to someone near or far, there's an application — a free application — to help you do that. If you want to create a Web site or wiki so your team can share its work with the world, Google Apps has you covered there, too.

Google Apps also offers a Google Apps Team Edition designed to help teams work together effectively. The utilities involved in the Team Edition are Google Sites, Google Docs, and Google Calendar. You can find out more about the Team Edition by going to www.google.com/apps/intl/en/business/team.html.

Zoho

Zoho (www.zoho.com) is an innovative company with a team of more than 120 developers pumping out collaborative, business applications you can use — free or for a low cost — online at any time. Dig around their Web site to find some applications that help you work more effectively as a team, and some pretty hefty business tools that enable you to track, work with, and report on people, projects, and processes.

Signing up for Zoho is free (just go to www.zoho.com) and you can use your existing Google or Yahoo! login instead of creating a new one, if you'd rather do that. (Reuse, after all, is a green idea.)

Finding the right kind of hardware to work with clouds

One of the great perks of using cloud computing is that because the applications are stored and run online, the capabilities of your individual system aren't as important as they are when you're installing Dreamweaver CS4 on your laptop and you need umpteen gigabytes of storage space and eleventy-six gigabytes of RAM.

More clouds to think about

Additional companies are already floating around in the cloud computing airspace. Most notably, you may be familiar with Microsoft's new initiatives, including Office Live Small Business (a collection of online business services and a free Web site), Office Live Workspaces (online document sharing, collaboration, and storage), and Microsoft Online Services, which all offer free or affordable applications online.

Amazon and IBM have teamed up to offer Amazon Web Services, a high-end Web-based IT solution for businesses that enables them to "rent" computing power and functionality on an as-needed basis. This kind of responsible scalability reduces both risk and cost for business and provides a smart green option. Find out more at http://aws.amazon.com/.

A reasonably fast (and green!) laptop would be a very nice match for any cloud computing application, which means you may be able to do more with less computing power (which is also a green idea).

Hardware manufacturers are beginning to take advantage of the lower processing demands for cloud computing by developing systems that provide access to the Web services without all the bells and whistles of full-feature computers.

A to Zonbu

The Zonbu computer (www.zonbu.com) is a tiny system with a small footprint — it uses only one-third the power of a normal (non-CFL) light bulb. The fast little system (1.2G processor) doesn't have any moving parts (not even a fan), so what is there to wear out?

Zonbu offers six USB ports, has built in Wi-Fi, and comes with its own cloud computing software, offering the following applications:

- ✔ Browser, e-mail, IM, and Skype
- ✔ Word processing
- ✔ Photo editing
- ✔ Web publishing
- ✔ Games
- ✔ Music and movies

This little green system already does a good job cutting CO_2 emissions, but just to take things completely down to carbon neutral, Zonbu buys carbon offsets to make up the difference.

The Moderro Xpack

The Moderro Xpack CPU is a small (paperback-sized, they say) unit that has a USB port for your keyboard and mouse, Ethernet and VGA cables, and optional Wi-Fi. This little system plugs into your monitor (and even has a little bracket you can use to attach it to the back if you really want to condense things) and draws only about 13 watts of power. The only moving part is a backup fan, so wear-and-tear is kept to a minimum.

The manufacturer also includes Moderro Browser OS — they call it "desktop-in-a-browser" — which is another form of cloud computing. Users can browse the Web and interact with all kinds of different Web services, while still using the Moderro OS to get things done. You can learn more at www.moderro.com.

Chapter 16

Making the Connection: Virtual Presence

*W*elcome to a world where thoughts are tangible things, where you can zoom around the world and participate in an event without leaving your office, where you can brainstorm and tell jokes and plan projects collaboratively, in real time, adding hardly any CO_2 to the atmosphere.

Think it's virtual reality? Think again — it's telepresence, the connection choice that's actually *better* than being there.

No matter what your industry may be, you doubtless have meetings to attend — sometimes with peers, sometimes with administration or employees, sometimes with students or faculty, sometimes with clients. Meetings mean conversation, connection, and — until recently — gathering in one place. And the getting-everybody-in-the-same-room thing meant travel costs, hotel reservations, and rental cars. And two of the three of those items meant *big* CO_2 emissions.

This chapter is all about how to achieve those great meeting goals — connection, collaboration, and creative and productive work — without killing the planet. And what's more, we show you that using these green technologies keeps more green in your budget, too.

Requesting Your Virtual Presence

Technology has come a long way since the early days of closed-circuit televisions, when, in order to take a distance learning course, you had to drive 30 miles to a central location (perhaps a school or an office) and sit in a room with a bunch of other adults, staring at a television on a cart while a talking head lectured you.

Yawn.

Today, easy-to-use software makes *telepresencing* — the ability to be in another location and participate fully, almost like you would if you were in the room — a real possibility and an affordable option for people all over the world. Telepresence works best when participants feel engaged in more than one sense — sight *and* hearing, for example — is involved.

Chapter 15 introduces the idea of *asynchronous conferencing,* which involves connecting with others in a way that doesn't involve all parties being tuned in at the same time: person-to-person e-mail, posting to an e-mail list, participating on a Web forum, or adding content to a blog or wiki, for example. All those ways of staying in touch — with clients, colleagues, or coworkers — offer flexibility so that you can contribute when the time is right for you.

Telepresence — the ability to communicate in real time, as fully present as possible — is *synchronous conferencing,* meaning that all participants are in contact with each other at the same time. Place is another matter, as the examples in this chapter show. When you are connecting in real time with others, you might use something simple, like instant messaging; Web-based, like Web chat; more formalized, like Web conferencing; or a big showy affair, like full video conferencing. Of course, you can also do the personal Webcam conferencing thing for video chats with friends and colleagues.

Getting Started with Telepresence

Your first mission — if you choose to accept it — is to decide which method of real-time communication you need to choose to accomplish your goals. If you simply need to chat with a coworker, you can pick up the phone or use instant messaging. To organize a brainstorming session, plan a new project, or assign roles and tasks (or check on project status), you can use a low-footprint Web meeting to share ideas, talk, or chat online.

If you're thinking training, perhaps a Webinar or a videoconference — both are a little more formal, with more startup work — is what you need. This section shows you some of the basics for meeting virtually and throws in some tips on making sure your virtual presence makes the same (or even stronger) impact than your real-world presence would.

The key is to think through your meeting, event, or communication first — and then find the tool to support it. It's out there. We're sure of it!

Messaging, instantly

All sorts of companies now offer instant messaging — the big two are Windows Live Messenger (or MSN Messenger) and AIM (AOL Instant Messenger). You've probably tried — and maybe tried to get away from — instant messaging already. It's the quick pop-up utility that somehow always appears in the lower corner of your screen at the worst possible time, like when you're demoing a new product for a client or trying to appear really busy for your boss.

Got message?

AOL Instant Messenger was a big hit early on — the instant messaging client is downloadable and runs on your computer whether you're an AOL sub-scriber. It's easy to use and has a small onscreen footprint. (See Figure 16-1.)

Figure 16-1: AOL Instant Messenger is free, simple, and fun, but maybe for after work.

If you don't have AIM, you can download it (for free!) and run it on your computer whether you use a Windows, Macintosh, or Linux machine. Simply go to `http://dashboard.aim.com/aim`, click Download, and click Run. The software should install smoothly, and you'll be ready to add contacts and send instant messages in minutes.

AIM also offers a version of Instant Messenger, AIM Express, that's completely Web-based, which means you don't have to download it to your computer at all. Find out more about it at `http://dashboard.aim.com/aim`.

To start a conversation with a friend who is online, you simply double-click the contact name, type a message in the box that appears, and click Send. The message goes immediately to your contact (who hopefully replies). It's a simple way to send a quick note: "Is our phone conference at 3 today?" or "Want to meet for lunch?"

In addition to having a quick real-time conversation, you can do the following:

- ✔ Play games
- ✔ Change your profile
- ✔ Create a custom away message
- ✔ Check your AIM mail
- ✔ Add utilities

Just a couple of years ago (which seems like decades, in computer evolution), AIM "Away" messages were all the rage. Students near and far seemed to be in a continual rush to see who could come up with the best/funniest/quirkiest/most original Away message. (For you baby boomers out there, an Away message is the message AIM displays when someone sends you an instant message and you're not available to receive it.) Is it possible that our love affair with the Away message led us to the ever-popular Facebook status update, and now, Twitter? Hmmm, interesting. . . .

Don't shoot the Messenger

Windows Live Messenger (formerly known as MSN Messenger or Windows Messenger) is another popular instant messaging tool that plugs into just about everything Microsoft. (See Figure 16-2.) In Chapter 15, we cover Microsoft Office Live and Office Live Workspaces, which small businesses can use to create free Web sites, organize business contacts, and more. Windows Live Messenger plugs right into the Office Live workspace (making it an easy way to contact coworkers and clients for business purposes), but it's also available as a free downloadable tool.

Want to get Windows Live Messenger? Simply point your browser to
`http://download.live.com/messenger` and click Download. In the
File Download dialog box, click Run, and the software installs on your computer. All things should be so simple.

Figure 16-2:
Windows
Live
messaging
is a little
more busi-
ness and
maybe a
little less
fun.

Windows Live Messenger offers a few features that make its use for business
a little more palatable than AIM: The Shared Folders feature, for example,
enables you to easily post files, presentations, and more into a Shared
Documents workspace where others on your team can download them easily.
You can also use Windows Live Messenger to make phone calls, set appointments, use a whiteboard, share applications, and, of course, chat.

Have Web, will meet

When your real-time business communication needs to go beyond the simple,
"Hey, what about this?" kind of question, you may be ready to tackle a Web
meeting. Web meetings give you a great way to save lots of things. They save

the time it would take to drive to a meeting, the carbon emissions that traveling requires, the trouble of reserving a meeting space, and all the preliminary work to gather the equipment you need. And that's just the tip of the iceberg.

Would you believe us if we told you that you could organize an international meeting of all your site managers throughout the world — and host it this afternoon? Web tools make it possible, and even easy, to get people together for brainstorming, a formal meeting, professional development and training, or something else entirely. You just bring your creativity and a little technical know-how, and the Web tools do the rest.

Case in point: Cisco's WebEx (www.webex.com). This simple but powerful Web meeting tool helps you set up a meeting, invite participants, and host a media-rich, engaged, and interactive meeting in a series of easy steps. You can show and view videos; work collaboratively on documents, presentations, and more; draw on a whiteboard; ask participants to take a poll; or just chat. The software is Web-based and has compatible versions for a variety of operating systems, so the attendees can use just about any kind of computer.

WebEx offers a free trial period in which you can host full meetings, capture content, and export everything you do, whether you sign up for the program. If you're at all interested, try it out: Hey, nothing ventured, nothing gained, right? At the very least, trying it out helps you find out more about what you and your coworkers need in terms of a meeting management tool. To try it out, go to www.webex.com, click Free Trial, and follow the prompts.

Penciling in a meeting with WebEx

Here are the steps for scheduling a meeting with WebEx:

1. **Click Host a Meeting in the navigation panel on the left.**

   A set of three submenu items appears.

2. **Click Schedule a Meeting.**

   The Schedule a Meeting page appears, as shown in Figure 16-3.

3. **Fill in the text fields as completely as you can.**

   Enter a descriptive topic for the meeting and assign a password to guarantee security. Specify the date, time, and duration of the meeting.

4. **In the Attendees box, type the e-mail addresses of the people you want to invite to the meeting.**

   If you prefer, click Use Address Book and create new contacts for those you hope will attend. (You may want to wait to do this after you make a decision about whether to buy the program — no point in entering all of this information if you plan to just let the trial expire.)

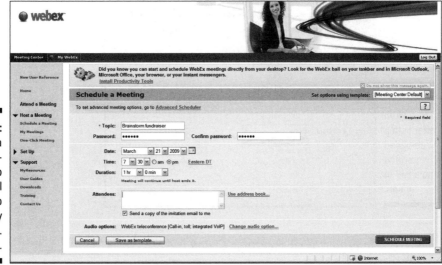

Figure 16-3:
Setting up a
Web meet-
ing is so
easy you'll
want to do
it for every
little thing.
Maybe.

5. Click Change Audio Options.

The Audio Options dialog box appears so that you can review and change, if necessary, the audio portion of the meeting. (See Figure 16-4.) By default, WebEx is set up to combine teleconferencing (where participants can phone in) along with the shared Web interface and applications. Choose your options and click OK.

6. Click Start Now.

An e-mail message is immediately sent to the recipients on your Attendees list, providing the following information:

Meeting topic

Date and time

Meeting number and password

The Web address for the meeting

The teleconference call-in number

Your e-mail address as the meeting host

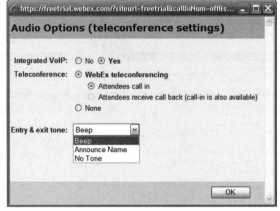

Figure 16-4:
Web meet-
ings often
offer both a
Web-based
interface
and a call-in
option.

Joining a Web meeting: C'mon in!

Pretend for a moment that you're one of the participants who is thrilled to receive the Web meeting invitation by e-mail. Your part is even easier than the message host. Here's what you do to join the meeting:

1. **A little in advance of the start time for the meeting (say, five minutes), click the link in the invitation e-mail message you've received.**

   This link takes you to a Web site that walks you through the process of downloading the software you need to join the Web meeting.

2. **After the software downloads, click the Join Now button.**

   A pop-up window appears, displaying the teleconference call-in number, the meeting ID number, and your participant number. To join the meeting on the call, simply call the teleconference phone number when you sign in online.

3. **Click OK.**

   The Web meeting begins and the host is alerted that you have joined. Your name appears in the participant list in the top-right corner of the page.

What can you really do in a Web meeting, anyway?

You know, there are two kinds of people in the world: those who like to go to meetings and those who don't. (Okay, that may be a bit of an oversimplification, but still.) If you're one of those people who hates to go to meetings — who thinks they are a waste of time, and you'd prefer to continue being productive at your desk — you will love Web meetings. And if you're a person who is an on-the-spot collaborator and thinks well in a group (and you love meetings), you will also love Web meetings. How can this kind of tool make everybody so happy?

If you have a focus and set objectives for your Web meeting, this technology really makes the most of your time, enables people to participate in a way that feels comfortable for them, and keeps ideas moving forward. What's more, you can save it all and use it later, so that even your scribbles and diagrams don't go to waste.

WebEx, for example, lets you do a number of things when the meeting goes live:

✔ You can display a document in the workspace so that everyone can see and review it together (by using the chat box or talking about it, if you're all phoning in).

✔ You can demonstrate a new product or design, show a PowerPoint presentation, or play a video.

✔ You can let everybody draw or write on a whiteboard together and then discuss their ideas. (See Figure 16-5.)

✔ You can let the whole group see your desktop, where you can demo new software, teach a process, or highlight new features in an existing program.

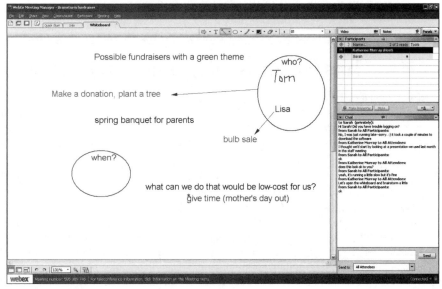

Figure 16-5:
Using a whiteboard is a great way to get the creative juices flowing. Visual thinkers really shine in Web meetings.

Don't let those good ideas (or really clever doodles) go to waste! You can save the contents of the whiteboard in UCF format (Universal Communications Format) by choosing File➪Save As. You can open and view the whiteboard UCF file by double-clicking the file in Windows Explorer. To find out more about UCF, go to `www.teleconference.att.com/resv/wmucffaq.html`. You can also sign up for a free trial of WebEx and watch the online demo to get a sense of how all the different features work together.

Get ready, get set, video conference!

Both Web meetings and some instant messaging tools enable you to use video to have some real face-to-face time in addition to audio and Web connection. For many of your work-at-home kinds of meetings, a simple but quality Webcam and the meeting or instant messaging software are perfectly fine. On the other hand, when you need to organize a bigger event that involves hosting executives and dignitaries from other companies (c'mon, you know you spruce things up for dignitaries), you may want to consider a more sophisticated form of real-time presence via videoconferencing.

True high-quality video conferencing means buying a video conferencing system with enough power to do what you need it to do. Professional video conferencing systems are available for meeting rooms (and they include large display and speaker systems, easy integration and management of users, and data storage and retrieval) and for interpersonal meetings.

Tips for successful video conferences

Try to keep it real. People respond to people, so even though the person looking into your meeting from Shanghai is really staring at a camera, encourage eye contact. It fosters better understanding.

Size does matter. Researchers are discovering that we relate to people in a video conference when they are close to our own size, generally speaking. This means that if the person participating in the meeting via videoconference is six inches tall or six feet tall on the conference room screen, a logic gap occurs. If your technology allows, try to arrange it so the person contributing appears in something close to real-

life size. It will enhance the understanding and connection going on in the meeting and can make the difference between whether people accept or resist the presenter's ideas.

Make sure the technology is transparent. The real goal with telepresence is not "Look how neat this technology is!" but rather "This meeting was so great; we forgot we were using fancy technology to pull it off." Work out the bugs ahead of time, make sure your audio is good, and test the video feed beforehand. Everything goes more smoothly if you work the tech glitches out in advance.

The best thing about the high-end option is the tons of CO_2 it saves when the director of your Shanghai office doesn't need to jet to Los Angeles twice a year for scheduled meetings. The planet Earth thanks you!

Reducing Your Carbon Emissions with Free Phone Service

You may have already heard about Skype, the traveler's friend. Skype is a free communications tool that you can download from the Web. It enables people and businesses, family and friends, strangers and lovers, to talk — free — from anywhere in the world. The trick to the free part is that in order to get that rate, you both need to be Skype members. (Don't worry — the membership is free, too.) If you want to call someone who is not a Skype member, you still can, but it will cost you (less, says Skype, than normal calling rates).

You just need to download the free software from www.skype.com, test out your microphone, set your audio levels, and you're good to go. Skype offers a version for each of the big operating systems — Windows Vista, Windows XP, and Mac OS X. Plus, it has other popular offerings, such as an app for the iPhone.

Skype also offers a pay-as-you-go program so that you can buy cheap minutes (still an odd concept) for your mobile phone or rack up some savings for international non-Skype calls to someone else's landline.

Getting started with Skype

Make sure you have your microphone and Webcam plugged in and ready before you get started. Depending on your system's capabilities, your microphone and Webcam may be built in; if that's the case, you don't need to do anything to prepare for using Skype. To prepare a microphone for use with Skype, simply plug the microphone in your audio port; to add a Webcam, plug it into an available USB port. If this is the first time you're using your Webcam, have the CD handy so you can use it to load the Webcam drivers if prompted.

Here's how to set up Skype. (It takes about 15 minutes.)

1. **Go to www.skype.com and download the version of Skype that matches your operating system.**

   The download instructions ask whether you want to run or save the software. You can either click Save and save the Skype installation files for later, or you can go ahead and click Run to run it now.

2. **When the software prompts you, start Skype.**

3. **In the Welcome Screen, click the Check Your Sound Works option.**

   The Skype window appears. Make sure your microphone is connected to the proper port of your computer.

4. **Click Call.**

   The system calls the Skype automated call center so that you can check your sound levels. (See Figure 16-6.) If you can't hear anyone speaking after a few seconds, turn up the volume on your computer.

5. **When prompted, speak into your microphone.**

   A status bar at the top of the call window shows you the length of the call and gives you a volume control so that you can adjust the volume.

Don't click End Call! After a few seconds, your voice will play back to you — if your microphone is working. Then the automated caller gives you instructions for adjusting your volume as well as tips to try if things don't seem to be working properly.

When all is said and done (literally), the automated caller hangs up and the call is ended. Now you're ready to use Skype by calling other Skype users.

Figure 16-6:
Calling
the Skype
automaton
lets you
make sure
your sound
equipment
works —
good to
know before
you start
calling folks
all over the
world.

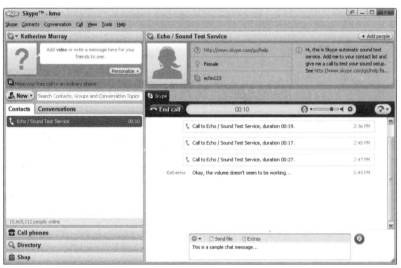

Adjusting your sound settings

If you haven't used your microphone in a while — or ever — check your sound settings in the Windows Vista Control Panel by choosing Hardware and Sound and clicking Sound. In the Sound dialog box, click Recording and click the Microphone selection. Click the Properties button and click Levels to set the microphone's sensitivity level. Click OK to close the dialog box.

You can also adjust the volume level by clicking the Volume control icon (a speaker) in the notification area and adjusting the volume slide to the setting you want.

Calling all Skypers

When you know your system works properly, the next task involves adding your contacts to your Skype list. The steps are simple.

1. **In the Skype window, click Contacts.**

   This displays the Contacts menu, which offers everything you need to add new contacts, import your contacts from Microsoft Outlook, Outlook Express, or Yahoo! (so that you have more people to call online), set preferences about contact information, and manage your contacts.

2. **Click Import Contacts.**

   The Find Your Friends dialog box appears.

3. **Select the check boxes of the program contacts you want to import, and click Search E-mail Contacts.**

   When the search is complete, Skype displays a list of your contacts who are currently using Skype.

4. **To add those people as contacts in your Skype list, click the check box to the left of each of their names and click Add Contact. If you *don't* want to add them, click Skip.**

   Skype then displays a list of all your contacts so that you can e-mail everybody, if you choose, and tell them to jump on Skype — and talk voice-to-voice for free.

5. **Customize the e-mail message Skype drafts for you, select the check boxes of the people you want to send it to, and click Send.**

   Or not. It's your call . . . literally.

If you think that a certain person is on Skype but you don't have him in your Contacts list, you can search for him by clicking in the Find a Specific Person text box and typing his full name, Skype ID, or e-mail address. Skype searches (quickly, too) and displays a full list of all the people in all countries on Skype who come close to that name or ID. Search the columns by country to narrow your search and then click the name of the person when you find him. A window opens automatically so you can send him a message right away and ask him to be your Skype buddy. Nice!

Presenting via Webinars

Here's a riddle for you: When is a Web meeting not a Web meeting? Answer: When it's a Webinar. *Webinar* is one of those postmodern words that mixes *Web* with *seminar*. When you have a large, organized training session — perhaps professional development, software training, or some other kind of professional, here's-how-you-do-it kind of event — consider using Web-based seminar software.

GoToWebinar (www.gotowebinar) is one example of a simple tool you can use to deliver all kinds of content in a collaborative Web format. GoToWebinar costs $99 per month but offers a free trial (and a lower-cost, GoToMeeting version for small businesses and individuals). You can create Webinars on the fly that include up to 200 people, or you can schedule larger events of up to 1,000 participants. This particular Webinar tool (the capabilities may vary with other products) makes it easy for you to

- Make presentations in a media-rich format.
- Record the presentation as a podcast.
- Moderate discussions.
- Lead training sessions.
- Make transcribed notes and documents available automatically to all participants.

So, what's the topic for your Webinar? Setting up a Webinar can be as simple as rolling out a new sales program to inspire your field sales reps. Or maybe you are hosting a Webinar for parents on how to apply for financial aid for their college students. Whatever your topic, with Webinar software like GoToWebinar, you can present the Webinar live and capture it as a full podcast for those who missed it. Here are the steps:

1. **Go to www.gotoWebinar.com and create a free trial account.**

   Click the Try It Free button and the site walks you through the process.

2. **Log in using your e-mail address and password.**

   The next page asks whether you want to launch a Webinar now or plan one for the future.

3. **Click Schedule a Webinar.**

   The Schedule a Webinar page provides a series of simple questions that enable you to set up the event quickly. (See Figure 16-7.) Enter the time and date, provide a Webinar name and description (remember that this information is used in marketing your event), choose your time zone, set audio options, and indicate whether you want participants to use passwords to access the Webinar.

4. **If you plan to share the Webinar with other presenters, click Specify Panelists.**

   Text boxes appear so that you can type the additional panelists' names and e-mail addresses.

5. **Click Save and Continue.**

   If your Webinar is part of an ongoing training program — perhaps an introduction to different software features at the same time each week — click the Recurs down-arrow and choose the time frame (Daily, Weekly, or Monthly).

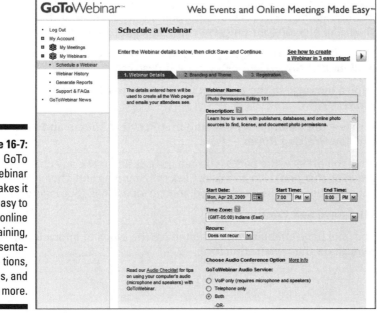

Figure 16-7:
GoTo Webinar makes it easy to do online training, presentations, classes, and more.

6. **On the Branding and Theme tab, you design the look of your Webinar. If you like, click Upload Logo to add your company logo to the site.**

   The logo image you upload must be smaller than 400 by 200 pixels in order to fit the logo space, so make sure your logo is the right size before you upload it.

7. **Click through the themes and choose the one that best fits the look you would like to convey.**

   The look and feel of the Webinar has an impact on the way your participants feel about the experience. Go for professional and friendly, and use colors and elements that help participants gain what they need (as opposed to distracting or overwhelming them).

8. **Click Upload Custom Image if you want to add your own photos or artwork to the page.**

9. **Choose the color for your Webinar waiting room (where participants gather before the Webinar begins).**

   Click the Standard Color drop-down arrow and choose the color from the list. Or if you know the hexadecimal number for the color you want, click the Custom box and enter that number.

   If your company has official branding elements — for example, a logo, letterhead, business cards, and a Web site — chances are that your designer knows the hexadecimal numbers for the colors used in the design. For branding purposes, you should have consistent colors on all company communications rather than, for example, four different shades of blue on four different communications pieces.

10. **Enter the presenter name, presentation title, and the company name (and upload the presenter's photo, if desired).**

11. **Type a message in the text box to welcome participants when they arrive.**

12. **Preview the Webinar by clicking first Preview Theme and then Preview Waiting Room.**

    After you preview the pages, you can go back and make any changes to the branding that you'd like to make: Click the Branding and Theme tab and choose other options. Looks good, though, doesn't it? (See Figure 16-7.)

13. **Click Save and Continue.**

    The final page enables you to customize the types of information you request on the registration form.

14. **Click the fields you want to include on the registration form, indicate whether you want registrants to receive replies immediately or after you approve their registration, and click Preview.**

    If you want registrants to go to another site — perhaps your business site — after registering, enter the URL in the box provided.

15. **Click Save and E-mail Me the Invitation.**

    An e-mail message is immediately sent to all panelists (as well as you, of course). Keep the e-mail where you can find it easily before the Webinar and use it to log in the day of the event.

GoToWebinar enables you to practice your Webinar before it goes live. Simply log in to your account, choose My Webinars, and click Practice.

Connecting with Remote Desktop

Microsoft's Remote Desktop Connection is one of those old standbys that isn't particularly pretty, but it gets the job done. Remote Desktop Connection creates a secure means for you to access your at-the-office system when you're working at home. And it's not a feature tied to a single desktop, instead it's an offering that entire businesses and organizations can use easily.

Check out this comparison chart of remote desktop software that is available for all different types of computers: `http://www.remote-desktop-control.com/eng/compare.html`.

Remote Desktop Connection makes it easy for you to connect to a terminal server or to another computer running Windows. Your system administrator or IT person at the office needs to give you network access and the necessary permissions to connect in-house.

To log in to your office system using Remote Desktop Connection, follow these steps:

1. **Click Start➪All Programs➪Accessories➪Remote Desktop Connection.**

    The Remote Desktop Connection box appears, as Figure 16-8 shows.

Figure 16-8:
Remote
Desktop
Connection.

Remote Desktop Connection
Remote Desktop Connection
Computer:
Connect Cancel Help Options >>

2. **In the Computer box, type the computer name provided by your system administrator (for example, `remote.example.org`) and click Connect.**

   After a moment, your desktop changes its appearance and displays the Windows Security dialog box. (See Figure 16-9.)

3. **Enter your username and password and click OK.**

   If you want Windows Vista to remember your connection (and you probably do), select the Remember My Credentials check box before clicking OK. Remote Desktop Connection accesses the terminal server, and as long as the required permissions are in place, all shall be well, and you'll be connected remotely. Simple, eh?

Figure 16-9:
Enter your
user ID and
password
to log in to
your system.

Windows Security
Enter your credentials
These credentials will be used to connect to remote.kdp.org.
administration\kathy
••••••••••••
Domain: administration
☑ Remember my credentials
OK   Cancel

Working remotely

If you are using Remote Desktop Connection to access the server in your workplace, chances are that all the applications that are available to you when you are in the office — for example, Microsoft Office 2007 applications, your company database, graphics or Web software, and more — are available to your through your remote connection. You should be able to navigate to folders and files in your own server folder or in any of the shared folders to which you have access.

The desktop will look different from your own personal office PC — that background showing your new puppy won't be visible, for example, because the space you're seeing is really server space on the terminal server, not your actual desktop on the computer on your desk at work.

Ending your remote session

When you are ready to close the remote connection, you can do it one of two ways:

- ✔ Click the close X in the upper right of the remote window title bar.
- ✔ Choose Start⇨Shut Down. When the Shut Down Windows dialog box appears, Disconnect is selected. Click OK.

The Remote Desktop Connection closes, and you are returned to your regular desktop.

Chapter 17

Your Green Small Business

*A*h, so you're an entrepreneur! One of those can-do, never-say-die, genius-starts-here kind of people. Good for you! You need that *chutzpah* in this economy. The good news is that there's always room for another good idea, and if the idea you want to grow (or are already growing) meets a need and distinguishes itself from the competition, chances are that buyers are waiting for what you offer.

But as you begin or continue that long climb to success, we want you to take some time to consider the planet that's giving you the chance to be the next big thing. The choices you make today — for your facility, your staff, your products, and your customers — can either help the planet or contribute to the problems that have her in a choke-hold. This chapter is all about the small and big things you can do to make your small business greener and improve the world around you at the same time.

Getting to the Heart of the Matter

Whether you are just starting your own business or you've been in business for years, you probably have at the heart of your efforts some kind of vision that is driving everything. Perhaps you have a passion for your industry and want to make a difference. Maybe you are building something to pass on to your children and grandchildren. Or you might be living out a dream of excellence, community, or industry. The list goes on and on.

Somewhere in the middle of that vision is the answer to the question "How is your business in partnership with the earth?" Depending on the nature of your industry, you may or may not see a direct connection. If you work in manufacturing, you use electricity, water, and perhaps oil and gas — natural resources — to accomplish your goals. If you work in a service industry, you rely on . . . let's see . . . electricity, water, and perhaps oil and gas — to do what you do.

You purchase products, maybe make products, and perhaps sell products. You use things and discard them. You create a space — for yourself or for many — and furnish it with items that promote (we hope) both comfort and efficiency. All those choices have green options and not-so-green options. Your awareness and choice as a business owner can make a big difference for the planet.

So how does your business work in partnership with the earth? It's a good question, and there are lots of ways to come up with — and act upon — good answers.

Trash to treasure

There's a great scene in the Cary Grant movie *Houseboat* (okay, confession, Katherine is a fan) where our hero demonstrates to his unhappy pre-adolescent son the cycle of life by pouring a pitcher of water onto a dock beside a lake. The water runs off the boards and into the water below. The water doesn't disappear, he points out; it just becomes part of something bigger.

In this way — scientists will tell you this too, but Cary Grant does it stunningly well — we know that energy is never used up and items don't go to waste — they really and truly just change form. They show up as something else.

So what are you doing with the items that you think you are throwing away? They may sit in landfills, which is a problem. They may leach dangerous chemicals into other peoples' water sources, which is a *really* big problem. Or they may be converted into paper, plastics, glass, and aluminum that can be used in helpful ways that sustain the planet.

Ah, that's nice — we knew we'd get to the good part eventually.

A major aspect of green business focuses on reducing the amount of waste you produce. Chances are that when you begin looking at green initiatives, you waste much more than you need to — and it's pretty mindless. You don't need something, so you throw it away. You printed 20 letters with the wrong letterhead? Just pitch it. What's 20 pages in the scope of a business day?

Well, green efforts cause you to pause a minute and look at those pages you just tossed. The back of the page looks perfectly useable. You could print the draft of your report on those pages. Or cut them up and use them for scrap paper. Or take them home for the kids to draw on. Or make origami in your spare time.

You get the idea.

Begin with the answer to this question: What is your waste management bill every month? How many pounds of garbage do you send away? Now see if you can reduce both those numbers next month, and by how much. It's a simple and powerful — and cost-saving — green effort. Nice. Let us know how you do.

The Good Housekeeping Green Seal of Approval

The Good Housekeeping Seal of Approval calls to mind an Ozzie-and-Harriet–style perfectly run home (when was the last time your laundry looked that good?), but did you know it's a real thing? Introduced in 1909 as a kind of consumer protection award, the Good Housekeeping Seal of Approval enabled consumers to know they were receiving quality products — soap, appliances, what-have-you — and that if they had problems with the items, the folks at Good Housekeeping would either replace the item or refund their investment in it. That's a pretty big deal — and a nice safety net for consumers.

The good people at Good Housekeeping are now working on the criteria for a Good Housekeeping Green Seal of Approval, which will carry on the same commitment to consumer education and protection while adding a few criteria. (See Figure 17-1.) Products qualifying for the green seal have to demonstrate all the qualities in the regular seal of approval, plus be made with earth-friendly materials, manufactured efficiently in a green way, and packaged and distributed with the earth in mind. Developers are still working on all the criteria, but it's a great effort at cutting through the *greenwashing* — businesses' attempts to grab some limelight and revenue by promoting green products and services that don't deserve the label. Watch for the Good Housekeeping Green Seal of Approval for products you purchase in the future, and if you run a small business, find out how you can seek out a Good Housekeeping Green Seal of Approval for the products you offer.

Figure 17-1:
The new
Good
House-
keeping
Green Seal
of Approval.

Greening Your Business: What Can You Do?

As you begin to think about how you can make your small business greener, you may wonder what you really need to do. How much paper can you conserve? How many light bulbs can you change?

But these items are just the tip of the quickly melting iceberg. Scan the following sections for green ideas for your new business or your already-thriving venture.

Greening your space

If you're just starting out and setting up shop for the first time, consider these possibilities in your setup choices:

❑ Use CFL light bulbs everywhere.

❑ Insulate, insulate, insulate.

❑ Use natural blinds (earth-friendly — made of bamboo — of course).

❑ Use natural light wherever possible.

❑ Consider solar power.

❑ Use natural flooring (or earth-friendly carpeting).

❑ Add an air purifier and keep it circulating, baby.

❑ Find out whether you can purchase electricity from renewable sources.

If you've already got an existing business and want to start greening it up, think about these low-cost ways to change your environment today:

❏ Put out recycling bins and let your staff know where to find them (and what to put in them).

❏ Add plants to your office — especially in the reception area, meeting rooms, and the lunch room or kitchen.

❏ Have your air quality tested; clean ducts; check air flow.

❏ Add light sensors to offices and rooms you don't use often — like conference rooms or meeting areas — so the lights turn off automatically when no one is in the room.

❏ Get an energy audit to help you find out how much energy your facility uses and where you can cut back.

Looking for green office supplies? Search no more! Here's a list of vendors offering green cleaning and paper products for your office: Marcal (www.marcal paper.com), Method (www.methodhome.com), Planet (www.planet inc.com), Seventh Generation (www.seventhgeneration.com), and Simple Green (www.simplegreen.com).

Landscaping for water conservation

In this book, we talk a lot about virtual space because it offers a great way to reduce energy use, drive less, and get more done. But because the earth is, after all, the original green space (well, to allow for the possibility of other universes, let's say "one of the original green spaces"), it's important to think about ways to make the actual facility you do business in as green as possible. One way to do this is to think about the way in which your office is landscaped. Do the trees help shade in summer and provide a break from wind, ice, and snow in winter? This can have an impact on the amount of heating and cooling you use, which ties directly to your energy consumption — and impacts both your bill and CO_2 emissions. Planting bushes, flowers,

and vines that are right for your climate helps with air quality and the beauty factor (which is vital for happy, relaxed employees).

One area that is getting more play in green awareness lately is the water-conserving landscape technique of *xeriscaping*, which focuses on designing landscapes with drought-resistant plantings to conserve water. Xeriscaping can save you a significant amount on your water bill, beautify your space, and cut down on the time and expense of landscaping services. To discover the seven principals of xeriscaping and find a listing of drought-resistant plants, visit this site: www.eartheasy.com/grow_xeriscape.htm#b.

Greening products and services

The materials that go into making and distributing your products come from somewhere — and go somewhere else. If you run a service business, you are using resources right and left, and using other peoples' products to do it. Where do these things come from and where do they go? Thinking through this question and considering your place in the link is a good first step toward greening your products and services.

A new business has another leg up here because it's easier to *start* green than it is to get greener in the middle of an established process. It's never too late to change, though. Here are some ideas to consider as you think about bringing the green to the items and ideals you offer clients and customers:

❏ Start at the beginning and think through the lifecycle of your product or service. How many supplies do you use? Where do they come from? Make a list.

❏ How many people does it take to make the product or offer the service you provide? Envision the product lifecycle and estimate the number of people involved in making it happen.

After you finish this evaluation, consider sending a green thank-you note (on recycled paper, of course) to everyone involved in getting your product or service out there. Sharing a little gratitude makes everybody's day brighter.

❏ Begin thinking about ways to green the list of supplies and materials you use. If the materials are already green, think about how far they travel to get to you. You may buy great recycled paper from Washington state, but what are the CO_2 emissions of the truck bringing it all the way to your office in New Hampshire?

❏ Consider whether all the folks touching your products need to be where they are to do it. Do you have employees who are driving long distances? Would it be a good green measure to give them the option of working at home a few days a week?

See Chapter 13 for good reasons to work at home and ways to ensure the job is still getting done.

❏ Get a green audit for your product or service to determine the CO_2 emission required to produce or offer it. After you have that number, you have something to work with. How can you reduce your footprint? You might be able to

• Reduce energy consumption using IT power-saving features.

• Unplug unused equipment.

- Reduce the size of your office space.

- Reuse materials and equipment whenever possible.

- Recycle everything you can.

- Consider alternative methods of heating and cooling.

- Purchase carbon offsets until you can expand your green efforts. (For more about carbon offsets, see Chapter 2.)

Eco-Friendly Reusable Bags (www.ecobags.com) is an awesome bag shop with just about every conceivable bag you could ever want for anything. Not only will you feel good about what you're offering, but your customers will take your green brand with them — free advertising! — everywhere they go.

Greening practices and people

One of the easiest and most fun aspects of greening a small business involves getting everybody on board. Sure, there may be naysayers — you know, the Eeyores ("If it *is* a good day . . . which I doubt,") — but for the most part, coworkers feel good about doing the environmentally kind thing.

Greening your practices is pretty easy to do if you make it a priority. Our workplaces get so busy that it's easy to push green initiatives to the bottom of the list, where they fall in the "someday when we have time" category. As we all know, that someday never comes unless you make it a priority. Incorporate green practices in your regular business routines, and it will become part of your culture. Here are a few ideas:

❑ Always use recycled paper to print unless the document is going to a client or customer.

❑ Always print double-sided unless the document type (a legal document, financial report, and so on) requires otherwise.

❑ Leave lights and computers (and other tech gear) unplugged unless they are in use.

❑ Institute work-at-home Fridays.

❑ Offer flex time so that staff can carpool and use public transportation to get to and from work.

❑ Make your green efforts visible with staff and celebrate benchmarks. (For example, "We reduced our paper purchase last month by 33 percent! Go team!")

❏ Help staff learn about and celebrate green efforts. As you find out about ways to green the workplace, you can share information with others to help them carry on the green effort at home. Add a green tip to your monthly newsletter; provide places for recycling, to make it easy; host a green lunch purchased with the amount of money you spent on energy-saving features last month.

❏ Make a plan. Table 17-1 is an example of a table you can use to help you plan the types of green efforts you'd like to add to your business. Invite everyone at work to participate and bring their own ideas and suggestions.

❏ Create your own green policies. The Environmental Protection Agency offers a Web page of resources (www.epa.gov/ems/info/index.htm) you can use to implement an environmental management system in your workplace. Whether you feel you need to be that elaborate, you can definitely get a team together to explore green efforts, write up work policies, and inspire others to get involved. Post your green policies in visible and logical places — by shared printers, in the kitchen, or close to the supply cabinet. Keep the message upbeat and focused on the positive change everyone is making by participating.

Table 17-1	Action Plan for Greening Your Busines		
Action	**Relevance**	**Deadline for Implementation**	**Items to Research**
Raise awareness of green initiatives among coworkers and clients.			
Buy Energy Star-rated appliances and computers.			
Calculate your business carbon footprint (and product/service CO_2).			
Celebrate small green successes.			
Buy CFL light bulbs.			
Create designs for your products that promote care of the earth.			
Give discounts to fitness organizations/health clubs.			
Do as much electronically and online as possible.			

Action	Relevance	Deadline for Implementation	Items to Research
Schedule an energy audit.			
Switch to environmentally friendly cleaning products.			
Purchase fair trade coffee and foods.			
Provide fresh air and water for everyone in your workspace.			
Landscape for energy conservation.			
Meet virtually (and often).			
Use minimal packaging.			
Use natural fibers wherever possible — in flooring, window treatments, cubicles, and so on.			
Employ natural lighting wherever possible.			
Use recycled bags, paper, and goods.			
Switch to soy inks.			
Purchase sustainably produced furniture.			
Work at home, virtually, or in combination.			

Residual outcomes

Some of the soft benefits of going green in your small business may not be immediately apparent, but you will see them eventually. Customers appreciate the recycled bags, even if they have to pay five cents more to get them. Your employees are proud to be part of a business that cares. Your organization carries itself a little taller because it's doing what it can. Mindsets begin to shift, bit by bit, and old patterns of disposability begin to dissolve. You'll notice people begin to think differently and start to hear folks talk more seriously about what they are using and what they're throwing away. When you hear the word *sustainability* pop up in a staff meeting, you'll know your business has a greener culture than it did when you started. Congratulations!

Putting Green Business in Context

Making the effort to go green is a good thing. (You've heard *that* refrain plenty of times by now!) But if you're a business owner, it's also important to go green for the right reasons. Greenwashing is everywhere, and consumers are catching on. Slap a respectable-looking green label on your bag of toxic waste and people might think, "Yeah, that's not such a great thing for the environment, but look — they're doing what they can!"

Although the temptation to overstate your green factor might be tempting because it's so hip right now (and we all need the business!), it's better to take the high road and stick with the facts. Your energy audit, your thoughtful exploration of the product or service lifecycle, and your time spent with your staff, family, and friends to think through (and then put into practice) green ideas gives you real data and real stories to work with. Share with your customers what you're doing now — not what you hope to do someday. Let them know how your product or service really is green, and where you're working to make it greener. And fight the temptation to turn green into a big PR event. Making green choices doesn't make us super world citizens or earn us gold stars. It's what we need to do to keep our planet inhabitable. That's not heroics — it's just plain common sense.

Here are some tips on how to share your green initiatives — in an authentic and straightforward way — with your vendors, friends, and customers:

- Numbers tell the story. Make yours good. How many miles did your employees drive to work before you started your green efforts? How many are they driving now?

- Compare your business CO_2 footprint this time last year with today's number.

- Share the number of green vendors you work with — and include their names and Web addresses.

- Show up on green forums on public sites and talk about why your business is going green (but mean it, even though it's free marketing).

- Include a tag line like "Please consider the environment before printing this message" at the bottom of your e-mail signature.

- Give to earth-care initiatives or carbon offset programs and let them use your name and company Web address in their promotional materials.

- Think of ways you can help your customers and clients learn more about green efforts — and then take the step and make it happen.

Discovering Four Simple Green IT Techniques You Can Implement Today

As the owner of a small business, you may be ultra-concerned with costs. You've got to balance what may be limited resources against the gains they produce. You may have staff, payroll, manufacturing, and marketing costs. Equipment costs — and the bankroll to maintain that equipment — are probably not a small chunk of your budget.

Even though buying green (as in all new Energy Star–rated equipment) might make you swoon, there are other things you can do to start getting greener right away:

✔ **Reduce what you consume.** Throughout this book, you discover techniques for educating yourself about how much energy you consume. With just a little refiguring, you can find the same numbers for your business. After you have a handle on the amount of power you're pulling and the CO_2 that's being generated as a result, you have what you need to plot a course of action. Ways you can reduce what you consume include these (and many others):

- Use power meters to find out where the power is going.

- Use smart power strips that turn off peripherals such as printers and scanners when they are not in use.

- Use power management on all your desktop and laptop computers.

- Use rechargeable batteries in mobile devices.

- Cut down on the use of paper, power, water, and gas.

- Meet virtually whenever possible to cut down on drive time.

- Let PDFs and other electronic files replace the hard copies you used to mail or take everywhere.

✔ **Reuse what you can.** Sure, it's in the budget to buy new printers and PCs every two years, but do you really need to do that? Could a simple memory upgrade and larger hard drive do the trick? Run the numbers to see what the cost savings are in relation to the new purchase. If in the long run it's a green thing (or just a smart thing) to go ahead and make the purchase, be sure to recycle your old systems responsibly.

✔ **Recycle the rest.** In Chapter 8, you learn how to prepare a system for recycling and discover who has recycling programs that keep CPUs and monitors out of hazardous waste piles. You can also recycle through continued use — donating your used computers to schools, nonprofit organizations, or friends in need of a new system.

✔ **Commit to green IT.** Making a real commitment to green IT means that you make a change in the way you approach technology in your business — as a tool to get things done effectively and in an earth-friendly way. Committing to green IT will mean different things for different businesses, but in general, it might look like something like this:

- Keep your eyes open for new green resources.

- Continue learning about green IT.

- When you replace equipment, buy green.

- Ask your vendors questions about their green commitment.

- Know what makes up the lifecycle of your product or service (and keep an eye on it).

- Commit to responsible recycling.

- Model your commitment by buying green, reducing use, and conserving what you can.

- Evaluate your technology needs and make a schedule for green purchasing points.

- Set up green policies and assessments so you know and can share how much energy (and investment) you're saving.

ReDO (`www.redo.org`) is a nonprofit organization with a mission of "promoting reuse as an environmentally sound, socially beneficial, and economical means for managing surplus and discarded materials." Not sure how you can reuse or recycle items you produce or use and throw away? Check out their site for ideas you can implement in your industry.

Seriously green

As you learn more about greening your small business, you will find ideas that are no-brainers (using CFL light bulbs, recycling, and buying green) and things that are, well, a little out there. Here's an idea for the *no-really-I-mean-it* green business advocate: a swamp cooler.

Perhaps not much more attractive than it sounds, a swamp cooler is a replacement for your typical CO_2-pumping air conditioner. The swamp cooler draws air into a chamber where it moves through pads soaked in water. The air then sucks up the water, which reduces its temperature (some say between 15 and 40 degrees). This type of air cooler uses much less energy and doesn't need one whiff of Freon. If you live and work in an area with relatively low humidity, this might be a possibility for you. Those of us in areas where the sweat drops off our laptops in July might need to wait for a different option.

Collaborating the Green Way

Collaboration is a key word in a new green workplace because duplication of effort requires more resources, more energy, more equipment . . . and besides, it's just not efficient. If you can create efficient sustainability in your business, your dollars will go farther and the planet will smile. Sustainability means making great choices with an eye toward the big picture — buying earth-friendly products, reducing your packaging, recycling wherever possible — and efficiency means accomplishing your goals in a straightforward way that doesn't waste a lot of time, steps, or money. Here are a few ideas for collaboration that can increase your green benefit:

✔ **Share resources.** One way to green your small business involves collaborating with others who offer complementary products or services. This might mean setting up shop in the same area — in the real world or virtually. It could mean sharing equipment, contractors, or even marketing lists. Collaborating can help you keep your expenses down and help reduce your consumption and make your purchases go farther, all at the same time.

Of course, don't overlook the obvious: sharing resources within your workplace! Printer sharing, fax sharing, share drives, and even office sharing can cut down on your power consumption and your square footage, both of which reduce your carbon footprint.

✔ **Combine efforts to cut green costs.** Is your small business hosting an event for your chamber of commerce? Are you working on a fundraiser for a local charity? Are your staff members looking for a volunteer opportunity? Think creatively to partner with other businesses in your area, keep your costs down, and reduce what you consume and throw away in the process.

✔ **Trade services, not incomes.** Say that your small contracting business is going gangbusters — everybody needs what you offer right now. A real estate office in your area needs some repair work on its awnings — and they can help you by whipping up a business postcard to put in the Welcome Wagon packets for all their new homebuyers. Is the trade worth it? Absolutely. Brainstorm possible partners for collaborating on projects or events, and do a little legwork to find out who to talk to about it. You can use a list like the one shown in Table 17-2 to get started.

✔ **Think virtual.** The Internet makes it possible to trade services easily without a lot of overhead. A marketing person can trade services with a designer — one designs the logo; the other gets the word out. An eye doctor, podiatrist, and orthodontist can all share a receptionist, a waiting room, and billing and marketing services.

Table 17-2	Collaborating the Green Way		
Action Item	**Possible Partner**	**E-mail Contact**	**Contact Date**
Plan marketing launch.	Biz Marketing	lisa@bizmarketing	9/1/09
Make packaging bid.	Green Box Packaging	tom@greenbox	8/15/09

Create Your Own Green Timeline

Given all the opportunities for greenness in this chapter, what are the take-aways? Your business is your call, and investing in green efforts is a choice and not a mandate. What kinds of changes do you want to make in your small business, whether you're just getting started or you've been at it for years? To help you get started brainstorming a green timeline (which we recommend you do with other business owners or with interested members of your staff or family so you have someone to be accountable to), here are some possibilities:

GREEN INITIATIVES FOR

Business name:_____

Date: _____

Point person: _____ E-mail: _____

FOUR THINGS to do immediately:

1. _____

2. _____

3. _____

4. _____

FOUR THINGS to do by this date next month:

1. _____
2. _____
3. _____
4. _____

FOUR THINGS to work on long-term:

1. _____
2. _____
3. _____
4. _____

FOUR THINGS to share with our clients and partners:

1. _____
2. _____
3. _____
4. _____

Finding Five Online Green Business Resources

As the owner of a small business, you are probably up to your eyeballs in details — trying to ensure a quality product or service, doing your best to put sound practices in place, creating a business plan, setting up accounts receivable and payable, managing data, buying materials, managing employees . . . the list goes on and on.

With so many choices to make and so many responsibilities, who has time to research every single vendor who makes a green claim? How do you know who is trustworthy and who isn't? Especially if you're going to pay a little more for green services, you need to feel confident that you're getting a good deal that will ultimately provide your customers with quality and the earth with a little more breathing power.

This section introduces you to five different sites that can help you find green businesses that are more than just talk. Each site takes a different approach, but collectively, they help you weed out the green spin from the real deal.

Greenpreneur.net

Greenpreneur.net (`http://greeenpreneur.net`), shown in Figure 17-2, sports the tag line, "The Future of Business," and on this site, you find a collection of relevant green articles tied to items in the news and how-to articles with information that business owners want to know. (For example, "Do It Yourself Business Energy Audit" is one of the most popular links right now.) You can also get a look at the sponsors on the site, read the blog, and look things up in the knowledgebase.

Figure 17-2:
Green-
preneur.
net offers
how-to's, a
newsletter,
blogs, and
more for
developing
sustainabil-
ity in your
business.

Green Maven

Type **green business** into Google and what do you find? No less than 220 *million* results. That's going to take a while to sift through! And when you narrow the list to something you can work with, how do you know that the businesses are really green? Green Maven (`www.greenmaven.com`) tries to take care of some of that work for you. (See Figure 17-3.) Green Maven, a green search engine, puts sites through an approval policy in which they "screen for green," looking for the following:

✔ Included sites must state their green values clearly on their home pages.

✔ The site submitted must be a quality site, complete and suitable for all family members.

✔ Certifications and third-party validations improve a site's chances of being approved but are not mandatory.

Figure 17-3:
To get listed on a green search engine or find vendors to support your green efforts, check out Green Maven.

Earth911.com

Earth911.com (http://earth911.com) is a great site dedicated to helping you find local resources that help you and your customers make good green choices and help create sustainability for the planet. Earth911.com (see Figure 17-4) has won more than 70 environmental awards and provides searchable, practical information to help you make green decisions about what to do with all sorts of materials: paper, metal, plastic, glass, hazardous stuff, electronics, and auto, household, garden, and construction materials.

Figure 17-4:
Earth911 is all about reducing, reusing, and recycling. Use the many resources on the site to carry out your best green efforts.

The Small Business Environmental Home Page

Yes, we know, this seems like a strange name for a site. But wait until you see all the resources available here. (See Figure 17-5.) The Small Business Environmental Home Page (www.smallbiz-enviroweb.org) offers all sorts of resources for small businesses who are concerned about compliance issues and creating an environmental management plan. You'll find everything from a how-to workbook to funding sources to state-by-state regulations, deadlines, and contact personnel. The site also offers more than 500 videos on best practices in environmental management for all sorts of industries. (How about "The ABCs of Integrated Pest Management" for starters?)

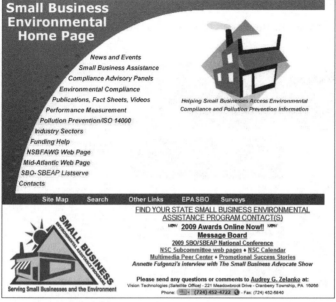

Figure 17-5:
The Small Business Environmental Home Page provides small businesses with tons of resources for green initiatives and environmental compliance.

Green America

The Green America site (www.coopamerica.org), formerly known as Co-op America, is a huge site full of how-to's, associations, and resources to help you find the information you need to make choices that support social justice and environmental concerns. (See Figure 17-6.) Green America is a nonprofit organization that focuses on using economic power — buying green — to work to improve sustainability and equity for everyone on the planet. Their vision statement says, "We work for a world where all people have enough, where all communities are healthy and safe, and where the bounty of the Earth is preserved for all the generations to come."

As a business owner, you can use this site to

✔ Search the Business Green Pages (or submit your own company for consideration).

✔ Learn about the Good Housekeeping Green Seal of Approval.

✔ Join the Green Business Network.

✔ Learn about the Green Business Conference, and much more.

Figure 17-6:
Green
America
offers
resources,
connections,
and the
Business
Green
Pages. Take
a look!

Part V
The Part of Tens

"Of course, according to green technology best practices, we'll replace that old broken washin' machine with a more energy efficient one that doesn't work."

In this part . . .

Ah, everybody's favorite — the *Part of Tens!* In this part of the book, you get a series of quick-look resources that help bring all your green efforts together. You take a look at what you can do in a quick and low-cost way to begin to make your computer more eco-friendly. Then you find out about big-picture resources for green knowledge — where you can go to find out what the scientists say and what policymakers think. (If you're wondering what that has to do with how you use your computer at home, we say "Everything!" Knowing what's happening in green initiatives — and hearing it from reliable sources — helps you see how much of an impact your individual choices really make.) This part also offers a collection of green shopping sites because we just know you're going to want to vote with your dollars when you can!

Chapter 18

Ten Best Ways to Make Your Computer Greener

*R*educe, reuse, recycle is a familiar refrain from green initiatives. This first chapter in the Part of Tens brings together a number of green techniques to give you the quick scoop on things you can do — right away — to begin making a green difference in your home computing.

To select these items, we decided to focus on the here and now, the low cost, and the practical. So even though investing in solar energy and powering your computer with what you capture on your roof might be a great long-term idea, you won't find that suggestion in this list.

If you're determined to go the solar power route (which we think is awesome), you might be interested in the Solio solar-powered charger found at The GreenTech Shop (`http://thegreentechshop.com`). This little charger is actually a hybrid, so it can store and convert energy from the sun or an AC outlet, but you can use it to power your mobile devices and go green.

Turn Stuff Off

Once upon a time in computerland, turning a system on and off repeatedly (meaning once or twice a day) took its toll on the hardware over time. Although technology has changed dramatically, becoming more flexible, more capable, and more adaptable to normal wear and tear, that once-upon-a-time story still lurks in the back of many people's minds.

It's time for a new story! Even if you have a system that is four or five years old, the computer you're using isn't going to wear out if you turn it off when you're away from your desk for more than a couple of hours.

And this isn't just for desktops and laptops. Turn off the monitor, the printer, the router, the Xbox, the Wii, every energy-gobbling thing (including the DVD player, the VHS player — good grief you still have one? — and anything that has a little flashing digital clock that never gets set properly). Even though by comparison the percentage of power your smaller devices draw is minimal compared to the energy they use in their active state, leaching 2 to 4 watts of wasted power continuously for weeks still adds up. If your device has an On light, has a self-charging mechanism, or shows any other signs of life, it is drawing some kind of power. Why waste it? Just let the thing charge up and then unplug it. It's kinder to the planet.

Of course if your device is scheduled to do an automatic backup or system scan in the middle of the night, leave it on so it can complete its maintenance processes. Or change your schedule so the quick maintenance techniques occur first thing in the morning while you're getting your coffee and saying good morning to your coworkers.

Manage the Power

No matter what kind of computer system you're using, your operating system has some kind of system to help you manage the power you use. Chapter 9 tells you all about this. Windows Vista, for example enables you to

- Choose or create a power management plan to suit different needs; see Figure 18-1
- Change the way your power buttons act
- Customize when your computer goes to sleep

Windows 7 takes a few more green steps by giving you additional power over your peripherals and helping you maximize your system resources by managing the power that's running things inside that mysterious gray box.

You can use Energy Saver settings in Mac's OS X to control when the system goes idle. (See Figure 18-2.) You will find the steps for using Mac power-saving features in Chapter 9 as well.

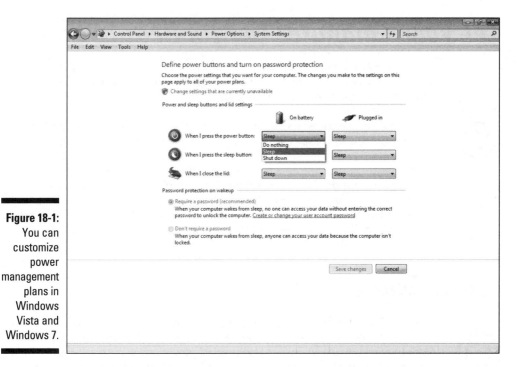

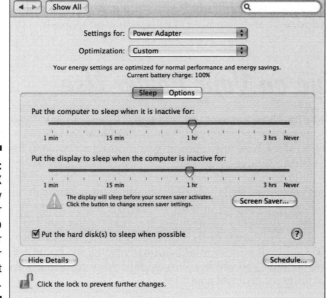

Let Your Computer Get Its Beauty Sleep

For those in-between work times, both Windows Vista and Windows 7 offer Sleep mode, which lets you easily and dramatically reduce the amount of energy your computer uses while remaining in a state of near-instant readiness.

Sleep mode is a great way to balance energy conservation with productivity because the system leaps back to life in only two seconds from a sound sleep.

What's more, your programs and data files are preserved in memory when you use Sleep mode. This differs from the Windows XP Hibernate mode, which offers a sometimes less-than-reliable method of taking a breather while preserving data and reducing power use. Find out more about Sleep, Standby, Hibernate, and other rascally modes in — you guessed it — Chapter 9.

Use a Smart Strip

Here's a simple way to reduce the energy your devices use right away: Get a smart strip. For a $25–$40 investment, you can get a surge protector that does more than just guard against an unexpected power spike. A smart strip includes special outlets that can sense when a peripheral is drawing power and when it's dormant, and by responding to the activity of the computer and peripherals, it knows when to turn off the outlet. This stops any power leaching that's going on when a peripheral is inactive. And that means you don't have to remember to unplug the device — or plug it back in when you want to use it.

Keep an Eye on Your Power Use

Knowing how much power you use is one of the best ways to keep energy consumption on your radar screen. A number of low-cost devices make it easy for you to track how much power you're using so you can figure out where you want to tighten your belt:

> ✔ **A smart power meter** is a device that plugs into your wall outlet; then you plug your computer into the meter. The meter tracks how much energy the computer is consuming and reports the number in kWh (kilo-watt-hours). Most meters are reasonably priced and can provide several reports that help you see which appliances in your home are costing you the most so you can begin to manage your consumption. Chapter 3 covers different types of smart meters.

✔ **A plogg** is a newer offering that combines a smart meter with the communication capability to send the data on a device's energy consumption to you wherever you might be. For example, if you are at work and want to get a power update from home, a plogg can send you a wireless message showing your power use. With some versions of the device, you can log in to a Web site and get access to your home power consumption data in real time. Ploggs for the home cost $95; you can find out more by going to www.plogginternational.com.

Look for the Energy Star

One of the easiest ways to make sure you're buying in an eco-friendly way (when you buy) involves looking for the Energy Star logo, which is shown in Figure 18-3. The Energy Star program is a collaborative venture between the U.S. Environmental Protection Agency and the U.S. Department of Energy. Only products that meet a stringent set of energy-efficient standards can display the Energy Star on their labeling. See Chapter 3 for more about using the Energy Star site to rate your own equipment and think through green purchases.

The Energy Star offers a comprehensive site where you can research all kinds of equipment and appliances to see whether they qualify for the Energy Star symbol. If they don't — steer clear!

Figure 18-3:
Look for the
Energy Star.

Boost Your RAM

Have you been looking for an excuse to increase your computer's RAM? Here's your green justification: More RAM helps speed your computer's processing power, which means less chunking to the hard disk and smoother processing all around.

Find out how much RAM you already have by right-clicking Computer and choosing Properties. The System Properties dialog box opens, and the amount of RAM on your system appears at the bottom of the General tab. On a Mac, click the Apple menu and then click About This Macintosh; the number in the Total Memory line tells you the amount of RAM in your system.

When you know how much RAM you have, go to your computer manufacturer's Web site to find out about the upgrade options for your particular computer model.

Adding a RAM module to your computer is a simple process. For the step-by-step procedure, visit Chapter 5.

Increase Air Flow, Reduce Heat

What do you do on a spring day when the house feels stuffy? (Oh, you didn't just say, "turn on the AC," did you?) Open the windows! This gets the air moving, cools things down, and saves the energy that the fan would use schlogging all that stale air around.

Your computer will thank you for the same kind of treatment. Make sure that your computer is well aerated. Here are a few ways to do that. (Put away the garden spikes!)

For your desktop computer:

✔ Allow several inches of ventilation space between the system unit and the back of your computer cabinet.

✔ Clean the back of the fan and dust around the back of the computer regularly.

✔ Make sure cables are organized and out of the way of the air flow.

✔ If you don't fear popping the lid on the system, check the cables inside the system unit to make sure they're organized so air can circulate easily.

✔ And while you're in there, blow any accumulated dust bunnies out of the inside of the computer. (Use the good old-fashioned birthday-candle-extinguishing method, though; stay away from using canned air.)

For your laptop computer:

- ✔ Get your laptop up off your lap (or bed, or footstool).
- ✔ Use a laptop tray, such as the Futura laptop desk from Lapworks, with ventilation slots to reduce system heat by up to 20 percent.
- ✔ Make sure the AC cord and other cables don't block the small fan outlet on the back or side of your laptop.

Check out the Futura laptop desk by going to Lapworks at `www.laptopdesk.net/laptop-desk-futura.html`.

Share Your Resources

So how many computers did you say you have in the house? Three? And how many printers, scanners, game systems, and cellphones? Uh-huh. We thought so.

One of the kindest things you can do for the earth right away — besides turning off and *unplugging* all the devices you're not using right now — is to share some of those resources.

With a small investment of time and effort in creating a home network, you can reduce the number of peripherals you use, cut down on your energy use, and share resources. Instead of purchasing and hooking up a printer for each computer system, for example, you can use one that all systems can access as needed. You can also share a single external drive, a DVD burner, a scanner — and even the same audio, video, and photo files by keeping your data in one central location. For ideas and how-to's on setting up a home network, see Chapter 12.

For the play-by-play on designing, setting up, and managing a flourishing home network, see Woody's *Windows Home Server For Dummies.* Other books with great networking info include two more by Woody: *Windows Vista All-in-One Desk Reference For Dummies* and *Windows XP All-in-One Desk Reference for Dummies*, 2nd Edition. And if wireless is your thing, take a look at *Wireless Home Networking For Dummies*, 3rd Edition, by Danny Briere, Walter Bruce, and Pat Hurley. Mac lovers should check out *Macs All-in-One Desk Reference For Dummies*, by Wallace Wang.

Recycle Responsibly

The last item in *reduce, reuse, recycle* is an important step that many people — *many* people — still don't know how to do. What should you do with that monitor you don't need anymore? What about the old laptop, your broken cellphone, or the digital camera that died two years ago?

Because toxic chemicals are still used in the manufacturing of computer plastics, boards, and capacitors, just putting a system in a trash bag and setting it out by the curb is a dangerous thing to do to the planet. Not only does the toss-it-out-with-the-trash method run the risk of seriously polluting your local environment, but it has global ramifications as well. Currently, millions of computer parts are exported illegally every year, ending up in remote villages in developing countries, where they're illegally burned for the metals, all the while releasing toxic chemicals into the air where children, families, and the whole environment is seriously threatened.

Most of the big computer manufacturers offer recycling programs so that you can easily return the computers and equipment you no longer need or use. Chapter 8 is all about what to do to prepare your computer for recycling, where to find a reputable recycler, and what you can expect to happen to your equipment after you donate it. Chapter 8 also explains other recycling options that help you reduce, reuse, and recycle.

Chapter 19

Ten (Plus) Online Resources for Green Info, Action, and Products

● ●

In This Chapter

▶ Getting the latest environmental news

▶ Consulting blogs from green living information

▶ Using social networking to promote change

▶ Accessing online save-the-planet tools

▶ Contributing to a green-living knowledge base

▶ Making buying decisions based on product ratings

▶ Shopping for green gadgets galore

● ●

*T*alk about green is everywhere right now — on the Web, on cereal boxes, on television, in books (yes, we know — you're holding one), and in magazines. Companies you never imagined as having any kind of interest in earth-friendly initiatives are suddenly promoting their new green products.

With all the resources available on the Web, it's hard to know where to start and which resources to turn to. In this chapter, you find great online resources for green news, tips, tools, how-to's, and more.

Staying Up to Date with Green News and Information

Because green computing and green living are such hot topics, more and more companies, organizations, and individuals are becoming involved in them. This section offers several sites you can turn to for information that helps you stay current with what's happening in the world of green.

The straight scoop on RSS

RSS stands for *Really Simple Syndication,* a kind of news feed that lets you know when new content has been published on a site you like. When the publisher updates the content of the page, you receive (by e-mail or in your Web browser, depending on what kind of RSS reader you use) the linked headline to the content as well as a brief description or introduction to the new information.

To sign up for RSS, you click the RSS icon and then either add the link (which is usually something like `http://www.anysite.com/rss`) of the displayed page to your Web browser or RSS reader.

Internet Explorer and Microsoft Office Outlook both support RSS feeds, so you don't need an additional RSS reader unless you want one. Here's a quick list of additional RSS news readers you can explore:

Newsgator (`www.newsgator.com/`)

FeedReader (`www.feedreader.com`)

FeedBurner (`www.feedburner.com`)

GoodCleanTech

www.goodcleantech.com

GoodCleanTech is a popular blog in the PC Magazine Network that offers all kinds of tips, how-to's, news, reviews, and more that help you bring green technology to your life in a variety of forms. This blog is a good one to grab via RSS so that you can scan the daily headlines. There's always something interesting at GoodCleanTech.

CleanTechnica

www.cleantechnica.com

CleanTechnica is part of the Green Options community of blogs and prides itself on offering readers current reflections on all the latest trends in clean technology. Whether you're reading about less-toxic electronics, renewable energy, or sustainable living, the articles are factual but not geekspeak. An added perk is that with just a click or two you can find additional posts on green lifestyles and green news.

Best Green Blogs

www.bestgreenblogs.com

If you're a blogger, or if you enjoy reading a variety of blogs, you'll love the Best Green Blogs directory. This site offers a huge collection of blogs, as well as a set of social networking tools (Twitter and Google Friends) that make it easy for you to gather and stay in touch with groups offering the green ideas you want to read.

DeSmogBlog.com

www.desmogblog.com

Do you customize your home page with RSS from your favorite blogs? Here's one to add to the mix: The DeSmogBlog Project. Depending on how long you've been tuned in to issues related to earth care, you may have already heard of DeSmogBlog. This site launched in 2006 and was quickly known as a source for reliable information about global warming.

Visit DeSmogBlog for current commentary on today's green headlines, as well as videos, research, fact sheets, and more.

Planet Green

http://planetgreen.discovery.com

Planet Green offers all kinds of articles and solutions designed to help you green your life. This beautiful site includes forums, videos, and social networking features, combined with how-to clips from Planet Green (the television network) to bring fresh green content for a wide range of interests. Be sure to check out the Tech & Transport area for content specifically related to green computing.

MSN Green

http://green.msn.com

The green living pages on MSN Green make living green easier by providing feature articles that are relevant to everyday life. From news to a green directory, shopping, and site tools, you'll discover all kinds of green ideas — including tech stuff — to help you live in harmony.

Greeniacs

www.greeniacs.com

If you're looking for a site that has a little bit of everything — articles, social networking, videos, blogs, shopping, and more — you may feel at home on Greeniacs.com. What's more, Greeniacs has a mission of providing nonpolitical, nonjudgmental, green info to anyone who's interested. Nice.

Sites for social action

If you're interested in getting involved in green social action from the comfort of your home computer, check out the following sites.

StopGlobalWarming.org: Stop Global Warming is an informational and advocacy site that combines public education campaigns with the opportunity to join a virtual march in support of green initiatives. When you visit the site, you're greeted with the current number of supporters participating in the virtual march. You'll also find a collection of resources that suggest practical ways to reduce your CO_2 contribution and to take action. It might mean writing to your mayor or watching a video clip, but you'll find all kinds of outlets for your advocacy urge.

Care2.com: Care2.com is a green community and lifestyle site that has millions (yes, millions!) of members. With how-to features, a wide range of topic areas, blogs, e-cards, a range of active communities, and the daily action, which gives you one green idea to try in your own life today, Care2.com encourages members to get involved and advocate for green issues.

WeCanSolveIt.org: WeCanSolveIt.org is the site of the Alliance for Climate Protection, a nonprofit organization founded by Al Gore. The objective is to start an effort that builds the political will to solve the climate change problem. The We Connect area of the site helps you find other We members in your state or region. The site also includes social networking features, solution articles, action alerts, and more.

11thHourAction.com: 11thHourAction.com is another multifaceted site that includes lots of how-to information, social networking, video, blogs, and more. The idea here is to create a vital community that is engaged in and fired up about acting on local, regional, and national levels.

Finding Tips, Tools, and How-To's

Finding out how to green your technology use and your life takes a bit of energy — yours! The sites and tools in this section give you a head start by providing solid green information on the latest environmental reports, utilities to help you understand more about your own energy use, and sites to get you started on the way to advocacy.

Alliance to Save Energy

```
http://ase.org/section/_audience/consumers
```

The Alliance to Save Energy has been around a long, long time. Longer than most of the jeans in your closet, we'd bet. The Alliance started in 1977 as a bipartisan effort in Congress, even before the U.S. Department of Energy was signed into existence by President Carter later that same year.

The Alliance sees energy efficiency as the key to a healthier world, a more stable economy, and enhanced energy security. The Alliance to Save Energy Web site offers a special section for consumers, with hands-on help such as

- ✔ Updated information about how to qualify for home- and car-efficiency tax credits
- ✔ Tips to help you cut your energy bills
- ✔ Tools for conducting a home energy audit

Climate Savers Computing Initiative

www.climatesaverscomputing.org

Climate Savers is a kind of do-everything site that gets you pumped up for green efforts and also gives you the tools to accomplish something. The site includes lots of practical how-to information, as well as advocacy suggestions, ways to save computing energy at home and work, and even a social networking component so that you can convince your friends to take action.

Make Me Sustainable

www.makemesustainable.com

Make Me Sustainable is a great lifestyle site that challenges you to commit to changing your habits to reduce your carbon footprint. You can use the carbon footprint calculator to determine where you have room for improvement and then pledge to take action. (We walk you through using the calculator in Chapter 2.) Make Me Sustainable has a social networking aspect that enables you to invite your friends, share goals, and create groups with similar interests.

Here a Wikia Green, there a Wikia Green

http://green.wikia.com

Everywhere a wiki wiki. . . . (Just had to say it.) It might not be too far-fetched to say that just about everyone who has browsed the Web has heard of Wikipedia. Jimmy Wales, one of the cofounders of Wikipedia — the hugely successful and mind-blowingly extensive (and sometimes not completely accurate because it's written and edited by us humans) wiki — has launched a wiki community called Wikia with the sole purpose of supporting green efforts and education. A *wiki* is a shared Web page or site that is open for all to contribute to and edit using online text tools. Wikia Green launched in 2008 and is a quickly growing source of green concepts, theory, practical writings, tips, science, shopping sources, and much, much more. When you're wondering how something is done, check out the special how-to section on the left.

Checking Out Online Buying Guides

When it comes to buying new stuff, what's the green thing to do? The answer depends on a number of factors, including whether you can reuse or recycle what you have and whether the new item you're considering is greener than the one you're replacing. The Web offers guidance on what products and companies are making a true green effort. Before you buy, check out these online resources to help distinguish true green initiatives from *greenwashing* (which is green talk without the thoughtful action to back it up).

Treehugger's Green Buying Guides

```
www.treehugger.com/buygreen
```

Treehugger is a popular blog reporting on all kinds of green and sustainable items. It features some great buying guides that can help you make green choices for computers and other electronics. Visit the site to review the buying guides as you're considering your next home computing purchase.

Green Electronics Council

```
www.greenelectronicscouncil.org
```

The Green Electronics Council is a nonprofit organization that promotes, supports, and rewards companies that design, create, offer, and recycle earth-friendly electronics products. GEC's largest project is the EPEAT (Electronic Product Environment Assessment Tool) program, which helps consumers evaluate which tech products actually live up to their green promises. EPEAT uses a three-tiered system to let consumers know how well products demonstrate the green characteristics they claim. Companies sign a factual-reporting agreement and submit their products for evaluation against 51 criteria (23 mandatory and 28 optional). Products are awarded a bronze, silver, or gold rating, depending on the results of the evaluation. To find out more about the EPEAT rating system, visit `www.epeat.net/Criteria.aspx`.

To find out more about how you can use EPEAT as a consumer to find green electronics, go to `www.epeat.net/Consumers.aspx`.

Looking beyond home computing

The focus of this book is bringing green ideas to your home computing. Several organizations are working to bring big green ideas to corporate and government initiatives. If the grand scheme of green piques your interest, the following sites are great places to start.

The Green Grid: www.thegreengrid.org

The Green Grid is all about advancing energy efficiency in businesses and data centers around the globe. (*Data centers* are large spaces housing servers; they process massive amounts of data and require similar amounts of power.) The Green Grid is a global consortium that wants to create useful metrics to guide energy-efficient business practices, improve data center performance, and promote energy-efficient standards, processes, and technologies.

World Resources Institute: www.wri.org

World Resources Institute is a think tank that encourages the practical application of research findings in initiatives that benefit the earth and people worldwide.

Virtual Energy Forum: www.virtualenergy forum.com

Virtual Energy Forum hosts — er, virtually — a huge, two-day, online-only event that encourages and rewards companies for changing to energy-efficient and clean energy-based practices. Although held for a limited time (albeit regularly), this event is a great place to tune in to the top-level discussions going on in the areas of energy management and alternative energies. Check out the site and mark your calendar.

Consumer Reports Goes Green

www.greenerchoices.org

Consumer Reports, the long-time consumer advocacy publication, has a healthy online green section that helps you evaluate green products, including calculators, computers, and AC power supplies. It's a resource you may want to visit before you get out the debit card and start your online shopping extravaganza.

Where to Shop for Green Products

Try the vendors in this list for green products and green ideas.

✔ **Buy.com (www.buy.com):** Offers a variety of green electronics products and shows you how to read EPEAT ratings for purchasing decision. Also, a new study by Carnegie Mellon University's Green Design Institute (March 2009) shows that purchasing online using Buy.com's e-commerce model uses 35 percent less energy and reduces carbon emissions when compared to a purchase at a store you drive to. Read the study, "Life Cycle Comparisons…: A Case Study of Buy.com," online at `www.ce.cmu.edu/GreenDesign`.

✔ **Green and Save (`www.greenandsave.com`):** It's not just a green shopping site — it's a movement. Claiming to build on a 20-year legacy, Green and Save says it adds two R's to reduce, reuse, and recycle, asking you to *rethink* and *retrain* as you learn new green habits. Find helpful articles in the Go Green area and computers in the Green Office section.

✔ **The GreenTech Shop (`www.thegreentechshop.com`):** For green-gadget lovers, the site offers radios, solar chargers, solar bags, lamps, and rechargeable batteries. If you're *really* a fan, friend The GreenTech Shop on Facebook or MySpace, or follow them on Twitter.

✔ **GreenShopper (`www.greenshopper.com`):** With a combination of information about the environment, encouragement for green shopping, and options for shopping locally or online, GreenShopper offers a variety of product categories (including computers and electronics).

✔ **Gaiam (`www.gaiam.com`):** Is the lifestyle blogzine that offers video clips, how-to articles (lots of how-to articles!), and event profiles, but it all leads you happily to the Gaiam store, where you can purchase earth-friendly products of all types.

✔ **MSN Green Shopping (`http://green.msn.com/shopping`):** The MSN Green includes a Shopping page that enables you to search for earth-friendly products in a variety of categories. Search results list product details as well as Greenzer scores on a scale of 1 to 10, to show how green each product rates.

✔ **Green Home Environmental Store (`www.greenhome.com/products`):** It's not a particularly compelling name, but this store offers quite a collection of earth-friendly computing products, such as disks, flash drives, rechargeable batteries, and compact solar power chargers.

✔ **Shopping Green on Yahoo! (`http://shopping.yahoo.com/b:Green%20Center:784718373`):** Browse the Yahoo! Shopping Green Center for items related to renewable energy, Energy Star appliances, rechargeable batteries, and more.

Index

• J •

• K •

• L •